BOOKS IN THE IGS BOOK SERIES NEW NON-ARISTOTELIAN LIBRARY

Korzybski, Alfred (2010). *Selections from Science and Sanity.* (2nd Ed.). Edited by Lance Strate, with a Foreword by Bruce I. Kodish. Fort Worth, TX: Institute of General Semantics.

Strate, Lance (2011). *On the Binding Biases of Time and Other Essays on General Semantics and Media Ecology.* Fort Worth, TX: Institute of General Semantics.

Anton, Corey (2011). *Communication Uncovered: General Semantics and Media Ecology.* Fort Worth, TX: Institute of General Semantics.

Levinson, Martin H. (2012). *More Sensible Thinking.* New York, NY: Institute of General Semantics.

Anton, Corey & Strate, Lance (2012). *Korzybski and...* (Eds.) New York, NY: Institute of General Semantics.

Levinson, Martin H. (2014). *Continuing Education Teaching Guide to General Semantics.* New York, NY: Institute of General Semantics.

Berger, Eva & Berger, Isaac (2014). *The Communication Panacea: Pediatrics and General Semantics.* New York, NY: Institute of General Semantics.

Pace, Wayne R. (2017). *How to Avoid Making A Damn Fool of Yourself: An Introduction to General Semantics.* New York, NY: Institute of General Semantics.

Lahman, Mary P. (2018). *Awareness and Action: A Travel Companion.* New York, NY: Institute of General Semantics.

Levinson, Martin H. (2018). *Practical Fairy Tales For Everyday Living, Revised Second Edition.* New York, NY: Institute of General Semantics.

Levinson, Martin H. (2020). *Sensible Thinking for Turbulent Times: Revised Second Edition.* New York, NY: Institute of General Semantics.

Mayer, Christopher (2021). *How Do You Know?: A Guide to Clear Thinking About Wall Street, Investing, and Life.* New York, NY: Institute of General Semantics.

Levinson, Martin H. (2021). *Practical Fairy Tales For Everyday Living, Revised Second Edition.* New York, NY: Institute of General Semantics. (In Spanish)

Levinson, Martin H. (2021). *Practical Fairy Tales For Everyday Living, Revised Second Edition.* New York, NY: Institute of General Semantics. (In Hebrew)

Mayer, Christopher (2022). *Dear FellowTime-Binder: Letters on General Semantics.* New York, NY: Institute of General Semantics.

Liñán, Laura Trujillo (2022). *Formal Cause in Marshall McLuhan's Thinking: An Aristotelian Perspective.* New York, NY: Institute of General Semantics.

Strate, Lance (2022). *Concerning Communication: Epic Quests and Lyric Excursions Within the Human Lifeworld.* New York, NY: Institute of General Semantics.

Korzybski, Alfred (2023). *Science and Sanity: An Introduction to Non-Aristotelian Systems and General Semantics* (6th Ed.) New Preface by Lance Strate, New York, NY: Institute of General Semantics.

Korzybski, Alfred (2024). *General Semantics Seminar 1937: Olivet College Lectures.* (4th Ed.) New York, NY: Institute of General Semantics.

Strate, Lance (2024). *Not A, Not Be, &c.* New York, NY: Institute of General Semantics.

Korzybski, Alfred. (2024). *Science et Sanité, une introduction aux systèmes Non-Aristotéliciens et à la sémantique générale.* New York, NY: Institute of General Semantics.

Levinson, Martin H. (2025). *Sensible Thinking 3: The Adventure Continues.* New York, NY: Institute of General Semantics.

Mayer, Christopher (2025). *The Unspeakable Level: Korzybski's Razor and Other Ways of Revealing.* New York, NY: Institute of General Semantics.

GENERAL SEMANTICS AND POLITICS

Corey Anton and Thom Gencarelli, Editors

INSTITUTE OF GENERAL SEMANTICS
New York, New York, USA

Copyright © 2025 by Corey Anton and Thom Gencarelli

All rights reserved. No part of this publication may be reproduced or transmitted in any form or by any means, electronic or mechanical, including photocopying, recording, or by any information storage and retrieval system, without permission in writing from the publisher.

Published by the Institute of General Semantics
401 Park Avenue South #873
New York, NY, 10016
www.generalsemantics.org

Interior Book Design by Scribe Freelance
www.scribefreelance.com

Cover image: Dom Heffer, 'Dumbos', 2024, Oil and Water based spray paint on canvas, 153 × 153 cm

ISBN: 978-1-970164-36-7 (Print)
978-1-970164-37-4 (eBook)
Published in the United States of America

Library of Congress Cataloging-in-Publication Data

Names: Anton, Corey editor | Gencarelli, Thom editor
Title: General semantics and politics / Corey Anton and Thom Gencarelli, editors.
Description: New York, New York : Institute of General Semantics, 2025. | Series: New non-aristotelian library | Includes bibliographical references and index. | Summary: "Designed for those discovering general semantics for the first time as well as for scholars who are well versed in it, this collection provides vital analytic tools for understanding the contemporary world of politics. It brings together essays that span a wide range of concerns, including the underpinnings of democracy, the challenges of media bias and the two-party system, the difficulties in thinking about money and inequality, the struggle against polarization, how to deal with conspiracy theories, and, along the way, provides ample resources for engaging in fair and rational dialogue. In today's world, where so many people are confused and disgruntled, and perhaps on the verge of giving up on the possibility of constructive political discourse, this collection is a breath of fresh air. It reminds us that hope is not lost so long as we are willing to openly and honestly think about what is going on. Essential reading for anyone interested in general semantics, the contemporary world of politics, and/or the connection between them, it is a collection not to be missed"– Provided by publisher.
Identifiers: LCCN 2025028885 (print) | LCCN 2025028886 (ebook) | ISBN 9781970164367 trade paperback | ISBN 9781970164374 epub
Subjects: LCSH: Discourse analysis–Political aspects–United States | Political culture–United States
Classification: LCC P302.77 .G47 2025 (print) | LCC P302.77 (ebook)

To Alfred and Neil

TABLE OF CONTENTS

Acknowledgements — xi

Preface
Thom Gencarelli — xv

Introduction: Setting the Stage
Corey Anton — 1

Chapter 1
Politics and General Semantics: Humanity, Time-Binding, Wealth, and Superabundance
Corey Anton — 9

Chapter 2
The Double Bind of Rational Political Discourse
Lance Strate — 43

Chapter 3
Modern Totems of our Imagination: The Economy, Inflation and Money
Chris Mayer — 107

Chapter 4
Media Bias, Two-party Politics, and the Two-valued
Orientation: Why the United States Finds Itself
on the Verge of a Second Civil War
Thom Gencarelli   119

Chapter 5
General Semantics and Constructive Political Discourse
Martin H. Levinson   137

Chapter 6
HashtagThis: #FreePalestine, Political Positions, and Social
Media Trends
Etai Eshet and Eva Berger   147

Chapter 7
Incitement and the Flash Mob
Susan Drucker and Gary Gumpert   153

Chapter 8
An Ounce of Prevention: General Semantics and
Conspiracy Theories
Joshua Clements   173

Chapter 9
Korzybski and Chantal Mouffe: General Semantics
Contribution to Agonism
Jermaine Martinez   195

Chapter 10
Myles Horton and the Highlander Folk School:
A Semantic Environment of Political Organization,
Activism, and Change
Ryan P. McCullough   225

Chapter 11
American Hatecore: Music, 'Jokes,' Race
Roy F. Fox   257

Chapter 12
Green Light: The Fact that Political Candidates May
Stretch the Truth in Broadcast Television Advertisements
Jefferson Spurlock   277

About the Contributors   281

Index   287

ACKNOWLEDGMENTS

The editors wish to thank a number of individuals who have been instrumental in helping us bring this book project to fruition, many of whom have also been part of our support system and thought community across the course of our careers.

First, we want to thank our 12 authors for their superb contributions to the book. An anthology is always and only measured by the sum total of chapters the contributors summon forth. Our authors' interest in and commitment to this project has been deep and wide from the very beginning. And their individual approaches to the subject matter, as well as their intentions, ideas, eloquence, and erudition indelibly mark these pages.

We need to graciously thank our publisher, the Institute of General Semantics, which has long served as the living room of our intellectual home. In particular, we thank Lance Strate, President of the IGS, for his continued support as a colleague, friend, and inspiration. We also thank members of the IGS Board of Trustees with whom we have worked so closely and for so many years, including IGS Executive Secretary Eva Berger, and Board members Nora Bateson, Margaret "Peggy" Cassidy, Susan Drucker, Ben Hauck, Dominic Heffer, Christopher Mayer, Mary Lahman, Martin Levinson, Jacqueline Rudig, Laura Trujillo-Liñan, and Gina Valenti.

We offer all appreciation to *ETC: A Review of General Semantics*, the IGS journal in which the chapters herein originally appeared as part of two special issues on the subject. We are especially indebted to the team that works so diligently to put *ETC* together, including Assistant Editor Michelle Kramisen, Book Review Editor Marty Levinson, Art Editor Dom Heffer, Journal Manager Phil Rose, and the entire Editorial Board.

All thanks also go to the IGS's little sister organization, the New York Society for General Semantics, including its President Peggy Cassidy and Vice President Teresa Manzella, and Members of the NYSGS Board of Directors including TC McLuhan and Michelle Shocked.

We would be remiss if we did not acknowledge the Players Club in New York City, which has continued to serve as host and home base for the annual Alfred Korzybski Memorial Lecture and IGS Symposium (as well as many other IGS and NYSGS programs), and wherein some of the chapters herein were first presented as works-in-progress.

All gratitude also goes to the Media Ecology Association – the alternate living room of our intellectual home – including all of its Officers and Board members. This includes so many people over the years. The current group, however, includes Robert Albrecht, Jeff Bogaczyk, Peggy Cassidy, Susan Drucker, Tiffany Gilliam, Fernando Gutiérrez, Julia Hildebrand, Christina Knopf, Jaqueline McLeod Rogers, Tiffany Petricini, Paul Soukup, S.J., Heather Stassen, Lance Strate, Matt Thomas, and Laura Trujillo-Liñan.

We cannot thank enough Dom Heffer for his specially-commissioned and beautifully conceived artwork that graces our cover. Likewise to Daniel Middleton and Scribe Freelance for their superb design and production work.

Corey would like to acknowledge family and friends as vital support staff, and he expresses the deepest of gratitude to Valerie V. Peterson for her boundless encouragement, keen insights, and indefatigable support. He wishes to thank his home institution, Grand Valley State University, for providing space, time, and resources for teaching and

ACKNOWLEDGMENTS

scholarship. Thanks also need to be given to Duquesne University, especially to Erik Garrett and Janie Harden Fritz. And, a note of thanks needs to be expressed to Northern Arizona University, especially to Jermaine Martinez. Finally, he wishes to thank Richard Lanigan from the International Communicology Institute. So many wonderful teachers, colleagues, and students, with their inspiring lectures, shrewd observations, and engaging questions, have fueled his thinking and research more than he can adequately express.

Thom is forever indebted and grateful to his teachers and mentors, James Chesebro at Queens College of the City University of New York, and Terence Moran, Christine Nystrom, Henry Perkinson, and Neil Postman at New York University. A special note is reserved here for teacher, mentor, and long-time friend Gary Gumpert – who passed away in November 2024, and whose final published work (of many hundreds) appears in these pages. He thanks all of his life-long friends and colleagues at Manhattan University and Montclair State University, and from the New York State Communication Association and New Jersey Communication Association. He thanks his students, from whom he learns something new and important every day. Finally, words can never express his gratitude for the love and support of his wife Alison, and sons Miles and Griffin, during all of the time he has spent locked away in his office and typing words on to a screen.

- C.A. and T.G.

PREFACE
THOM GENCARELLI

In the summer of 2017, I was on vacation with my family when I met a couple from the United Kingdom – from London, to be exact. The husband was an investment banker, and we ended up having quite an interesting, extended conversation about global politics and economics. It was during this conversation that I first heard the words come out of my own mouth: that "the U.S. seems headed toward another civil war."

That conversation was the very first thing that came to my mind when Corey Anton first approached me about the idea for this project. I thought, in particular, about that modifier before the word "war." What does it mean for a war to be "civil," or that a war *can be* civil?

I, of course, went back to examine the roots of the term, which begins with the U.S. Civil War during the 1860s. The first thing I discovered is that the use of the term to describe that war did not come into common usage until the 20th Century. It comes from the Latin *bellum civile*, which means "a war between or pertaining to civilians." (This also explains the use of the term "Antebellum South" for the period before that war.) Thus, the use of the word civil, in this case, refers to the fact that the two armies at war with one another were raised from among civilians of the same country.

The terms "civilization" and "civics" obviously come from this same root. Civics, in fact, comes from the Latin *civicus*, which means "relating to a citizen," and is defined as "the study of the rights, obligations, and responsibilities of citizens in a society."

However, when I have thought about the notion of a civil war I have always been drawn to the particular connotation of the word civil as it relates to the notion of being "civilized." In fact, there are *three* connotations at work here. One is the idea that to be civil means to be polite and courteous, and there is nothing polite or courteous about men killing one another. (I am also being deliberate, and not sexist, in using the word "men" in that last sentence.) The second is the cultural idea and ideal that means to become educated, to become more developed as individuals and as a culture, and to aspire to our best – toward whatever greatness we humans might achieve. Finally, there is the legal connotation: that civil *law* is not about adjudicating matters of criminal action or behavior but about the social order, about fairness, about what is right and just.

All of this brings me back to Alfred Korzybski. Bruce Kodish's book, *Korzybski: A Biography* crystallized for me how Korzybski's project, which became general semantics, arose from the horrors he witnessed as an officer during World War I and his attempt to help us avoid such things ever happening again in the course of human affairs. Of course, the war in which he fought came less than a half century after the end of the U.S. Civil War.

To me, then, the essential question becomes this: In the face of myriad wars across the globe *since* World War I, *can* Korzybski's teachings help us achieve the simple measure of sanity that is a true and lasting peace and coexistence among peoples, nation states, and sovereign territories here on this small speck of space dust that is all we human beings have ever known?

Lately I have been reading Heather Cox Richardson's "Letters from an American," which give me hope. Richardson is a professor of U.S. history at Boston College who specializes in the period leading up to the Civil War, the war itself, and the reconstruction. She offers up hope because she presents what I will call a *thermostatic* rather than cyclical view of history: that when things tip too far toward one end of the political spectrum, it is we citizens who become the source/force that leads us away from extremism and fanaticism and back toward balance. (Such a perspective dovetails nicely with the thermostatic view of education originally posed by my great mentor Neil Postman.)

In this moment of political polarization in the United States, I would like to think that the citizens who have chosen a "side" do not truly hate one another and will not come to hate one another. I would like to think that we can agree, in a civil way, to disagree. I would like to think that this side taking will not eventually lead to violence – which all too often tends to beget more violence in response. I would like to think that saner heads will prevail, at long last, and come to realize and accept that killing one's fellow human being in the name of some mandate or idea or ideology or order from above is never sane nor justifiable.

I would like to think that this book can make some small contribution to helping us – and helping us to think – in this regard.

INTRODUCION:
SETTING THE STAGE
COREY ANTON

In various discussions—some at recent conventions, some with board members of the Institute of General Semantics, and some on public social media sites such as Facebook—I have heard people bemoan the failure of those who study and promote general semantics (GS). They suggest that those who know of it, who understand it and practice it, fail to bring it to the masses. They speak of a potential, not-yet-realized claim that the world would be a better place if those who knew about it were more adept at helping people find it, understand it, practice it, etc. They suggest that not enough has been done to bring GS into people's daily lives, to show that it is much more than an academic discipline. They further claim that, given its importance and relevance, GS has been spread neither widely enough nor far enough.

Even more pointedly, some claim that many current political quandaries and disputes can be handled and/or largely alleviated, if more people understood basic principles and practices of GS. It is almost depicted, at times by some people, as if GS needs to be taught at all schools across the country. It needs to become part of the basic core curriculum of junior high and high school, and, if that were to happen, political woes and psychological strife would be greatly reduced. The general sense is that, on the one hand, U.S. society seems less sane all the time, and, on the other hand, GS is what people need most but are not getting.

These concerns seem even more pressing as we acknowledge that there are some people, largely academics in communications or psychology or related fields, who have heard of general semantics but who think of it is a museum piece, a relic, something which has historical significance, but which is not of serious relevance to today's world. They suggest that GS is passé, outdated, and no longer that useful. Some have accused it of being "cultish" and dabbling in "pseudoscience." I have heard younger scholars say, "'General Semantics?' Isn't that something from the 1950s?" Clearly, GS is not as visible as it might be and is not widely recognized as highly relevant to today's quandaries and troubles.

Indeed, how well have those who know of GS updated or advanced (or even sought to popularize) the system? How well have current general semanticists brought GS into the current milieu? Admittedly, there have been some advances within GS such as "E-prime," "neuro-linguistic programming," and "radical general semantics," and there have been a few significant scholars such as Martin Levinson, Bruce Kodish and Lance Strate who have made GS more contemporary, but, as a whole, how well have GS scholars answered the critiques of cultism and pseudoscience?

To what extent is GS rightfully (and/or wrongfully) dubbed "outdated"? How different, if at all, was the science during the heyday of GS than the science of today? Was GS_{1950} something different, more relevant and useful than GS_{2025}? Given the time period when GS began, might GS practitioners need to know something about attribution theory, the actor-observer bias, balance theory, cognitive dissonance theory, the Dunning-Kruger effect, the economics of attention, mortality salience studies, neuro-imaging sciences, media ecology, the spiral of silence, terror management theory, etc.? And/or, might people need, now more than ever, to update GS and integrate its insights, and, ultimately, demonstrate its relevance to everyday life?

INTRODUCION: SETTING THE STAGE   3

Now, at the least, if we are to believe (accept as a fair map): that there are increasing rates of depression and anxiety among young people, that teen suicide rates have spiked upward in the last decade, that authoritarian regimes are on the rise globally just as democratic ideals are waning in the U.S. and abroad, that disparities between rich and poor have never been wider, that large parts of the U.S. have overturned 50+ years of abortions rights, that forms of hypocrisy can be found in abundance just about everywhere you look, etc., then, what does GS have to say to all (or any) of it?

What are the particular issues or cases where principles and concepts of GS would offer meaningful and relevant direction? Is it possible to get GS on the main stage and bring it to the rescue to many of today's ills?

Some Questions to Consider

Perhaps the above remains too vague and too sweeping, too inclusive and too general. Maybe more targeted focus would help. How about some questions that might give further orientation as well as finer nuance: How useful do people find GS for both individual problems *and* collective quandaries? Said otherwise, in contrast to (or in addition to) any personal benefits that GS might provide for individuals with psychological maladies, does GS offer practical instruction within socio-political realms? Even more specifically, how, exactly, would today's political climate be different if more people understood and practiced basic principles of general semantics? Which people, if any, would be better off and how so in particular? To what extent does general semantics unmask pretenses, shed light and give insight? Where, specifically, do we find the science and where do we find the sanity within GS?

Does the whole of general semantics, "the system" taken in total, have any natural inclinations to either "the political right" or "the political left"? That is, would those *most well versed* in GS, those who actually know and practice it, have any political inclination at all? Would they be more likely to have a bend or leaning that moves them, at least generally speaking, in a conservative direction, a progressive direction, or a libertarian direction? Do we find no political inclination at all?

Let me try it this way: Aristotle makes it clear that rhetoric, as he understands it, remains morally neutral: it can be used for good or ill, depending upon who uses it and to what end. Can the same be said of the Non-Aristotelian system that is GS?

Or, if the above still remains too abstract, too mired in "intensional" thinking, how about some lower-level policies or laws? If someone were well versed in GS how might they talk about, and/or encourage others to think about, the common debate regarding abortion? What principles, concepts, devices, tenets or practices would inform one on how best to think about that debate? Should one be pro-life or pro-choice or something else? Have any particular technological advances brought new facts to light that are relevant to this debate?

How about the prevalent U.S. political discourse about the 2nd amendment? What positions and formulations would likely be advanced by those most well versed in GS? Does it matter that the bullet was invented in 1847, nearly 60 years after the 2nd amendment was passed in 1789? What would the GS response be to the often-stated claim that "The only thing that stops a bad guy with a gun is a good guy with a gun"? Are such absolutist and reifying statements not highly problematic?

Which particular policies and practices, enacted where and in which particular ways, have most helped people to achieve a saner society? For example, if the map is not the territory and the word is not the thing, then what is to be said of "fake news"? Would those schooled in GS be less likely to believe fake news? Are there defenses against fake news? What resources does GS provide for determining what should be believed or what should not be believed?

Does GS offer science and sanity to peoples' concerns over gender identity and LGBTQ rights? How about the "Me Too" movement?

INTRODUCION: SETTING THE STAGE 5

What would be a representative GS response? Might concepts such as indexing, dating, and non-allness assist here, or no?

If someone wanted to draw upon well-known general semanticists to respond to any or all of the questions listed above, I think we can agree that Alfred Korzybski would not offer the exact same advice as would S. I. Hayakawa, who, in turn, would differ from Wendell Johnson, Irving Lee or Samuel Bois, and none of them would likely offer the same advice as Neil Postman or Christine Nystrom, etc. And even Korzybski$_{1916}$ is not Korzybski$_{1946}$ etc., but then, where does that leave us? Could different people bring "the same principles" of GS to an identical issue only to reach very different conclusions regarding the nature of the issue and how to best handle it? Does this line of questioning imply that GS thereby becomes less potent, less universal, as it is diminished by a thousand qualifications (limited to this person, here at this time, with this particular vantage of selection of a changing phenomenon, etc.)?

Now, as already alluded to several times, if someone were to insist that most individuals well versed in GS would likely begin by suggesting that all of the above is simply too abstract, too intensional, too much mere verbalism, we might accept the wisdom, but then, again, I must ask, where do we practically go on from here? I mean, the insight that "the map is not the territory" does not admonish us to abandon map-making, but rather, to continue to make and use maps but to be aware of their many reductions and limitations. Said more critically, when does reluctance to generalize become its own form of impotence? On this note, can there be such a preponderance of facts, such an overabundance that "to me-ness" can become problematic? For example, can people take the facts involved in the January 6th events on the U.S. capital, and with the expression "to me," come to very different conclusions regarding how to understand what happened?

How about these: are people well versed in GS better suited for (or more competent at) handling political discourse? Can they talk about the political issues of the day without falling into either/or thinking, jumping to conclusions, suffering inappropriate semantic reactions, and/or polarizing social relations?

Which concepts and principles of GS, which authors and books, are most suited to help people out of their political quandaries and assist them in avoiding further trouble? How, specifically, do concepts such as "non-allness," "to me-ness," "consciousness of abstracting," or devices such as "indexing," "dating," "hyphens," and "etc.," aid in addressing and handling difficult situations and complex social problems? For example, if we avoid the "is of identity," substituting the expression, "She is a Democrat" with "She voted Democrat in the last three primary elections," how, exactly does that help?

Might it be that those well versed in GS are simply more likely to eschew political discourse, especially if it traffics in high-level abstractions? Perhaps people who are most versed in GS simply avoid political discourse in polite company? Is avoiding the folly of such talk a main piece of wisdom offered by GS? If yes, well, then, what does *that* mean? How is that any better than simple folk wisdom or etiquette advice?

Lest the above series of questions be misunderstood, I wish to stress that I do believe that GS has much not-yet-realized potential. I believe that consciousness of abstracting and awareness of the kinds of biases built into language choices and habits are vital for alleviating some of today's social ills. People need to be as aware as possible of how they abstract, categorize and label; they need to be aware of the differences between facts, inferences, and hearsay, just as they need to appreciate the biases inherent in media forms. They need to be aware of elementalism and forms of misplaced concreteness, and they must try to avoid hastily made over-generalizations and unfounded assumptions. In a word, they need to grow ever more *extensional*.

To that end, the essays collected here take up many of these ideas, along with many other issues related to politics. The collection, which began as a call for papers and then produced a double-issue on "general semantics and politics" within the journal *ETC: A Review of General*

INTRODUCION: SETTING THE STAGE 7

Semantics, provides a great deal of insight and direction for those who wish to understand how general semantics relates to politics.

The chapters included here cover topics such as: grasping how economic quandaries relate to political sensibilities, understanding the conditions and practices that undergird democracy, revealing the shortcomings of the two-party system, illustrating the need for constructive and civil political discourse, documenting the role that flash mobs play in political movements, offering defenses against conspiracy theories, showing how political activism and social change best proceed, presenting strategies for taming socio-political antagonism, uncovering the role of racial tensions within political biases, and revealing how to assess political candidates' broadcast advertisements.

Across the lot, these essays bring the principles and practices of GS into the 21st century. They show how GS offers a great deal for those who seek refuge from political unrest, and they provide needed resources thinking about (and engaging in) political action. They powerfully demonstrate the value and relevance of general semantics today.

CHAPTER 1

POLITICS AND GENERAL SEMANTICS: HUMANITY, TIME-BINDING, WEALTH, AND SUPERABUNDANCE
COREY ANTON

Growing Extensional

Of the many concepts within GS, one of the most important concerns the distinction between "intensional" and "extensional" orientations. People mainly traffic in the former, and they often require training to grow into the latter. And, even after significant training, people occasionally will slip into intensional orientations, at least to some degree.

For the most part then – and more often than they would like to believe – people respond and act in ways that are overly intensional. They confuse their ideas for facts of the world; they take their thinking about things to be fair substitutes for the things themselves. It is not uncommon for people to take the feelings that subtly accompany their thoughts and judgments as proof of the veracity of their thoughts and judgments. Overlooking this basic fact regarding human symbolic activity, people routinely make emotionally laden judgments and use vague abstractions, and, all along, they feel confirmed by their "gut sense" of things. Animated by some level of emotion and sentiment, people get caught up within their sweeping and/or encompassing generalizations, and they often do so in self-gratifying ways (see Ellen Langer, 1992).

Take, for example, how people talk about any major city (e.g. "New York," "Los Angeles," "Hong Kong," etc.). Without ever having been to a particular city, people can, and commonly do, talk about that city and take their words in earnest. They take themselves seriously; they believe what they are saying despite having no direct personal experiences with said city. Because they have read articles, seen pictures and movies, and they have talked with people, often friends and relatives, who have been there, they somehow are able to take their own talk about these cities seriously. But even those people who have visited a city for lengths of time, how long would it take them, and how much would they have to directly experience, to become familiar enough to speak with confidence and authority? Evidently, it matters very little. Said simply: regardless of whether people have no, little, or much experience, many feel some level of confidence when they make their judgments and verbal assessments.

When people feel that what they say about something sums it up a definitive way, they are being intensional. It is easy for people to become semantically stubborn and to take how they feel about something as proof of what they say about it. This is partly why dialogue can be difficult: people who are lifelong residents of a city can have significantly different experiences of that city. Hence, they can disagree about how a city should or could be summed up. They know it from their vantage and networks, their particular relations with particular others in particular places at particular times. They know not "the city," but rather, how it appears "to them" at present. Making a distinction between talking about "how things *are*" and talking about "how things *appear to someone"* is vital to growing extensional, just as is recognizing that appearances are partial and have a limited shelf life.

When general semanticists admonish people to recognize that "the map is not the territory," they are pointing out the need to stay vigilant in recognizing the shortcoming of human judgments and symbolic representations. With symbols and abstractions people easily confuse themselves. They treat limited experiences and oversimplifications as if they were adequate summations of vast territories. With training in GS, people can become more extensional. They can learn: (a) how to attend to discrepancies between maps and territories, and (b) how to study structural relations between their words, feelings, judgments and experiences.

No one is wholly intensional, nor is anyone wholly extensional. That said, when people are caught up in their ideas without checking to see if the ideas correspond to reality, they are being intensional. When people mindlessly believe what they hear (or think), when they thoughtlessly rely upon abstractions, hearsay and definitions, they are practicing intensional orientations. When people bear intensional orientations, they are not merely misinformed and acting upon abstractions. They also are emotionally animated in their beliefs and commonly believe that they are correct because of their feelings. Accordingly, they feel no need to seek out information that challenges or contradicts their taken-for-granted worldview.

In contrast, when people learn how to refrain from believing everything that they hear, see, say or think, they are becoming extensional. Likewise, they are bearing a more extensional orientation when they give conditional status to their beliefs and when they pause to reflect upon their own judgments. When they openly seek to learn more about something, when they avoid assuming that they know everything that is to be known about something, when they delay their reactions to others' statements and deeds, they are growing more extensional. In a word, becoming more extensional means bringing adequate skepticism to one's beliefs; it also means subjecting beliefs (both one's own and others') to scrutiny and interrogation.

Consider, as another example, marijuana, pot, cannabis. (Notice how the different words carry different connotations and valuations). Many people who have never tried the drug, who have never been around anyone using it, and who have read very little scientific information about it, may, depending upon context, express rather strong opinions about it. This is being intensional. I am reminded of many well-meaning nuns where I went to grade school. They sought to educate pupils. They were trying to help, but, that granted, they were grossly misinformed and seemed to allow their feelings and beliefs to substitute for scientifically checked information. There are other people, those who have personally used it, those who have been around others using it, and those who have read a good deal of scientific information about it. They too might express rather strong opinions about the drug, but, if they are growing extensional, they remain open to evidence that is counter to their beliefs. They are willing to hear out claims and learn of facts that run against their current assumptions and orientations. They are willing to accept that they do not know all that there is to know, and they are willing to change beliefs accordingly.

The point of growing extensional is not to become so open minded that one's brain falls out, but rather, it is to learn how to keep in mind the fact that we chatter noises and often take our pronouncements way too seriously. We allow feelings, beliefs, assumptions, and symbolic representations to cloud over our relations with reality and with other people. These are marks of the childhood, perhaps the adolescence, of humanity. Growing extensional amounts to growing up; it means learning how to take responsibility for judgments. Growing extensional, one might say, means bringing a scientific attitude to ourselves within everyday life; it means trying to be more scientific in all aspects of knowing, judging, thinking, acting, etc. It is to speak with hedges and qualifications. It is to acknowledge uncertainty and retain a sense of deep humility. To begin, we simply admit that we commonly are overly intensional in our orientations, and, from there, we learn how to become increasingly extensional.

Now, given what has been said about growing extensional, the key question is: how extensional can people grow regarding humanity itself? This question, turned toward humanity, is slightly different than questions regarding cities or cannabis, for we, ourselves, are the very phenomenon in question.

Whatever lies outside of our direct experience is easily subject to intensional orientations. But does that mean that what is closest to us is thereby grasped extensionally? I think not. Surely we can (and often do) misunderstand ourselves. We can have erroneous or malformed views about ourselves. We can have opinions about what it means to be human without trying to verify for ourselves in a deep way if our orientations and assumptions are correct. And, to make matters worse, just as in the examples already mentioned (i.e., cities and drugs), people routinely take their feelings about things as evidence for the veracity of their beliefs. Furthermore, they act upon their beliefs in such a way as to make them seem and feel true. Such practices easily produce self-fulfilling prophecies and well illustrate what Korzybski meant by "logical fate." People basically take their feelings about their beliefs as proof for the trueness of those beliefs, and, thereby, entrench and institutionalize them. And, in tandem, people commonly take historical precedence as confirmation of inevitability. As Pula says in his *Guide for the Perplexed*, "Once a premise is accepted, we are 'fated' to reach related (derived) conclusions. Accepted assumptions have consequences" (p. 97). For these reasons, it can be challenging to grow extensional regarding humanity.

Seriously, how are people to understand themselves? Is it even possible to grasp, in a precise and non-self-deceiving way, how humans "fit" with the rest of the cosmos? What would it look like to grow extensional regarding humanity?

One of Korzybski's main achievements was precisely this kind of grand re-imagining of the human condition. He distinguished different classes of life, and, in doing so, he left a wealth of what sadly seems to me to be fairly unappreciated material. People have yet to come fully to terms with his many insights; they have yet to bring the full relevance of his claims into the 21st century.

Humanity and Human Wealth

To help people grow more extensional regarding humanity, I first, as a kind of precursor, need to stress once again the importance of being cautious regarding "either/or" thinking. I already underscored that people are not *either* intensional *or* extensional in their orientations; they are varying degrees of both. I here must preemptively address a couple of other places where dichotomous thinking can become highly problematic.

People commonly fall into forms of "either/or thinking," whereby an issue is considered in oversimplifications, often with all the good on one side and all the bad on the other side. One form appears wherever people suggest that "you" are *either* "with us" *or* "against us." Much contemporary political polarization moves around that dichotomy. But more subtle forms deserve consideration. I believe that the subtler forms, rightly approached and carefully considered, help to demonstrate the relevance of GS to political discourse and to help people grow extensional regarding humanity.

The two more subtle forms are: the tendency to dichotomize "personal effort" and "initiative" on the one hand, with "luck" and "good fortune" on the other hand. The other tendency is to set up an either/or framework for understanding the relationship between "self" and "other" and/or between "individual" and "collective." I begin with the latter and then move to the former. Then, considering these two in more detail, I review Korzybski's thinking on time-binding and its relation to economics. Growing extensional with regard to humanity amounts to resisting, as best as possible, the dichotomies addressed here while also attending to the kinds of wealth implied in time-binding. Finally, I consider some of the main takeaways for grasping contemporary politics and political discourse. As economic concerns and sensibilities undergird a good deal of political thought, I seek to show how economics, understood within GS, offers needed resources for thinking most broadly about politics.

Either/Or Fallacy Applied to "Individual" / "Collective"

Korzybski maintained that animals abstract but they are unaware of that fact. They experience events and objects in their environments but are not aware of the "process level of reality" underneath, nor are they aware of the possibilities of multiple verbal levels of abstraction (see Korzybski, 1993). Humans, in significant contrast, can gain "consciousness of abstracting." They can realize that their objects of sensory experience are comprised of sub-microscopic processes, and also, they can understand that those objects can be talked about at different levels of abstraction (e.g. description, inference, etc.). One of the main tasks of GS is to not confuse map and territory. We need: (a) to become aware of the various ways in which we cannot access the process level of reality directly, and (b) to acknowledge that we always deal with various abstractions, reductions, simplifications, etc.

In this context, then, the question that might reveal some relevant assumptions within political leanings is: which has a greater claim to primacy, which should be taken as more fundamental, the individual or the collective? *Which is the lower level of abstraction, which the higher?* That is to say, are individuals fundamentally real and society merely an abstraction of some individual's consciousness? Or, are collectives fundamentally real and individuals a kind of abstraction out from collective life? Which comes first (or is logically prior), the individual or the collective? Can there be either "self" or "other" without both? Perhaps people are social in their being, but, by thoroughgoing detribalization, they have created the appearance of a self-sufficient and independent individual. Or, conversely, perhaps concrete individuals, through various means of communication, have created the appearance of a society that is somehow more than individuals but is only an illusion.

The problem with the above lines of thinking is that any individual/collective split suffers from "*elementalism*," meaning that it is a confusion generated when we try to verbally tear asunder what remains inseparable outside of language and thought. We ought to grasp how they, "individual" and "collective," cannot be separated except verbally or in the imagination. Nevertheless, these questions lurk in the background of many political discussions. Just as one simple example, some libertarian narratives, at least broadly construed, suggest that individuals were free and unfettered until "the state" appeared and denied individuals their rights and liberties. Such a depiction underestimates the kinds of tyranny practiced within traditions and families (see Harari, 2018). Roughly speaking, prior to the emergence of the modern state, parents could do whatever they wanted with their children. They could beat their kids senseless, sell them into slavery, sell daughters as would-be brides, etc.

The key point in this context is to avoid the either/or logic altogether. People are both collective and individual, each dimension going all the way down (see Anton, 2001). All collectives are of made of individuals, and, yet, individual human beings never precede the collective that socialized them in their humanity. There simply is no way to settle it without rounding it out and oversimplifying it, and, thereby, confusing map for territory. One cannot separate individuals from collectives any more than one can separate space from time. Human existence as we know it is always *historically* constituted, which means buoyed in the wake of past others, both individual and collective.

Perhaps the best strategy is to admit the merits of each side, and to recognize that, depending upon context and issue, either could be depicted as primary and fundamental, but that the whole situation is also more complicated than that. Korzybski's notion of the "*time-binding class of life*," as I try to show later, precisely manages to find the way to humbly and gratefully accommodate both collective and individual without succumbing to "either/or" thinking.

To believe in everything or to believe in nothing, both are equally maladjusted and immature. The more difficult assignment, the one involved in growing up, is learning the limits of thoughts and beliefs as well as deciding what to believe and what not to believe. People must learn to assess how much confidence, realistically appraised, they ought to have regarding judgments-feelings-beliefs.

Either/Or Fallacy Applied to "Effort" / "Luck"

When people think about who deserves what, or when people reflect upon how much they personally have earned what they have, or how rightfully entitled they are to their socio-economic status, they commonly imagine that *either* they worked hard for what they have, *or* they were lucky. Two inverse correlates are: (a) "people don't have much of anything *because* they didn't work hard," and, (b) "people don't have much of anything *because* they have been unlucky." I am suggesting that many people incline toward a variety of either/other thinking when they abstractly think about how people's lives turn out. It is easy for someone who has become successful in some area to attribute that success to initiative, effort, competence, etc., but, obviously, there are other factors in addition to hard-work and good fortune. Effort and luck are not mutually exclusive, nor are sloth and misfortune mutually exclusive.

Keeping these two either/or fallacies in mind, I now review Korzybski's early articulation of the different classes of life. I show how this definition of humanity, as the time-binding class of life, provides ample resources for understanding the contemporary political world. Grasped in the right way, it undercuts "either/or thinking," and it aids in understanding key dynamics at play in political discourse.

The Time-Binding Class of Life

People struggle to think clearly about political issues for many different reasons. One main reason, I have been suggesting, amounts to shortcomings in self-understanding. It is not easy to grow extensional regarding humanity. We tend to look at ourselves through our assumptions and preconceptions; it is hard to apprehend our nature without prejudice. By the time we start to seriously inquire into our basic nature, we already have been shaped by our culture and its beliefs and language practices. Accordingly, it is easy to assume that common sense offers an adequate account of humanity. For some people, this means individuals are assumed to be immortal souls temporarily trapped inside physical bodies. For others, it means that humans are no different than any other animal. And note here that these different assumptions are not merely "beliefs." They become world-views and reality-tunnels that filter, shape, and color experience. These are also the source of many different kinds of self-fulfilling prophecies. Without realizing it (or the extent of it), people can act in ways that seek to validate their beliefs and assumptions as true or correct.

But the more we are honest with ourselves and the more informed about history and the world we become, the easier it is to recognize cultural beliefs and assumptions. Humanity simply does not "fit" within zoological classifications all that well, partly because of the wide variety of cultures across space and time. There is no particular *human* habitat, no particular *human* courtship or mating practices, no specifically *human* diet, no particular *human* religion. People around the world and throughout history have lived and died in so many different ways; human interests and beliefs, sexual practices and orientations, eating practices, goals and aspirations, sensibilities and values, all have been so different (for an interesting illustration, see Korzybski, 2002, pp. 47–49). But, and this cannot be underscored enough, it is not merely the wide variety of cultures and cultural practices across the globe and throughout history; it is the fact that humans across the lot are *time-binders*.

Humanity represents a different *dimension* within life. One of Korzybski's insights was to grasp the mathematically rigorous differences between a "point," a "line," a "surface," and a "cube." From there, he postulated that human life, in terms of time-binding, involved something structurally similar; he realized the existence of different dimensions. Korzybski writes:

> We can represent the different classes of life in three life coordinates. The minerals, with their inorganic activities would be the Zero (0) dimension of 'life' – that is the lifeless class – here represented by the point M.
>
> The plants, with their 'autonomous' growth, to be represented by their ONE DIMENSIONAL line MP.
>
> The animals, with their 'autonomous' capacity to grow and to be active in space by the TWO DIMENSIONAL plane PAM,
>
> The humans, with their 'autonomous' capacity to grow, to be active in space AND TO BE ACTIVE IN TIME, by the THREE DIMENSIONAL region, MAPH.

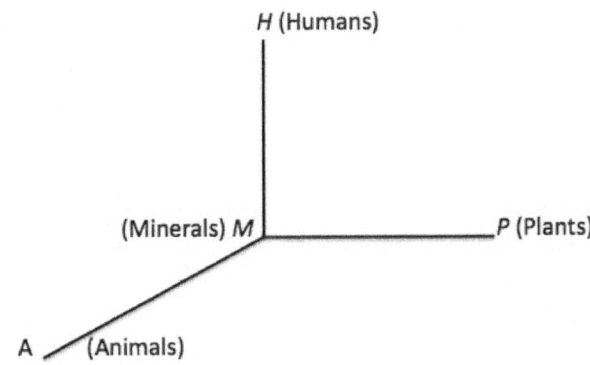

> Such diagrammatic illustrations must not be taken too literally; they are like figures of speech – helpful if understood – harmful if not understood. (1921, p. 61).

Different kinds of mathematical entities have their own properties. Moreover, the properties of a cube include those of point, line and surface, but they add something not found in any of these others. As Korzybski writes, "If we take, for example, a volume – say a cube – we see that the cube has surfaces and lines and points, but a volume is not a surface nor a line nor a point" (1921, p. 53). Hence, more than the "chemistry-binding" of plants, and more than the "space-binding" of animals, "time-binding" calls for radical re-discovery of what it means to be human. As Korzybski suggests, "… to treat a human being as an animal – as a mere space-binder – because humans have certain animal propensities, is an error of the same type and grossness as to treat a cube as a surface because it has surface properties" (1921, p. 60). He continues: "Applying animal standards to time-binding beings is like applying inches to measuring weight" (1921, p. 147). And, again, "… if we are studying the relations between surfaces and solids, it is fatal to mistake solids for surfaces; just so, too, if we stupidly confuse humans with animals" (1921, p. 151).

So what, exactly, are those dimensions or properties that come along with humanity but which are not there for mere space-binders? Well, as already mentioned, we can identify language and communication technologies. Humanity is distinguished by kinds of "symbolic transformation" and "abstraction" that undergird thought and culture alike (Dewey, 1988; Langer, 1942; Cassirer, 1944). Humans dwell within semantic environments. The human, as a time-binder, is the most malleable of creatures, the most subject to its own socio-historical/ cultural tampering. This means that language and symbolic activity paved the way for the incorporation of various communication technologies (alphabet, money, calendar, print, mirror, photograph, radio, television, computer, internet, etc.). Within all of these we also could include the worlds of art, mathematics, music, and science. I will be touching more upon these shortly, but, for now, to display Korzybski's contribution, I address various meanings of "wealth." The phenomenon of "wealth," I try to demonstrate, provides an exemplar of "properties" which emerge only with the time-binding class of life. The notion of time-binding, said otherwise, calls for a thorough re-evaluation of the phenomenon of wealth.

Animals may have conditions of more or less abundance, but that remains qualitatively different than the kinds of "surplus" found within humanity. Animals simply do not have "wealth" as we know it. Humans, on the other hand, have many different kinds of wealth, and wealth is not merely abundant resources used for survival. As Korzybski writes: "Properly understood, wealth consists of the fruits or products of this time-binding capacity... Animals do not produce wealth" (1921, p. 113). Only time-binding produces wealth.

Time-Binding and The Meaning of Wealth

We can advance how GS bears relevance to political discourse and politics by reviewing Korzybski's notion of time-binding, especially as represented in three chapters from *Manhood of Humanity*: "Wealth," "The Capitalist Era," and "The Survival of the Fittest." What is needed, I believe, is a review, appraisal, and updating.

Korzybski calls for a more extensional orientation to humanity, and to wealth in particular, where he writes

> ... let us, in so far as we can, regard the familiar terms – wealth, capital, and money – as unfamiliar; let us deal with them afresh; let us examine open-mindedly the facts – the phenomena – to which the terms relate and ascertain scientifically the significance the terms must have in a genuine science of human economy. (1921, p. 99)

Basically, he is asking people to carefully interrogate the degree to which their ideas regarding wealth and humanity are more false to facts than extensional. How well does our thinking about wealth capture the phenomenon? In his move to a more extensional orientation toward humanity and wealth, Korzybski furthermore suggests that: "It is necessary to analyze current conceptions of wealth, capital, and money – the childish conceptions of them – in order to reveal their false stupidity and folly" (1921, p. 100). He adds: "Many definitions of wealth, capital and money are to be found in modern books of political economy – definitions and books belonging to humanity's childhood" (1921, p. 100). In suggesting that people need to grow up and re-conceptualize the phenomenon by attending to it more honestly and in terms of time-binding, he is, once again, advocating a more extensional orientation to humanity.

In some ways, the many different benefits of culture, starting with language itself, are what we ought to include in our notions of wealth most broadly construed. We are the "wealth-producing" class of life. Korzybski identifies two kind of wealth, one he calls "material" and the other he calls "knowledge," both of which have "use-value." He further delineates these by suggesting that "The first kind perishes – the commodities composing it deteriorate and become useless. The other is permanent in character... The one is limited in time; the other unlimited in time; the former I call POTENTIAL USE-VALUE; the latter, KINETIC USE-VALUE" (1921, p. 114).

A more extensional view of things thus reveals two different kinds of use-value that emerge from time-binding: by "potential use-value," we mean all of the artifacts, antiques, heirlooms, homes, buildings, roads, bridges, irrigation canals, material things, etc. that have been left in the wake for others to use and enjoy. Some of these can be useful for a rather long time, even if they do breakdown, require repair, etc. Some of these are more or less personal possessions while others are collectively shared riches. In additional to those "potential use-values," there are what Korzybski calls, "kinetic use-values." These include immaterial forms of wealth such as ideologies, knowledge, languages, maneuvers, methods, practices, and techniques. They are sources of countless benefits for humans. Further clarifying his distinction, Korzybski writes:

> All potential use-values left to us by the dead are temporal and differ in utility. Many potential use-values are found in museums and have very limited value today in practical life... Kinetic use-values are permanent in character, for, though they may become antiquated, they yet serve as the foundation for the developments that supersede them, and so they continue to live in that to which they lead. (1921, p. 120)

Human wealth is, therefore, so much more than large stores of "money." It is also more than merely individual possessions and resources. Korzybski rejects traditional definitions of both wealth and capital because he sees that the phenomenon of time-binding enervates the integrity of the distinction. As he furthermore states:

> The fundamental importance of time as a factor in the production of wealth – the fact that wealth and use-values of wealth are literally the natural offspring of the spiritual union of time with toil – has been completely overlooked, not only by the economics, but by the ethics, the jurisprudence, and the other branches of speculative reasoning, throughout the long period of humanity's childhood. (1921, pp. 116–117)

Contrasting that childish position, he outlines a more extensional orientation where he claims

> ... wealth consists of those things – whether they be material commodities or forms of knowledge and understanding – that have been produced by the time-binding energies of humanity, and according to which *nearly all of the wealth in the world at any given time is the accumulated fruit of the toil of past generations* – the living work of the dead... This fact, of supreme ethical importance, applies to *all* of us; none of us may speak or act as if the material or spiritual wealth we have were produced by us; for, if we be not stupid, we must see that what we call *our* wealth, *our* civilization, everything we use or enjoy, is in the main the product of the labor of men now dead, some of them slaves, some of them 'owners' of slaves. The metal spoon or the knife which we use daily is a product of the work of many generations, including those who discovered metal and the use of it, and the utility of the spoon. And here arises a most important question: Since the wealth of the world is in the main the free gift of the past – the fruit of the labor of the dead – to whom does it rightly belong? The question cannot be evaded. Is the existing monopoly of the great-inherited treasures produced by dead men's toil a normal and natural evolution? Or is it an artificial status imposed by the few upon the many? Such is the crux of the modern controversy. (1921, pp. 115; 124)

So here we have it. Although we as space-binders can divide things up and claim ownership, there are ancient others, long since dead, to whom we *all* owe an immeasurable debt for the wealth we enjoy. Our common lot is one of immense indebtedness to the labors, toil and sacrifice, of the now dead. This is partly why political divisions, animalistic spatial divisions, are somewhat dubious and highly immature.

Obviously, it would be a mistake to speak in broad abstractions regarding "capitalists" and "socialists." The terms "capitalist" and "socialist" are too abstract, and each category holds a wide range within it. But, that acknowledged, I would suggest that, roughly speaking (and oversimplifying of course), some capitalists wish to gain the wealth of the dead and keep it for themselves while some socialists wish to disperse the wealth equally to all. It is as if such capitalists underestimate how much the wealth came from the toil of others now dead, while such socialists underestimate the need for accrued wealth to be rightly used by living people if the wealth is to continue to benefit humanity. In either case, Korzybski, I believe rightly, asserts, "Whether we be capitalists or socialists or neither, we must learn that to prey upon the treasure left by the dead is to live, not the life of a human being, but that of a *ghoul*" (1921, p. 133). To grasp the time-binding class of life, we need to appreciate how much we in the present are indebted to all of the others who came before us.

For too long people have made a virtue of selfishness, called it natural to humans. They then unwittingly proceeded to create institutions that invite personal greed and selfishness and cast them as honorable principles of human conduct. Not only did people, over many centuries, create institutions that enabled them to practice greed and selfishness in the name of "proper behavior," but many even assimilated popular notions of Darwinian "survival of the fittest." Unfortunately, this lowers humanity down to the level of animals.

> … We shrug our shoulders in acquiescence and proclaim greed and selfishness to be the very core of human nature, take it all for granted, and let it pass at that…, but it belies the characteristic nature of man… to call SUCH a class a *naturally* selfish class is not only nonsensical but monstrous. (1921, pp. 142–143)

And, to make matters even worse, those who own major communication networks – who have the power to amplify their voices – have often helped to distort truth, to misinform and systematically hide from the obvious facts of time-binding (see Korzybski, 1921). They come to have a vested interest in promulgating a narrative that oversimplifies the relationship between individual and collective and the complex dual nature of effort and luck.

People have learned to treat themselves as animals in a "rat race." They assume a "stab and grab" world, where people imagine that they "*deserve*" what they have; they believe that people earned their wealth (or deserve their poverty). Some people are wealthy and accomplished, and they have worked hard to get what they have, but they also may underestimate the amount of luck, fortunate circumstance, and sheer caprice within their lives. They may have been born into families of great affluence and may have had their parents buy them out of difficulties and set them up for success. Not everyone gets that luxury. There are others who have worked hard but were not rightly connected, some who had illnesses or sick family members. At the least, we need to appreciate that *no one can rightfully claim control over where and when they were born.*

People need to fully grasp how much of what they enjoy and what they call their own is actually the product of the effort and work of people now deceased. We dwell in the wealth that is left in the wake of the departed. Look around your room right now. Carefully examine any object that you see. Ask yourself: how did it get here? How long has this been in existence? What made is possible? Pens and notepads are illuminating: the ability to read and write, the capacity to take notes and plan things out on paper, none of these are one's own inventions. Not one of us "invented" writing; none of us invented pen or ink, nor paper. So much know-how was required, so much passing down over many generations. We, those fortunate enough to live in the modern western world, simply take these things for granted.

When we speak of "survival of the fittest" within the animal kingdom and within humanity we are significantly changing the meaning of the expression. The "fittest" of humanity refers to "the finest," "most excellent" forms of potential and kinetic use-values, gathered across generations, which are so much more than personal possessions or accrued capital. As Korzybski suggests, "Survival of the fittest, where *fittest* means *best* in science and art and wisdom, is a *natural* law for mankind, the time-binding class of life" (1921, p. 154). People need to grow up and see that resources and money need to be used not solely for private consumption and personal indulgence, but rather, for further producing the best potential and kinetic use-values. Again, it's vampiristic and ghoulish to consume without attempting to generate more and better use-values.

People do seem to live as ghouls. They seem so inclined to take more than they need, despite that fact that they are not any better for it. People need to understand how wealth relates to the commonly made philosophical distinctions between "having" and "being." People want to have wealth, want to own a great deal, but they seem not to grasp what it means to be wealthy. One can have lots of stuff but not be wealthy just as one can have somewhat meager material possessions and still be very well off.

I perhaps here need to make a very brief digression on the history of money and economic exchange (see McLuhan, 2003). Money, in its earliest forms, existed as things, commodities, staples, material goods, something of value in its own right (e.g. potential use-values). Early barter economies traded in food or products or services. Even precious metals (e.g. gold or silver) were physical materials, and, as such, they were stores of work already accomplished. Then came paper money, representative money. People want representative money not for itself, but rather, because of what it represents and can fetch. Representative money thus serves instrumental ends. That is to say, people want representative money because they want all the goods and services that money furnishes. In the twentieth century, as print money was removed from the gold standard, it has become nearly synonymous with information, digitalized representations of stored labor and credit, (i.e., the promise of future work to be done). This means that money has become largely a kinetic-use value. Money, and economic exchange, has grown into agreed upon techniques for exchanging values and representing stores of work, hence the proliferation of local and regional currencies. The history and evolution of money is a story of a transition from the dominance of potential use-values to the reign of kinetic use-values, a transition that includes an exponential growth in kinetic use-values. This has significant implications. Part of what is at stake, in this context, concerns the differences between using money in service of creature comforts and using money in service of time-binding relevance and purpose.

Should we, then, be inclined toward either "democratic socialism" or to "trickle-down economics?" Using Korzybski's ideas as my frame, I suggest that we strive for what could perhaps be called *"time-binding economics"* or *"wisdom economics,"* which has elements of both "the left" and "the right" embedded within. People need to understand their time-binding nature. They must realize that wealth, both possible use-values and kinetic use-values, are robbed of their usefulness if they are stagnant and not part of the perpetuation of further trans-generational wealth. This means that hoarding money is just as ill advised as is evenly distributing it to everyone. It also means that each person assumes adulthood only as they take on the heroic task of trying to generate the most excellent use-values in their own consumption of already existing wealth.

Wealth and the Age of Superabundance

Korzybski's account of the relationships between humanity, time-binding and wealth makes clear that the twenty-first century begs for the adulthood of humanity. People need to grow up, sooner rather than later. The age of superabundance is upon us, and it is not an unrelenting good for all (also see Anton, 2024). Admittedly, we, those living in the current United States, live in an age of unprecedented comfort, convenience, ease, and safety. Never before have individuals used less effort to have so much delivered to them and provided for them. Middle-class life in the United States and in most parts of the modern industrialized world resembles life that only royalty could imagine throughout antiquity. People live with centralized heating and cooling, indoor plumbing, electricity, running hot water, and refrigeration. They enjoy fruits and vegetables shipped from around the globe. Nevertheless, the age of superabundance includes the possibilities for mass self-indulgence and cultural decadence as well as possibilities for extreme social inequality. People in the age of superabundance may be serious trouble both to themselves and to others. In the age of superabundance, greed and selfishness are toxic all around. This is partly why people, now more than ever, need to grow extensional regarding humanity. They need to understand their nature as the time-binding class of life and they need to see it for its implications regarding political economy.

As already suggested, language is the ultimate gift of human wealth. It is the supreme exemplar of kinetic use-value. Babies are not born speaking the particular language they will come to know as their "mother tongue." Language is part of the real but not physical culture that is bestowed. It is handed down, generation after generation (Langer, 1942). This also means that human babies are born incomplete in a more thoroughgoing way than other animals. Humans are the most plastic of beings, and they have the most prolonged maturational periods. This is not without consequence. It means that the phenomenon of language can elude comprehension because it is learned from others; people routinely assume that language stands primarily in the service of communication and/or practical ends. On the contrary, although it is learned from other people, language equally (or perhaps primarily) helps to build the architecture of articulate thought and enables individuals to gain various degrees of conscious control over aspects of cognition and mental life. In a word, language is inherently collective as well as individual: to speak is to speak a language that one did not invent, and yet, each person has a unique lexicon and uses language somewhat uniquely. Moreover, brain development and command over cognitive resources partly depends upon language acquisition. Language, then, is no mere window dressing upon mind. It is partly how foresight, reflection and recollection come into being (Dewey, 1988). Language helps to generate an internal workspace for consideration of possible states of affairs (see Dehaene, 2014).

Language makes humans the wealthy animal. To learn language, to fall into a particular culture, is to gain otherwise unimaginable wealth, and none of it is private property. Language exemplifies *shared* wealth, a wealth given freely across eons. We potentially slip into an under-appreciation of language and time-binding if we suggest that humans are simply animals who "have" language. That makes it seem as if language is simply one more attribute or characteristic of an animal, a potential use-value rather than a kinetic use-value. It is not that language makes us time-binders; it is that only organisms who are in time as we are would have need for language (see Herder, 1966). And, there is a spiral of influence that goes from the human to the environment and from the environment to the human (see Korzybski, 1993). This is partly what is meant by the notion of time-binding. To be human is to bear the wealth of socio-historical-cultural existence.

Language has helped to make a world that now requires language. And literacy illustrates this point even more so: phonetic literacy, as a technique for apprehending the spoken word, helps to extend and amplify the riches provided by language. It enables new modes of cognition and of thinking about thinking (see Olson, 2016). But, note, only in literate societies can someone be illiterate. More will be said on this in a moment but the point here is that through time, language and literacy paved the way for countless communication technologies upon which people and societies today depend. Communication technologies such as calendars, clocks, computers and cell phones have revolutionized the modern world. The last 150 years have witnessed an unprecedented growth in human wealth. Many young people today, even those in lower or middle-class United States, enjoy entertainments such as music, videos, video games, other forms of engagement that occur at the push of a button.

Consider some of the wide ranges of wealth available to the general public today. As I write this, I am listening to Blue Lake Public Radio, which is broadcast locally in West Michigan, though people anywhere in the world can tune-in online. The station just played some fine symphony selections from Dmitri Shostakovich, followed by some compositions by Gustav Mahler. Such exquisite programming floats in the airwaves, available to anyone who has a radio or Internet connection. Many young people today listen to Pandora, Spotify, or Radio Garden. They select the kind of genres or artists they desire and can tune into to a wide array of music, and it is all either free or relatively inexpensive.

People can go to YouTube and gain knowledge regarding just about anything: they can pick up tips from a five-star chef on how to cook a standing-rib roast; they can learn how to program in java script; they can learn how to hang drywall; they can learn how to do intermittent fasting; they can learn a wide range of yoga poses; they can learn how to change a *Moen* faucet head. Beside the wealth of such kinetic use-values, YouTube provides a wide array of materials that are ends to be enjoyed in their own right (e.g. potential use-values). People can listen to music, watch stand-up comedy, watch movies, documentaries, interviews, listen to lectures, etc. The amount of material available for no cost other than a computer and Internet service is truly staggering, and I am not even including the streaming services such as HULU or HBO or Amazon Prime.

Another example of superabundance comes from comparing encyclopedia sets to Wikipedia. Encyclopedia sets were once a staple of middle-class life. They were fairly expensive but were assumed to be a reasonable investment because of the wealth of information they contained. Today, with Wikipedia at their fingertips, anyone with Internet access can go to the site and find amazingly rich information. Imagine printing out the entire contents of Wikipedia, compiling it into a collection that would be the equivalent of an Encyclopedia set. What would be the size and cost of such a set? Wikipedia, obviously, is an amazing collective wealth. Note that it is crowd-sourced, collectively generated and shared. The general point is that modern media forms provide an abundance of both kinds of wealth: material prosperity to be enjoyed in its own regard but also a wide range of repeatable techniques and procedures.

Another way to get at superabundance is to consider the proliferation of generative artificial intelligence systems for creating images. Programs such as "Dall-E 2," "Midjourney," and "Stable Diffusion" produce stunningly beautiful images. By typing in a few prompts, people can create images that rival some of the most beautiful art. It is truly astonishing and breathtaking (also see Anton, 2023). Across the past few centuries, some people have spent oodles of money on art, some of which is of dubious artistic merit, but the high cost has been accepted because the art was "rare" or produced by a "famous" artist. When people fetishize art in this way, when they spend millions of dollars for a painting or sculpture so that they can personally own it, they are not being "fittest." Generative AI image technologies, as more and more people come to use them, make of every person a potential artist. They enable anyone with Internet access to personally generate some of the most sought after forms of material wealth throughout Western history: beautiful works of art. Said otherwise, generative AI systems radically diminish the scarcity of art.

Perhaps one of the most interesting cases of superabundance here regards "Alpha Fold," Google's AI for determining the folding of proteins. According to a recent conference presentation, Alpha Fold has accomplished in a few weeks what would have taken 400 million years of research, and scientists can now accurately predict the folding of 200+ million different proteins, basically all known proteins! (See ColdFusion's YouTube video, *Google Strikes Back*"). It is hard to know, exactly, what this means for the future of healthcare, disease prevention, etc. but, at the least, it means massive change. Furthermore, who will have access to such technologies? Will they be available for all or only for the few? Are such discoveries equally useable for good as for ill? What will happen if AI systems somehow make possible endless renewable energy, or, what if they create blueprints for inexpensive technologies that can desalinate ocean water and make it potable? These questions point to nebulous and hard to predict consequences, and they will be even more so if and when advanced AI systems crack basic laws of physics and quantum mechanics, biochemistry and evolutionary biology, etc.

I suggested above that the age of superabundance should not be taken as an unrelenting good, especially if humanity remains in its childhood of self-understanding. At this juncture, it perhaps would help to consider some of the ways that today's superabundance poses challenges and difficulties.

The older generations sometimes disparage younger generations for not being interested in employment. They lament that young people today "do not want to work" and that they "expect something for nothing." People also commonly comment that this generation, the millennials, will be the first generation in a long time to not be better off than their parents. Even if this is true in some senses (teen suicide rates, rates of depression and anxiety, incarceration rates, rates of home ownership, etc.), there are other metrics (longevity, hygiene and sanitation, child labor, rates of violence, etc.) that show how everyone in the modern industrialized U.S. is basically better off than all previous generations (see Tupy and Pooley, 2022). Moreover, even if there is a growing disparity between the "rich" and the "poor," the poor in the U.S. have never had it better, especially if we consider the proliferation of kinetic use-values. It is hard to keep everything in proper perspective when the baseline keeps rising.

Part of the trouble here is that many who express concerns about the younger generation seem to under-register how much work and living conditions have changed. This is part of the meaning of superabundance: young people today, assuming that are not utterly destitute and struggling to survive, have comforts and conveniences largely unknown prior to the 20th century. They live as minor deities, enjoying diversions available at the snap of a finger. It seems ever easier for people to be pleasurably distracted and amused (see Postman, 1985). People now enjoy forms of entertainment that were simply unimaginable a century or two ago. Music streaming services, social media platforms, and multiplayer online video games are just some of the distractions available. But it is more than that.

Imagine having a time machine, taking a camera back 200 years and photographing nothing but people's hands over the last two centuries. I think such photographs would be quite revealing. Hands, generally speaking, have changed significantly. In the past, they were thick, rough, and weathered. They were gnarly. People often had scars, injuries or missing digits and fingers. Today things are different. People type and text message; they are basically paper-pushers and information-movers. Their hands have grown soft and the skin on their hands has never been thinner. Many peoples' hands hardly have been worked, as many people have never known manual labor or experienced physical hardship and/or danger on the job.

The above can be addressed in different terms and from a different angle. Such an angle change is necessary because these issues are highly complex. The thin skin of today's hands also means that many jobs have been streamlined and made more efficient. Jobs have more automation in today's world, and in many ways people's jobs have increasingly been reduced to pushing buttons or moving information. Additionally, a good deal of the personal element, the slow and natural pace of activity and interaction, has been designed out from the job in the name of efficiency and increased productivity. Work for many people is less social and less enjoyable. It is less spontaneous and more routinized. It is often less meaningful too, as competence and skill have taken a backseat to automated technique and technological innovation.

Perhaps not surprisingly, people have never been so sedentary. In the U.S. we face an obesity epidemic. People simply do not get enough exercise and they have an almost limitless amount of food conveniently available. The age of superabundance means many people routinely eat "drive-through fast food," which often carries massive caloric loads of fatty and sugary foods. Superabundance means more choices, greater range of available products. It also means that many people consume super-processed foods that are quick and easy, hot and ready to go.

Some of these observations also require a little emendation. Both forms of wealth (i.e., potential use-values and kinetic use-values) are subject to kinds of inflation. One the one hand, it is commonly known that antiques (i.e., potential use-value), especially ones in mint condition, can fetch a high price at auction. Also, artifacts and relics, even ones not fully functional, can command large sums of money for their acquisition. But, on the other hand, people may attend less to the kinds of "symbolic inflation" that accompanies kinetic use-values. It is perhaps because kinetic use-values become environmental that their inflation commonly travels below attention. Moreover, this is also part of the problematic underbelly to the age of superabundance.

By the term "symbolic inflation," I refer to the practices, techniques and procedures of a given generation, which enable forms of improvement, but, in turn, elevate demands upon those who would engage them and perpetuate them. What was achieved and bestowed becomes a necessity soon enough; what was a hard won and novel accomplishment can in time become a baseline expectation for all. This point cannot be overstressed. It is, as already mentioned, clearly evident in literacy, but it also can be found in countless areas of everyday life.

Allow me to offer an illustrative example. It is somewhat cherry-picked but I believe that it serves as a useful metaphor for changes that have happened throughout the entire culture in a relatively short time. Compare the performances, the actual movements, that earned a gold medal in gymnastics at the 1960 Olympic games to those that earned a gold medal at the 2016 Olympic games. Go look for yourself. Clearly, demands upon Olympic athletes have elevated significantly. But it is not just Olympic athletes who have been pressed into ever greater and more demanding feats. The same could be said for all of athletics today. My father was a collegiate athlete. He went to college on a baseball scholarship, but he also played college football. Today, this is impossible: collegiate athletes, to retain their scholarships, must sign papers where they agree to not play in other sports, as they might get injured. Moreover, the professionalization of sports means that many athletes have been training in their respective sports since they were children. Sports today are ultra-competitive. Look at the U.S. football players from the 1970s and compare them to the football players in 2023. In the 1970's many of the players look like "normal" guys, of relatively average size. Today, not so much. Many have been in weight-training programs their entire lives and some have taken steroids to bulk up. It is not uncommon to see some guys who are gigantic.

It perhaps also helps to make some distinctions regarding the kinds of demands implied by different kinetic use-values. Consider the wide range of techniques and methods that are available on YouTube. People can learn just about anything and everything imaginable, from how to do magic tricks to how to start a fire in the wild. But notice the difference between, on the one hand, a recipe (which can be easily followed and executed) and, on the other hand, recommendations on how to play the violin or juggle five clubs (both of which require dedication, practice, and maybe even skill). This is an important difference, and one that makes a difference. The age of superabundance means that some of the kinetic use-values are from people around the world; the "competition" occurs at a global scale. Internet information enables people to gain access to the "best of the best" in countless different areas. They can see what is possible (and what is happening) outside their local and regional environments. This often serves to elevate competition, but also can discourage some people from even attempting, given how talented some people seem to be. Watching video after video of other people performing amazing feats of talent, self-disciplined tricks, or expert stunts can be inspiring for some people, and yet, it can encourage in others attitudes of resignation and feelings of irrelevance.

In the age of superabundance people are easily positioned to become bystanders, onlookers, listeners and spectators who sit on the sidelines of life. This is partly why Marshall McLuhan, in *Understanding Media*, subtitled his chapter on the phonograph: "The Toy that Shrank the National Chest." Before the proliferation of recorded music, everyone was inclined to sing and make music as best as they could. After recorded music saturated peoples' lives, the division between musician and non-musician grew thick, and many people stopped thinking of themselves as "singers."

So many forms of engagement and entertainment are mediated and made possible through electricity. They commence when someone turns "on" some electronic gadget. With so many "on" buttons in their lives (TVs, radios, computers, streaming services, etc.), people gain access to worlds that "go on" without them. Hence, some children today are content to watch videos of other children playing with toys. Some watch others play video games while some watch other children open birthday presents. Pornography consumption is high, and yet people in general are not having as much sex as they used to have. It may be the case that some young people have watched so many different acts performed by expert sex workers (i.e., "porn stars") that they have come to believe that they personally would be unable to "live up" to such sex. Porn consumption may also contribute unwittingly to performance anxiety, which perhaps leads some individuals to give up on sex with other people altogether. At the least, it encourages shallower forms of intimacy and aligns with "hook-up" culture.

The techniques and practices of yesterday bring with them expectations, demands, and protocols of tomorrow. There is also the issue of the material world already having been divvied up among those who came earlier. The world has much of its material wealth, prime real estate for example, already divided up and owned. Many young people somewhat feel as if they are caught playing a game of Monopoly where the other players have had a head start and all of the properties are already owned by the other players. They are left to play it out, moving around the board, with very little opportunity for purchasing any of the properties.

Concluding Remarks

People sometimes try to capture the sense that "no amount of money ever seems to be enough" by saying, "Well, the more you make, the more you spend." To which, others, those who want more money, likely respond: "Exactly, I want to *spend* more!" Here, in this context, it helps to reflect upon the expression, "*Money doesn't buy happiness.*" This expression means different things depending upon who says it, to whom, and in what context. It could mean something along the lines of "accumulating capital in excess results in diminishing returns of happiness," which is very different than something along the lines of "people who do not have the basic necessities of life have not been denied happiness and therefore should learn to be content with what they do have."

Many people have so much and yet (or maybe because of it) they remain deeply unhappy. Korzybski offers what he calls "the extensional theory of happiness," which amounts to having minimal to no expectations (2002, pp. 89–92). Expectations create the conditions for unhappiness and disappointment. But perhaps cultural progress and advancement, the benefits that come from time-binding, are thereby subject to being unappreciated. People, being a bit ghoulish and/or immature, take the accomplishments of previous generations as granted and then expect too much. Dennis Gabor (1972) suggested that his theory of happiness is that people fail to appreciate what they get without effort. Along similar lines, Antoine de Saint-Exupery (1950) wrote that he always preferred people of the monastery to people who live a secular life. The former, wholly without worldly possessions, are not any happier than the latter, but, he suggests, they are much less likely to be fooled as to the source of their happiness. He also adds a key piece of wisdom: "... those who content themselves with luxury bought from the merchants are none the better for it – even though they feast their eyes only on perfection – if, to begin with, they themselves have created nothing" (1950, p. 31). If we are to grow up and grow extensional regarding humanity, we may need to move away from "individual consumer capitalism" and make more and more room for "collectivist producer capitalism" (see Anton, 2010a, pp. 133–135).

In the age of superabundance, when AI systems will soon be able to do just about anything with a few computer keystrokes, *there will be little to do other than cultivate yourself.* AI systems might be able to help you build your vocabulary, but they cannot be your vocabulary, or, you literally don't know what you are talking about. AI systems might be able to offer diet and fitness advice, but they cannot eat for you, nor can they do the needed exercise on your behalf. AI systems might be able to give instruction and useful tips on how to play a musical instrument, but they cannot bestow a virtuoso's competency upon you: such mastery comes only with practice and dedication.

If people are ever to grow up, they must do a better job of *sharing* and *taking turns* (see Anton, 2020). They need to appreciate how much they stand indebted to the labors of those have come before them. Making sure that everyone has basic health care is more important than providing more luxury for the wealthy. Why? Well, there is a basic law of diminishing marginal utility. As Barry Schwartz nicely sums it up: "As the rich get richer, each additional unit of wealth satisfies them less" (2016, p. 69).

Along the shoreline on Lake Michigan, one can find many extravagant and expensive houses. Some of these mansions, worth millions of dollars, are occupied a couple of months a year. When I see such homes, I think that this could be wonderful if and only if there were not so many homeless people, if only people had access to affordable housing and healthcare. According to Bernie Sanders' Facebook page, "In the Cayman Islands, there is a modest five-story building that is home to 18,857 companies. Either this is one very crowded building, or it is a phony address used by 18,000 plus corporations for one purpose: to avoid paying taxes to the United States of America" (2020).

The problem here is so obvious. People are doing well but avoiding carrying their portion of shared burdens. Even as they suspect that their actions are morally questionable, people do what is legal. Because so many people confuse morality with legality, we need better laws, less childish laws, ones that make wealthy persons more socially accountable (see Anton, 2010b).

Take the current crises regarding the possibility of either cutting social security benefits or raising the age of retirement to 70 years old. How can these possibly be the solutions when so many billionaires and multimillionaires avoid paying taxes? There is nothing wrong with some people being paid extravagantly so long as there are basic care and housing for the elderly and indigent.

People need to understand that after a certain amount of comfort and convenience, they can only get so happy from such things. Basic care for all, rather than extravagance for the affluent, seems the most mature and sane response. This is not to shake a finger at those who own more things than others; it is to ask them how well they understand themselves and how they connect to all that is. People all need the courage to ask themselves how fittingly or passionately have they produced high-quality "use-values," both potential and kinetic, given all that that they have received gratis from those others, now dead, who have come before them.

References

Anton, C. (2001). *Selfhood and authenticity.* SUNY Press.
Anton, C. (2010a). *Sources of significance: Worldly rejuvenation and neo-stoic heroism.* Purdue University Press.
Anton, C. (2010b). *Valuation and media ecology: Ethics, morals, and laws.* (Ed.). Hampton Press.
Anton. C. (2020). *How non-being haunts being: On possibilities, Morality, and Death acceptance.* Fairleigh Dickinson University Press.
Anton, C. (2023). *A.EYE CANDY: A museum of imaginary robots and other digital delights.* Institute of General Semantics.

Anton, C. (2024). "Key Technologies in the Rise of the Age of Superabundance," *Explorations in Media Ecology: The Journal of the Media Ecology Association*, 23(4): 349–363

Cassirer, E. (1944). *An essay on man*. Yale University Press.

ColdFusion. (2023, May 18). *Google strikes back* [Video]. YouTube. https://www.youtube.com/watch?v=Qa4K7XsRO0g&t=763s

Dehaene, S. (2014). *Consciousness and the brain: Deciphering how our brain codes our thoughts*. Penguin Books.

Dewey, J. (1988). *The later works of John Dewey, 1925–1953. Vol. 1: 1925. Experience and nature*. Southern Illinois University Press.

de Saint-Exupéry, A. (1950). *The wisdom of the sands* (S. Gilbert, Trans.). University of Chicago Press.

Gabor, D. (1972). *The mature society*. Praeger Publishers.

Harari, Y. N. (2018). *Sapiens: A brief history of humankind*. Harper Publishing.

Herder, J. G. (1966). *Essay on the origin of language* (A. Gode, Trans.). University of Chicago Press.

Langer, E. (1992). "Interpersonal Mindlessness and Language," *Communication Monographs*, 59(3), 324–327.

Langer, S. K. (1942). *Philosophy in a new key: A study in the symbolism of reason, rite and art*. Mentor Books.

Korzybski, A. (1993). *Science and sanity: An introduction to non-aristotelian systems and general semantics* (5th ed.). The International Non-Aristotelian Library/Institute of General Semantics.

Korzybski, A. (2001). *Manhood of humanity* (2nd ed.). Institute of General Semantics.

Korzybski, A. (2002). *General semantics seminar 1937: Olivet College lectures* (3rd ed.). Institute of General Semantics.

McLuhan, M. (2003). *Understanding media: The extensions of man*. Gingko Press.

Olson, D. R. (2016). *The mind on paper: Reading, consciousness, and rationality*. Cambridge University Press.

Postman, N. (1985). *Amusing ourselves to death: Public discourse in the age of show business*. Penguin Books.

Pula, R. R. (2000). *A general-semantics glossary: Pula's guide for the perplexed*. International Society for General Semantics.

Sanders, B. (2020, March 6). In the Cayman Islands, there is a modest five-story building that is home to 18,857 companies. Either this is one... [Facebook status update]. Facebook. https://www.facebook.com/senatorsanders/posts/10158753809202908/

Schwartz, B. (2016). *The paradox of choice*. HarperCollins Publications.

Tupy, M. L., & Pooley, G., L. (2022). *Superabundance: The story of population growth, innovation, and human flourishing on an infinitely bountiful planet*. Cato Institute.

*Note: I wish to thank Thom Gencarelli for support and encouragement, and I wish to thank Barry D. Liss and Jermaine Martinez. I also need to express deep thanks to Valerie V. Peterson. I should acknowledge, too, that an earlier version of this paper was presented at the 2023 Alfred Korzybski Memorial Lecture and Symposium.

CHAPTER 2

THE DOUBLE-BIND OF RATIONAL POLITICAL DISCOURSE
LANCE STRATE

Introduction

The year was 1992, a presidential election year in the United States, and I was teaching a graduate course on media ecology. One of the books assigned for the class was Neil Postman's *Amusing Ourselves to Death: Public Discourse in the Age of Show Business*, published in 1985, and the discussion turned to the effects of television on election campaigns. As we considered the negative impact of the electronic media on American politics, one student asked, *will democracy survive*? The response came to me quite spontaneously, and I answered almost immediately, *has it*? The question was left hanging in the air; to this day, it remains suspended by all accounts. The first question, *will democracy survive?*, presupposes that democracy has survived so far, and the second question, *has democracy survived?*, presupposes that democracy did exist at one time. This in turn suggests a third question, *did democracy ever exist in the first place?* These questions form the basis of continued philosophical and sociological inquiry and debate. From the standpoint of general semantics, however, they are not altogether meaningful and therefore problematic for the simple reason that democracy is a high level abstraction, one that is lacking a universally agreed upon operational definition. What is abundantly clear is that the term democracy is often invoked in a vague and ambiguous manner, that it represents a category applied to a wide variety of types of government and politics, that these different types of government and politics themselves change and evolve over time, and that the term is often used to refer to or include phenomena closely related to and yet distinct from democracy itself, such as the rule of law, values such as freedom, equality, and justice, and the idea of the open society. My concern here, I hasten to add, is not with definitions of democracy or taxonomies of different kinds of democracies. For my purposes, I find it sufficient to invoke Abraham Lincoln's eloquent expression that democracy amounts to *government of the people, by the people, and for the people.* Admittedly, this rhetorical formulation is a far cry from an operational definition, but its association with the American republic is significant, in that my focus is on democracy as has been established via the United States Constitution, and similar forms of western-style liberal democracies, however imperfect they may be.

Moreover, my purpose in this essay is to consider the relationship between democracy and reason, that is, between democratic politics and rational political discourse. As a product of the Enlightenment, modern democracy emerged out of a particular kind of semantic environment, a particular type of media environment. What then has happened as the semantic and media environments that gave birth to democracy have been changed and transformed? This was very much a concern for Postman (1985), who argued that the television medium has had a deleterious effect on American politics and government. If anything, these concerns remain and have grown with the expansion of television via cable, satellite, and streaming services, and the addition of the internet, the web, social media, and mobile devices (Strate, 2014). As we near the end of the first quarter of the 21st century, many consider us now to be experiencing a crisis of democracy, and express a very real fear that it is in decline and in danger of disappearing altogether. In this context, my intention here is to contribute to our understanding of politics and the open society, with the fervent hope, to invoke Lincoln once more, that democratic government *shall not perish from the earth*.

General Semantics and Politics

Postman's (1985) familiarity with general semantics contributes to his analysis of the effects of television on American politics, as can be seen by his emphasis on public discourse (see also, Postman, 1992, 1995, 1999; Postman, Weingartner, & Moran, 1969). His former colleague, S.I. Hayakawa, was the most successful popularizer of general semantics, and went on to serve a term as a United States Senator from California. Another prominent scholar associated with general semantics, Anatol Rapoport, is often considered the founder of Peace Studies. And the author of the first popular book on general semantics, Stuart Chase (1938), coined the phrase *new deal*, which Franklin Delano Roosevelt adopted as the slogan representing his economic policies (Chase, 1932a, 1932b). Indeed, the introduction of general semantics itself, via the publication of Alfred Korzybski's *Science and Sanity* (1933/2023), is commonly grouped together with other scholarship devoted to the analysis and criticism of language and symbols in the early 20th century following the First World War; this sudden interest has been attributed to the newfound concern regarding mass communication (including the new medium of radio broadcasting), the growth of advertising and the public relations industry, research and applications in the area of public opinion, and innovations in mass persuasion and propaganda. While certainly relevant, these associations obscure the fact that general semantics is more broadly concerned with epistemology and empiricism, and that it all started with an attempt to apply science to society.

Stemming from his background in science, technology, engineering, and mathematics, Alfred Korzybski advocated for a technocratic form of government in his first book, *Manhood of Humanity*, originally subtitled *The Science and Art of Human Engineering* (1921, 1950). What was needed, he argued, was government based on reason and evidence, as could only be administered by individuals with the appropriate training in empirical research methods, in other words, scientists and engineers. He pointed to the amazing progress that had been made in science and technology over the course of the modern era, taking off during the Enlightenment and leading to the Industrial Revolution. This was in sharp contrast to the tragic persistence of irrationality in all other aspects of human relations, and its concomitant expression in the form of hatred, bigotry, exploitation, oppression, persecution, violence, warfare, and the like. His immediate motivation, as commonly cited, was his direct military experience serving during the First World War, and the broader understanding of the horrific nature of that conflict, leading to the desire, shared by many others at that time, to find a way to prevent such catastrophes from ever occurring again.

As I have discussed at length elsewhere (Strate, 2022a, 2022b), Korzybski was also particularly concerned with the social, political, and economic disruptions of the early 20th century, especially the challenge represented by new totalitarian forms of government, primarily following the Bolshevik Revolution and establishment of Soviet Communism in Russia, as well as the beginnings of fascism in Italy. He was far from alone in looking to technicians for salvation; for example, the noted economist Thorstein Veblen in his scholarly work, *The Engineers and the Price System* (1921), explored the idea of a governing soviet of engineers (the Russian term soviet meaning council, and this coming from before the time that the term took on the extremely negative connotations it gained during the Cold War). Indeed, Marxist ideology was put forth as social and economic theory, and the kind of government pioneered in Russia and the Soviet

Union was referred to as *scientific socialism*; the slogan popularized by Karl Marx, from each according to his ability, to each according to his needs, is decidedly a call for a rational approach to social organization. That the deterministic view that Marxian theory was based on was rendered obsolete by the revolution in relativistic physics associated with Albert Einstein was not lost on Korzybski. The accompanying notion of a *dictatorship of the proletariat* was also inconsistent with government based on technical expertise, which was why Veblen argued that it was not the workers but the technicians who could possibly oust the capitalists who own the means of production. It was not surprising, then, that Korzybski and others sought for an alternative approach that would provide a rational distribution of resources and responsibility within the relatively conventional framework of liberal democracy.

Industrialization had greatly increased the complexity of modern societies, and favored greater centralization, either via business and industry or by government. Modernity also was associated with a shift in outlook from tradition and the past to progress and the future (Strate, 2011), and this naturally led to calls for centralized planning. The Soviet Union demonstrated the potential for planned economic development through their achievements in rapid industrialization, amplifying arguments for centralized planning in the western world, especially following the Stock Market Crash of 1929 and the ensuing Great Depression, which was taken by many as evidence that capitalism was a failed system. Thus, the new deal that Stuart Chase (1932a, 1932b) advocated amounted to a call for revolution, hopefully non-violent, predicated on a shift towards collectivism and government control. As he put it, "the shift of ambition and the goal of success toward public service, science, research, the arts, industrial management, statesmanship, and away from sheer accumulation, would be the happiest and most welcome change which could happen to contemporary civilization" (Chase, 1932a, p. 201). In addition to being influenced by Korzybski, Chase also drew on Veblen,

John Maynard Keynes, and Henry George. The idea of centralized planning was not limited to economic development as, for example, Korzybski's contemporary, Lewis Mumford, was a leader in the urban planning movement, and a cofounder of the Regional Planning Association of America.

For Korzybski (1921, 1950), the main motivation was to eliminate the irrational element governing society, and while his technocratic vision was idealistic, if not utopian, it was also partly prophetic. His specific proposal was to establish government agencies run by specialists with expertise in specific sectors to determine the best course of action based on objective assessments of factual evidence; significantly, their function would not be to rule or control, but rather to advise, augment, and adjudicate within an otherwise democratic government. And in limited fashion, this is the kind of shift that occurred when Franklin Delano Roosevelt became president of the United States. With the understanding that elected Congressional Representatives and Senators lacked the expertise and resources needed to legislate on the vast number of complex matters that the federal government needed to oversee, responsibility was shifted to the executive branch through the formation of a multitude of agencies charged with producing and promulgating regulations for their specific areas of concern. Whether Korzybski's proposal had any role in this is unclear, but his ideas were certainly part of the zeitgeist of that period. The approach to public administration that Roosevelt instituted, sometimes referred to as *the administrative state* (Waldo, 1948), has been criticized as overly bureaucratic and less democratic in that it moves regulatory decision-making from the legislation to the executive branch of government, and has come under extended attack from conservatives and populists. But it is very much consistent with Korzybski's desire for government based on time-binding principles (aka general semantics). And while it is not immune from political and economic influences that interfere with a strictly rational approach to administration, those same influences also allow for democratic oversight and citizen participation. No clear alternative seems to have been proposed, apart from a return to laissez-faire approaches, which in turn have been criticized as irrational and resulting in a variety of social harms, including economic failures and crashes, environmental degradation, extreme inequality and political unrest. While opponents of the administrative state have sought to label the system as socialist, it is best understood as a form of liberal democracy; laissez-faire government and centralized bureaucracies with an established civil service and centralized planning are both varieties of the open society. Open systems, including open social and political systems, are characterized by their ability to change in order to meet changing circumstances, to grow and evolve to meet new challenges posed by their environments.

Korzybski's (1921, 1950) vision was made manifest via Roosevelt's New Deal, but at the same time Korzybski came to realize that the extreme version of technocracy, placing the engineers in charge of government, was not a panacea, as he concluded that, outside of their areas of specialization, technologists and scientists could be just as irrational as anyone else. This led him to shift his emphasis from the social to the psychological, as he developed the system he dubbed general semantics, the implication being that both a polity and a leadership schooled in general semantics would be the best means of establishing government based on rational thought and action (Korzybski, 1933/2023). Inspired by the scientific revolution associated with Albert Einstein, who introduced the world to non-newtonian physics, supported by non-euclidean geometry, Korzybski (1950, 2023) characterized general semantics as a non-aristotelian system. In doing so, he was mainly concerned with Aristotelian logic, an approach based on deductive reasoning, one that consequently proved to be easy to integrate into a variety of religious and theological systems; Aristotelian logic, as exemplified by the syllogism, was also in many ways inimical to the inductive reasoning and empirical method that served as the foundation for modern science. But we can also extend the concept of the non-aristotelian beyond Korzybski. For example, the theory of evolution based on natural selection, as put forth by Charles Darwin and Alfred Russel Wallace, along with the discovery of genetics attributed to Gregor Mendel, also associated with Hugo de Vries and William Bateson, as well as the identification of the DNA molecule by James Watson and Francis Crick, based on research by Rosalind Franklin, constitute a non-aristotelian approach to the biological sciences; Aristotelian biology posits species as permanent and unchanging, again a perspective easily integrated into various religious and theological systems. In this respect, Jean-Batiste Lamarck might be considered the progenitor of non-aristotelian biology, given that he was a proponent of evolution, albeit one in which acquired traits could be inherited (Bateson, 1972).

Aristotelian Politics

If we posit the possibility of a non-aristotelian approach to the political sphere, it would make sense to first consider what Aristotelian politics entails. In doing so, we might take a hint from the fact that Aristotle was employed by Philip II of Macedon to tutor his son Alexander III, better known as Alexander the Great. As is the case for all scholarship, Aristotle's understanding of politics was influenced by his personal experiences and the circumstances of his life, which include Alexander's conquest of Athens and Aristotle's close connection to imperial Macedonian rule there, as well as Aristotle's exile from Athens following Alexander's untimely death. This is coupled with his education by Plato, who was notorious for his anti-democratic views and authoritarian politics. Karl Popper (1945/2022) characterizes Plato's views as totalitarian, arguing that they constitute the philosophical basis of 20th century Communism, fascism, and Nazism. According to Popper, while Aristotle is critical of some of Plato's minor excesses, his politics are largely consistent with the authoritarian mindset of his mentor:

Aristotle's thought is entirely dominated by Plato's. Somewhat grudgingly he followed his great teacher as closely as his temperament permitted, not only in his general political outlook but practically everywhere. So he endorsed, and systemized, Plato's naturalistic theory of slavery: 'Some men are by nature free, and others slaves; and for the latter, slavery is fitting as well as just ... A man who is by nature not his own, but another's, is by nature a slave ... Hellenes do not like to call themselves slaves, but confine this term to barbarians ... The slave is devoid of any faculty of reasoning', while free women have just a little of it. (Popper, 2022, p. 220)

Popper goes on to explain:

But the theory of slavery is only one of Plato's many political ideas to be adopted by Aristotle. Especially his theory of the Best State, as far as we know it, is modelled upon the theories of the *Republic* and the *Laws*; and his version throws considerable light on Plato's. Aristotle's Best State is a compromise between three things, a romantic Platonic aristocracy, a 'sound and balanced' feudalism, and some democratic ideas; but feudalism has the best of it. With the democrats, Aristotle holds that all citizens should have the right to participate in the government. But this, of course, is not meant to be as radical as it sounds, for Aristotle explains at once that not only slaves but all members of the producing classes are excluded from citizenship. Thus he teaches with Plato that the working classes must not rule and the ruling classes must not work, nor earn any money. (But they are supposed to have plenty.) They own land, but must not work it themselves. Only hunting, war, and similar hobbies are considered worthy of the feudal rulers. (p. 221)

Beyond the elitism characteristic of Plato and Aristotle, their fundamental position is that the good of the state is paramount, eclipsing any consideration of the good of the individual, and that the obligation of the individual is to serve the good of the state. This anti-democratic stance is consistent with modern totalitarianism, not the least in viewing the state as an organic unity, which is to say as an organism in which each individual citizen is a part of the whole, akin to an organ or cell. There is also a naturalism at work here, in the notion that different classes of people find their natural position as slaves, workers, warriors, and rulers, paralleling Aristotle's science in which species are permanent and unchanging, and substances seek out their natural place, so that air and fire move upwards and earth and water downwards. Aristotle's metaphysics informs his politics as well, in that he follows Plato in his attempt to establish the ideal form or formal cause of the state, while emphasizing the final cause that moves states naturally towards realizing their potential, the end towards which they are inevitably drawn to (for more on formal cause and final cause, see Anton, Logan, & Strate, 2016; Aristotle, 1998; Campbell, 1982; Deacon, 2012; McLuhan & McLuhan, 2011; Strate, 2022c; Trujillo Liñán, 2022). Aristotle's essentialism is consonant with his reliance on deductive logic, as opposed to the fuzzy logic of inductive and empirical methodologies.

The political philosophy of Plato and Aristotle was in many ways reactionary rather than revolutionary, specifically a reaction to the invention of democracy as a practical form of government; their criticism and attack was directed against the Athenian democracy developed over the course of the 6th century BCE by Solon and Cleisthenes, followed in the 5th century by Ephialtes and Pericles. Although Plato and Aristotle's efforts to undermine Athenian democracy did not yield the results either philosopher hoped for, that system of government was largely undone by Aristotle's student, Alexander the Great, and nothing comparable was established for nearly two millennia. And while the philosophers are often held up as champions of reason, they were preceded by the pre-Socratics from the Greek colonies in Asia Minor, who introduced the first forms of theoretical science. Also known as the Ionian Physicists, they included Thales, Anaximander, Anaximenes, Anaxagoras, Archelaus, and the pre-Socratic philosopher often invoked in general semantics circles, Heraclitus, as well as Parmenides, and significantly, the appropriately named pre-Socratic philosopher Democritus, who is best known for his contributions as an Ionian physicist in introducing the theory of atomism, but was also a proponent of the parallel ideas of individualism, egalitarianism, and equalitarianism. The parallel here is between the idea of the atom as the basic unit of matter and the citizen as the basic unit of the polity, and it seems more than coincidence that science originates in the same culture as democracy, and during the same century, the 6th century BCE.

Similarly, in the modern era there is a clear link between science and democracy, both seen as key components of the Enlightenment or Age of Reason. Enlightenment philosophy is generally said to begin in the 17th century with Baruch Spinoza, René Descartes, Francis Bacon, Gottfried Leibniz, Thomas Hobbes, and John Locke; Locke was key to the development of liberal democracy in theory, followed in practical application by the intellectual leaders of the 18th century American Revolution, Benjamin Franklin, Thomas Jefferson, Alexander Hamilton, Thomas Paine, John Adams, James Madison, etc. The emergence of modern science mostly occurs in the 17th century following the astronomical breakthroughs of Nicolaus Copernicus, with Johannes Kepler, Galileo Galilei, and Isaac Newton, as well as Francis Bacon, John Locke, George Berkeley, and David Hume. More than the accumulation of scientific discoveries, modern science supplanted Aristotelian logic with a new emphasis on induction and empiricism.

Modern democracy and science, as primary manifestations of the Enlightenment, form the basis of what Popper (2002) terms the *open society*, in contrast to authoritarian and totalitarian societies that follow the political logic of Plato and Aristotle, and their modern inheritors, starting with G.W.F. Hegel. Popper explains that Hegelian dialectics and historicism are extensions of Aristotelian logic and metaphysics, and that they formed the basis of right wing ideologies such as fascism and Nazism. Karl Marx famously gave Hegel's approach a materialistic twist, and his dialectical materialism formed the basis of left wing ideologies associated with the Communist forms of government operationalized by Lenin, Stalin, Mao, and others. Francis Fukuyama (1992) famously employed a Hegelian approach when he declared an end to history following the fall of the Soviet Union in 1991, a conclusion that proved to be somewhat less than accurate, not to mention problematically Aristotelian. In contrast to Fukuyama, Postman (1999) argued for the need to retrieve and reclaim the Enlightenment commitment to reason, expressed metaphorically as *building a bridge to the 18th century,* if we want to retain our democracy in the 21st century.

At a minimum, it is painfully apparent that there is tremendous agita today over the challenges to liberal democracy, given the resurgence of authoritarianism in various parts of the world, the failure of democratic revolutions to take hold, the introduction of what Viktor Orbán termed *illiberal democracy,* and the relative success of populist movements in the United States, the United Kingdom, France, Italy, and elsewhere. While there is good reason to view western-style democracy as resilient, at least in the west, owing to the continuity of the American experiment if nothing else, the election of 2016 and the failed insurrection of January 6, 2020, has shaken our confidence in the stability of our system. Admittedly, that confidence was based on a very selective view of the history of liberal democracy, and we need only recall events such as the American Civil War and the Great Depression, the original sin of slavery and the war against the indigenous peoples of the western hemisphere, and the myriad injustices visited upon individuals on account of their race, ethnicity, religion, gender, and sexual orientation, to disabuse ourselves of that notion. And as much as we can point to real progress in regard to the American experiment, we have also borne witness to the failure of democracy to take hold in many other nations. It is sobering to recall that soon after the U.S. won its independence from the British Empire, there was the disastrous outcome of the French Revolution giving way to the Reign of Terror and the dictatorship of Napoleon Bonaparte. Disappointments abound, not the least being the failure of democracy to take hold in Russia, first after the

Russian Revolution led to the abdication of the Tsar, and again after the fall of the Soviet Union. We have seen democratic revolutions sputter and fail in China, following the Tiananmen Square protests of 1989, and authoritarian rule extended to the once free city of Hong Kong. And we have seen the promise of the Arab Spring in recent years fail to deliver stable democracies in the Middle East. At best, we can conclude that establishing and maintaining democratic governments is far from easy or effortless, certainly not automatic. Democracy, it seems, goes against the grain of human beings, as a social species, to form hierarchal relationships, engage in territorial behavior, and employ aristotelian approaches to social-political-economic organization.

The Paradoxes of Democracy

The enemies of the open society are legion. The external threats are myriad. But there are also challenges intrinsic to democracy itself. Plato and Aristotle were aware of the paradoxes posed by open societies, and this informed their critical assessments and attacks on democratic government. Many of these paradoxes are rooted in Aristotelian logic and rigid adherence to absolutes. For example, there is the paradox of using democratic processes to curtail or liquidate democratic government, the paradox of political freedom allowing some citizens to limit or eliminate the freedom of others, the paradox of the principle of toleration being used to protect intolerance, etc. These are examples of the kinds of paradox easily dealt with by reference to Alfred North Whitehead and Bertrand Russell's (1925–1927) theory of logical types, so that democracies can adjust the rules of the game but not so much as to undermine the entire system, individual freedom is upheld so long as it does not interfere with the freedom of others, and tolerance of intolerance is allowed as long as intolerance does not infringe upon the basic requirement of tolerance.

Zac Gershberg and Sean Illing (2022) provide a modern spin on this ancient argument, one that allows for greater complexities and contradictions, by linking the paradox of democracy to the paradox of free speech:

> The great myth of America culture, then and now, is that democracy is built on free expression, both spoken and printed. Though wrapped up in shibboleths from the marketplace of ideas, such a myth is not without its advantages. There is wisdom in the notion that free expression is its own justification, as a matter of principle and as a check on power. The price, however, is sometimes high. Truth won't always win out, and the public sphere can't be contained. This is a lesson perpetually relearned when novel media technologies flood the information space. (p. 131)

While noting the disruptive impact of broadcasting in an earlier era, Gershberg and Illing (2022) are primarily responding to the more recent introduction of digital technologies, online communication, and social media. In contrast to those who see transparency as a panacea, invoking the metaphorical shibboleth that *sunlight is the best disinfectant*, they note that free speech and new media have led to a flood of disinformation, paralleling Neil Postman's (1992) earlier arguments about contemporary technology breaking down established methods of gatekeeping and filtering. The problem, they note, is that "democracy is a political culture without foundation" (p. 259), going on to explain:

> In the end, democracy offers free expression and the possibility that power might be checked. Those opportunities may not be fully taken advantage of, but they constitute democracy's claim to superiority over technocracy or aristocracy or authoritarianism. Unfortunately, there's no guarantee of escape from communicative anarchy. There are some who hope we can escape from Plato's cave of ignorance, that reason and the right institutions are all we need. Yet there is no "outside world," no refuge from bad outcomes or dangerous demagogues – only the volatility of open expression. (p. 260)

They go on to note that freedom of speech can be threatened by too much freedom of speech, as "institutions that reinforce power hierarchies are still in place, but their ability to constrain the communicative space has been thoroughly diminished," and that "the so-called crisis of democracy isn't really a crisis of democracy; it's the explosion of illiberalism and a loss of elite control over flows of information" (p. 260). The result is a chaotic public sphere in which the left and the right both engage in efforts to limit discourse, engaging in public shaming, bans and censorship campaigns, and cancel culture, facing off against provocateurs, trolls, and fakes both deep and shallow. And as Gershberg and Illing (2022) explain:

> When we say that speech has never been freer, we mean that there have never been fewer barriers to entry in public discourse. There are now more voices, more perspectives, and more platforms that ever before. One of the many consequences of this cultural environment is the struggle over where to draw discursive boundaries and what sort of social sanctions are permissible when those boundaries are transgressed. What was previously unsayable will become commonplace, and what was previously acceptable will be challenged and even culturally suppressed in favor of new discursive norms. (pp. 260–261)

The problem they continue to return to as the paradox of democracy is the paradox of free speech, a paradox that is intensified by the speed of communication in the contemporary American media environment, the volume of information that is transmitted, and its enhanced accessibility:

> A culture of free speech has never been self-securing, and now we have been forced to negotiate the perils of such liberty in real time. All the speech policing, oddly enough, may not signal the short-circuiting of a free society so much as its natural outcome. To say that the age of liberal democracy is dead is to say that the liberal-democratic rhetorical style of discourse no longer reigns

supreme.... what was once the dominant mode or style of communication – in the mid- to late twentieth century, in particular... now finds itself as but one option among many in a public sphere characterized by convergent media. And there are now more voices and styles competing for supremacy in the public sphere. The conceptual mistake, then, is to assume that freedom invariably leads to more liberalism, or that a free society will naturally reinforce the conditions that sustain it. (p. 261)

From a systems view, the problem of openness is also readily apparent. Systems cannot be entirely open to their environment, as their boundaries are what give the system its identity, making the system a separate entity in relation to its environment. For a system to organize itself, it must achieve a measure of closure, the process of forming a boundary and closing itself off from its environment is essential for autopoiesis (Luhmann, 1982, 1989, 1990, 1995; Maturana & Varela, 1980, 1992). While the universe in its totality is considered a closed system, as there is nothing outside of it, systems generally need to be at least a little bit open in order to take in whatever they need to maintain themselves (e.g., nutrients in the case of living systems). Media of communication function in a similar manner, performing the essential function of surveillance of the environment, as well as coordinating responses to the environment, while also shielding us, at least in theory, from being overwhelmed by the chaos of the environment, filtering out what is superfluous, unwanted, and harmful – hence, it could be said that the medium is the membrane (Strate, 2018). In this instance, the systems view emphasizes the ecological value of balance (Strate, 2014, 2017) against the extremes of Aristotelian absolutes (of openness and closure). Time is also a factor, one that is often overlooked, as systems oscillate between states of greater and lesser openness and closure, an insight that sociologist Orin Klapp (1978) emphasizes. In this sense, the perceived paradox of openness parallels Zeno's paradox of Achilles and the tortoise, in its disregard for the factor of change over time.

Meta Levels to Democracy

Whether it is the problem of disregarding logical typing or ignoring the factor of change over time, the solution to most paradoxes is to move up in levels of abstraction (Korzybski, 2023) to one or more meta levels. Doing so does not immediately solve all of the real world problems that plague us, but it does help to clarify our concerns and focus our critical faculties. To this end, I have devised an Open Society Pyramid model to help visualize the relationships involved:

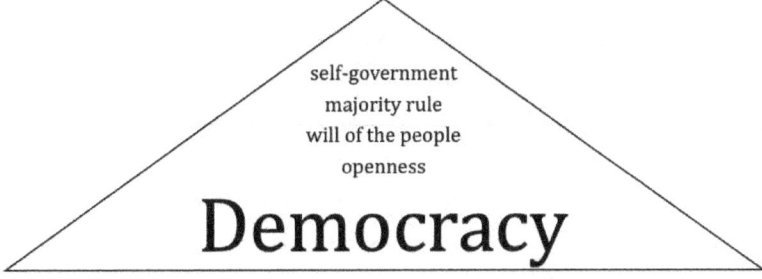

Figure 1 The Open Society Pyramid: Democracy as the Basis

Figure 1 represents the open society based solely on democracy, with its attendant elements of self-government, majority rule, the will of the people, and openness (aka free speech). This view of democracy, boiled down to the concept of the consent of the governed, is commonly considered the basis of political power, authority, and legitimacy (Ellul, 1964, 1965), as well as routine decision-making. Generally viewed as the foundation of liberal democracy, on its own it has the potential to descend into the tyranny of the majority, mob rule, the madness of crowds, and ultimately self-destruction. These vulnerabilities were clear and present within Athenian democracy, so that the criticisms of Plato and Aristotle were not entirely without merit. Tracing the origin of democracy back to ancient Greece, Gershberg and Illing's (2022) understanding of the basis of democracy is consistent with the ancient critique:

> Democracy proceeds from the freedom and equality to raise one's voice among others in public. *Isonomia*, or the equality before the law, comes later. The liberty of *isegoria* is how democracy can furnish the right of *isonomia*. *Isegoria* provides the communicative and cultural environment of democracy.... So long as any one citizen among the demos can address others, society can proceed openly – allowing for the people and their representatives to talk and consider what to do. (p. 30)

This perspective on democracy emphasizes its relation to the development of rhetoric in ancient Greece, and the specific way that it evolved within that culture. It represents a relatively simplistic view of self-government in which the citizenry consists of a relatively small group of people, one that excluded women, slaves, and foreigners, within a specific locality, ancient Athens. In this setting, all of the citizens could know one another, at least by reputation, all are expected to take part in deliberations, and all communications are delivered in person via public speaking. Without in any way detracting from the significance of this achievement in the ancient world, and its importance in the development of modern democracy, it does represent a limited form of democracy, one that is particularly vulnerable to the contradictions and paradoxes outlined by its critics.

The problem, I would suggest, also lies in semantic reactions to the term democracy. As a god term in modern western cultures, much of what is associated with democracy, and much of what the term often is used to refer to, is not merely self-government, majority rule, the will of the people, and openness. Democracy also refers to the rule of law. And while Gershberg and Illing (2022) suggest that *isonomia* comes after *isegoria* in ancient Greece, widening our scope makes clear that the idea of equality before the law precedes freedom of speech in the ancient world, having its origins in legal texts dating back to the third millennium BCE, such as the Sumerican Code of Ur-Nammu and the Babylonain Code of Hammurabi, leading to the

Mosaic Law of the Israelites. Gershberg and Illing are hardly alone in taking a narrow view of western culture as originating with ancient Greece, followed by ancient Rome; the Eurocentric bias that traditionally privileged Classics in school curricula and that informs the history of rhetoric and rhetorical theory has been widespread within liberal arts education. The philosopher Leo Strauss (1967) famously pointed metonymically to the distinction between Athens and Jerusalem, both serving as the primary legs upon which western culture stands; while ancient Greece gave us philosophy, natural science, and theater, as well as democracy, ancient Israel, the older of the two, provided the basis for monotheism via the Abrahamic religions that dominate much more than the west, as well as narrative history as expressed within the Torah and other Hebrew scriptures, and systems of ethics and law. What Jerusalem represents would not be non-aristotelian in Korzybski's (2023) sense, but rather pre-aristotelian, albeit also capable of integrating Aristotelian logic within a theological frame. As a parallel to Athens, Jerusalem also might point the way towards a non-aristotelian politics.

Moreover, I would argue that not only is the rule of law an essential component of democracy as we have come to understand it, but it also represents democracy's meta level. Functional democracies require some form of legal framework or constitution, the rules of the game so to speak; this would include protections for minorities against the excesses of majority rule, and guarantees of human rights. Of course, there must be mechanisms for making adjustments to the legal framework, based on democratic decision making, so there is interaction between the levels such that the lower level can modify the meta level. But such alterations and amendments would typically require considerable effort and general consensus. Rule of law is therefore arguably more vital to a functioning democracy than majority rule, which potentially can descend into extremes of populism. We can therefore add this meta level to the Open Society Pyramid model:

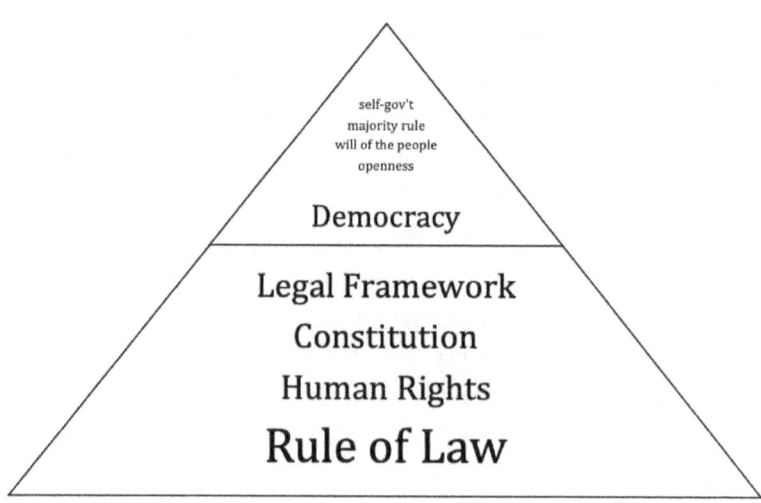

Figure 2 The Open Society Pyramid: Rule of Law as the Basis

Figure 2 indicates that a legal framework and/or constitution, based on human rights and rule of law constitutes the basis of democracy within an open society. Indeed, freedom of speech and the equal rights of citizens to participate in public discourse and political deliberations can only be guaranteed by the rule of law, however much they might be accepted as custom. This two-tiered model may be sufficient for our needs, and it is typically the case that references to a meta level are confined to only two levels, as in communication and metacommunication (Bateson, 1972, 1979; Watzlawick, 1976; Watzlawick, Bavelas, & Jackson, 1967). For Korzybski (2023) and within general semantics, however, levels of abstracting can continue upwards without any discernable limit, and in regard to this discussion I believe that legal frameworks have, and need, their own meta level. By this I mean that a set of basic principles are required on which to base a legal system. Principles might otherwise be referred to as values, and within deductive logic as the basis of first premises. They are what Thomas Jefferson was referring to when he opened the Declaration of Independence with the proclamation, "We hold these truths to be self-evident, that all men are created equal, that they are endowed by their Creator with certain unalienable Rights, that among them are Life, Liberty, and the pursuit of Happiness." In this most fundamental statement of American democracy, we again see the primary influence of Jerusalem as opposed to the purely secular humanist tradition derived from Athens.

The values most basic to democracy would be the abstract notions of freedom and equality. As principles, they are generally accepted as "truths" while the tension that exists between the two are usually ignored. But taken to their logical ends, the value of freedom includes the freedom to excel in some way that results in a measure of inequality, whereas the need to establish equality requires some measure of restrictions on freedom. The inherent opposition between freedom and equality corresponds to two other oppositions. One is the opposition between individualism and community, freedom aligning with the rights of the individual, equality aligning with an emphasis on the group and communal needs and preferences. The second is the opposition between capitalism and democracy, freedom and individualism aligning with the right to pursue happiness via the accumulation of material wealth and power, democracy being based on equal status when it comes to voice and vote, and a sense of civic virtue and commitment to serve the greater good. While the contradictions are generally ignored, and American culture leans in the direction of freedom, individualism, and capitalism, as opposed to equality, community, and democracy, all of these values co-exist with the American political and cultural semantic environment.

Claude Lévi-Strauss (1969) argues that polar oppositions are resolved by a third mediating element (as in the Hegelian dialectic of thesis, antithesis, and synthesis), and I would suggest that in this case, the mediating term is *justice*. Apart from reconciling the contradictions that would otherwise exist, justice is fundamental for both Jerusalem and Athens, and frequently invoked within the Torah and Bible. Justice is more basic that the rule of law, given that prior to the development of codified law, judges ruled on disputes, drawing on traditional sayings and stories and their own personal experience. In this sense, then, justice is situated on a meta level in relation to the rule of law, and otherwise would be essential for an open society. We can therefore add this additional meta level to the Open Society Pyramid model:

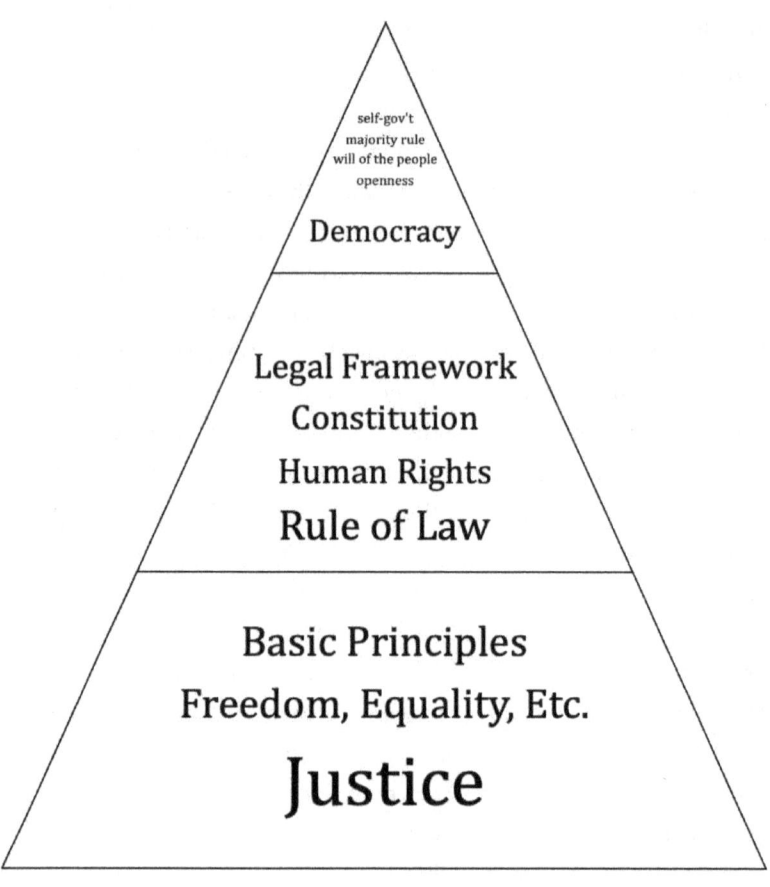

Figure 3 The Open Society Pyramid: Principle of Justice as the Basis

While basic principles such as freedom, equality, and justice may seem sufficient on their own as fundamental values, or self-evident truths, they can also be seen as dependent upon a fourth meta level. In order to work with principles or premises in Aristotelian fashion, and to acknowledge the importance of data and evidence with more modern frameworks, and thereby to properly work within a legal framework and a democratic political system, the most basic requirement for an open society, as Popper (2002) maintains, is *reason*. To function as an open society, there must be citizens capable of and committed to using reason as the basis of their decision-making processes. There needs to be a profound faith in reason, a belief in reason, and an emotional attachment to reason that itself does not need to be justified by reason. Following Gödel's notion of incompleteness, reason cannot justify itself, otherwise we wind up with another form of paradox; instead, reason would seem to be the base upon which all else is built.

With this in mind, it follows that yet another meta level is needed for the Open Society Pyramid model:

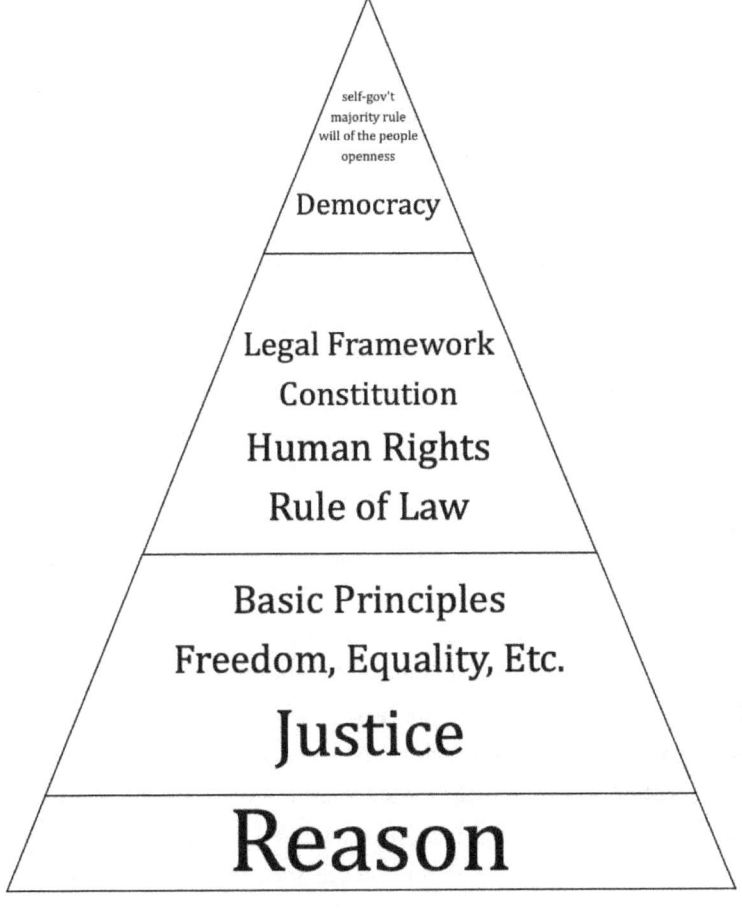

Figure 4 The Open Society Pyramid: Reason as the Basis

While logically these are meta levels, which implies the metaphor of moving up from lower to higher levels, we can also visualize these relationships as beginning with reason as the foundation on which basic principles are built, on which in turn a legal framework is built, which forms the basis of democratic government. In regard to what may seem like mixed metaphors regarding direction and placement, note that the Korzybski's (2023) famous Structural Differential model depicts higher levels of abstraction as descending from lower levels.

The Reason for Reason

Having invoked *reason* as a high level abstraction, at least some clarification is necessary. It is also important to acknowledge that there has been a tradition in western intellectual history of cultural bias when it comes to discussions of reason; this particularly extends to the historical emphasis placed on the Enlightenment and the *Age of Reason*. The claim, whether stated outright or implied, that the term *reason* can only be applied to western civilization, or more specifically to secular western civilization, or modern western civilization, implying in turn that all other cultures are essentially irrational, has been rightly criticized as ethnocentric. Indeed, it has also been criticized as anthropocentric, as other species also exhibit the ability to engage in a form of reasoning. Like any other word, the term *reason* can be defined in more than one way, and there is no one correct way to do so, and it should come as no surprise that some definitions have been contested, given the generally positive connotations associated with the word. In its simplest sense, reason could be equated with cognition, a biological function associated with all manner of lifeforms (as well as other systems engaged in information processing). In a slightly more limited sense, reason can be connected to the ability some species exhibit to engage in learning, modifying their behavior to adjust to changes in their environment. And especially as we move into the animal kingdom and focus on species with nervous systems, the ability to engage in planning and problem solving is often equated with the concept of reason. More generally, reason is typically equated with thought, with the activity of thinking, which is a product of neurological activity centered in the brain. Reason is further distinguished, however, by the ability to delay responses to stimuli, to think before acting, to inhibit kneejerk responses and replace reflexes with reflection, to respond with symbol reactions rather than signal reactions. Behavior of this sort is particularly present in vertebrates, and very much a characteristic of mammalian life, including primates and hominids. The fact that we refer to our own species as *homo sapiens* implies that our defining characteristic has to do with wisdom or knowledge, in other words, with reason, at least in potential. It is that exactly that potential that general semantics seeks to unlock and maximize (Korzybski, 1950. 2023).

However much humanity is distinguished by our brain power, what truly makes us unique is our capacity for language and symbol use. This suggests that reason may have at least as much to do with human communication as it does with our cerebral qualities. The need to engage in coordinated action and maintain social cohesion is a common thread binding all manner of social species, including primates. The origins of symbolic communication and its presence or absence among our evolutionary ancestors is, for the most part, lost to the mists of time, but it is certainly the key to human survival, and the overall success of our species. With this in mind, reason is also equated with talking rather than fighting, with using words instead of resorting to force, with dialogue rather than conflict, with persuasion in the place of coercion, argument in place of combat. Reason therefore is associated with the peaceful resolution of differences and disagreements, with negotiation, reconciliation, and understanding. Language certainly facilitates cognitive functions such as planning, problem solving, and learning, as well as enhancing cooperation and social cohesion (Burke, 1950; Dunbar, 1996; Duncan, 1962, 1968), and is the key to the time-binding capacity that Korzybski (1950, 2023) argues is the defining characteristic of the human class of life. Symbolic communication is also closely associated with our capacity for empathy and self-reflexiveness (Mead, 1934), and theory of mind (Baron-Cohen, 1995; Frith, 1989; Strate, 2022c), the assumption we typically make that others have a mind similar to our own, all of which are profoundly linked to the concept of human reason.

Insofar as reason can be understood as being closely related to communication, it follows that changes in the ways that human beings communicate are related to changes in the ways that we reason, and changes in our understanding of what reason entails. And to better understand these changes, we need to draw on the media ecology approach (Strate, 2017, 2022c). We can thereby understand that in the absence of the written word, oral cultures are dependent on individual and collective memory for their time-binding function, and on the mnemonic techniques used in the service of preserving and passing down knowledge. Reason, therefore, would be strongly tied to adherence to tradition, evaluation being based on consistency with traditional thought and practice; it follows that oral cultures would be characterized by a conservative bias, favoring the conservation and preservation of hard won knowledge, and therefore a significant degree of aversion to novelty (Ong, 1982). The phrase *rhyme or reason* would have particular resonance here, as the poetic quality of language would reflect its relation to reason. To be memorable would also mean to be *musical,* and in preliterate Greece the term musical had the added connotation of being educated, in much the same way that the term *literate* has a similar connotation for us, education in that culture being based on the memorization of the songs of Homer (Havelock, 1982). Reason would be tied to sayings, proverbs, and aphorisms, and to narratives, expressed concretely in the form of agents performing actions rather than as abstract concepts (Havelock, 1963, 1978, 1982, 1986; Ong, 1967, 1982). This would emphasize reasoning by analogy and metaphorical thinking, based on the similarity and appropriateness for the situation at hand of a given saying, fable, or parable. Moreover, oral cultures are also extremely group-centered, so that reason would emphasize human relations, such as can be found in the wisdom literature of tribal cultures (the term literature being something of a misnomer for oral traditions maintained in collective memory). This would favor reasoning based on consensus, and consistent with the need to maintain social cohesion and collective memory.

I want to emphasize the fact that members of oral cultures are not inherently unreasonable or irrational, or lacking in the ability to make logical deductions or draw conclusions based on evidence. Simply put, just as the oral mindset differs from the literate mindset, so does the concept of reason within these different types of media environments. In part this is due to changing emphases in regard to language, symbol use, and modes of communication. But this is also due to the fact that the invention of writing provided a set of resources that were not previously available, that in turn enabled new modes of thought and new possibilities for the gathering, distribution, and preservation of knowledge that were hitherto unavailable. And the effects were arguably revolutionary, albeit taking effect gradually over an extended period of time. In its most basic sense, writing vastly increased our capacity for time-binding by providing a means of accumulating and storing knowledge outside of the human mind with its limited memory capacity, allowing for a much greater amount of knowledge to be passed on from one generation to the next, thereby enabling significant human progress (Korzybski, 1921, 1950). Time-binding, however, involves more than just the conservation of knowledge; it also incorporates its evaluation, and in this writing was revolutionary as well. Storing knowledge in visual form outside of the individual's mind made possible *the separation of the knower from the known*, to use Eric Havelock's (1963) happy phrase, and freed from the necessity of memorization, individuals were able to view their thoughts and traditions from the outside, in relatively objective fashion, and thereby to criticize and correct them. This opened the door to new kinds of reason.

Speech requires a concrete setting involving a specific time and place, and particular participants who are talking and/or listening. Writing liberates speech from its situational context, allowing individuals to engage in language-based communication across space and time, making it possible for messages to be received by readers unknown to the writer, receivers that senders never intended to communicate with. Writing thereby decontextualizes the spoken word, rendering it increasingly more abstract. Additionally, in allowing verbal expression to break free of the necessity of mnemonic techniques such as poetry and narrative, writing gives rise to more abstract forms; for example, Goody (1977) notes that the list is a new form made possible by writing, in which the formulaic combination of subject and predicate, not to mention epithet, can be separated, leaving only a sequence of items free of any context of action or motion. The kinds of formulas familiar to us from a song like "The Twelve Days of Christmas," such as eight maids a'milking, seven swans a'swimming, six geese a'laying, is reduced to a list format as

- 8 maids
- 7 swans
- 6 geese.

Even before the development of fully formed systems for representing the spoken word via visual markings, the invention of numerical notation opened the door to new forms of reason associated with digital form and function, mathematics representing the core of what came to be known as *rationality*, as in *ratio*, and *rationing* (which requires some form of division). Notably, the introduction of separate characters with numerical value, numerals, represents an important step forward in abstraction. Notational systems typically start out by repeating the same mark over and over in one-to-one correspondence with the number of objects being counted. For example, if you have five chickens, you repeat the symbol for chicken five times on the writing surface (Schmandt-Besserat, 1996). But once a separate symbol is introduced to represent the number *five*, it becomes possible to conceive of five not just as an adjective, a description, but as a noun, a phenomenon in and of itself, the abstract quantity we know as 5 – a member of an oral culture would ask, *five what*? With abstract thinking, it becomes possible to talk and think about other abstractions, not just something that is *good* but *the good* in and of itself, not just someone who is *just* but *justice* in and of itself (Havelock, 1978, 1986). Decontextualizing speech makes possible increasingly more abstract forms of expression (Goody, 1977, 1986, 1987), and the abstract thinking that is associated with the literate mindset (Ong, 1967, 1982) becomes the basis of a new concept of reason.

In this way, the written word was a necessary precondition for the introduction of codified law (Innis, 1951, 1972; Logan, 2004), the abstract listing of rules and regulations, which in turn gives rise to a different kind of reason from that which prevails in oral cultures. Rather than reasoning based on analogy, codified law requires a more digital form of categorical thinking. For example, for a judge evaluating a case involving the death of one person at the hands of another in a nonliterate culture, analogical thought would invoke a narrative such as the biblical story of Cain and Abel, and the judge would consider whether the case at hand is sufficiently similar to that story, or of a different nature. By way of contrast, a judge working with the new form of digital thought made possible by literacy and required by written codes of law could render a verdict based on a commandment such as, you *shall not murder*, which would involve deliberating on whether the particular case being tried fits into the general category of murder or else is a member of some other category (e.g., accident, self-defense).

Abstracting involves categorizating and generalizing, which also involves leaving out details as we move increasingly higher in level of abstraction. Literally taking something out of something else, abstracting is thereby closely related to analysis, which involves breaking things down into their component parts. It follows that abstract thinking is closely related to analytical thought, another byproduct of writing. For example, breaking utterances down into separate characters started us down the road to analytical thinking, intensifying as those characters evolved from logographic to syllabic to alphabetic writing systems (Havelock, 1982, 1986; Logan, 2004; McLuhan, 1962, 1964; Ong, 1967, 1982). It is no coincidence that the Ionian physicists introduced the concept of atomism following the introduction of the alphabet, a writing system that breaks down all linguistic sounds into a basic set of units. Coinage too follows the introduction of alphabetic writing, breaking all goods and services down to a basic set of monetary units, both serving as the model or metaphor for presocratic speculation about the basic building blocks of matter. This represents the beginnings of theoretical science, which was followed by the beginnings of democracy, breaking down the polity into the individual unit of the citizen, the atom of society. The separation between the knower and the known also created the potential to put some distance between the individual and the group, as reading to oneself, even if read out loud as was almost always the case in antiquity, the reader is instantly transformed into an individual occupying a private conceptual space. In simpler terms, the separation of justice from judges, in the form of written legal systems such as the code of Hammurabi and the Torah of Moses introduced the idea of individuals being equal before the law. A commandment such as *you shall not murder* does not specify who it applies to, and therefore by implication applies to everyone. In this way, individualism, rule of law, and democratic government all emerge within the literate cultures of antiquity, albeit somewhat separately and incompletely.

The introduction of alphabetic literacy did not immediately or completely undermine adherence to tradition. Although we are instantly transformed into individuals occupying a private conceptual space when we are reading to ourselves, reading in the ancient and medieval world was almost entirely done out loud, often in a group setting. Reading at that time was also limited by the very small number of written texts that were available, conferring upon them an authority that was near unassailable, especially with the introduction of the concept of the sacred text and canon. Also, the literate mindset resulted in what I would characterize as the madness of Plato, his view that abstract concepts or ideal forms are more real than concrete, material phenomena, indeed that abstractions are the only things that are real (Strate, 2022). Presumably, abstract thinking was still a novelty in ancient Greece, and it is not unusual for individuals when introduced to something new to fall in love with it in obsessive fashion. This same mindset made possible the introduction of Plato's dialectic and Aristotle's logic, with their emphasis on deductive reasoning.

Moreover, Aristotle was much concerned with taxonomies, which were a natural response to the knowledge explosion brought on by writing and alphabetic literacy (Hobart & Schiffman, 1998). As he set about trying to organize all the information that had been preserved in written texts, he worked out techniques for categorizing phenomena, and this was the practical basis for Aristotelian logic (Strate, 2011). From a modern standpoint, the volume of knowledge and information was limited, so that Aristotle could believe that he had perfectly systematized all that was available, and that he had access to absolute sources of authority. For this reason, deductive logic alone was sufficient for secular and polytheistic philosophers, and for the Abrahamic theologians who adapted his approach to their own systems of belief. Also significant was the fact that they had access to relatively few texts, relied heavily on oral communication, and to a large degree on memory as well. In this way, ancient alphabetic literacy formed the basis of both theology and ideology, and in general the Aristotelian modes of thought that remain influential to this day.

Reason in Context

Popper (2002) uses the term *reason* to refer to more than the rationalism of Plato and Aristotle, which is to say more than deductive logic, but also, and most importantly, in keeping with modern science, reliance upon data and evidence, induction and the empirical method. Reason also requires an openness to criticism, testing, refutation and falsification, which begins with an openness to opposing points of view, to making your own reasoning available to others, to comparison and contrast, to public debate and disputation, and to relatively objective means of obtaining support and verification. While this explanation falls short of the concrete requirements for operational definitions, and therefore runs the risk of reification and idealization (Johnson, 1946; Postman, 1976), this basic understanding of reason is consistent with Korzybski's (2023) emphasis on scientific method as the basis of general semantics. And if reason in general is intimately associated with language and symbolic communication, and reason in the ancient and medieval sense is linked to alphabetic literacy, it follows that reason in the modern sense is also connected to a particular mode of human communication, and a particular type of media environment, one that differs from our original oral media environment and the chirographic media environment of antiquity and the middle ages: the typographic media environment (Strate, 2017). To a degree, this represents a further evolution of human reason rather than a complete break with the past, as the full potential of literacy was present beforehand but not fully unlocked until after the invention of the printing press with moveable type in 15th century Europe (McLuhan, 1962; Ong, 1967, 1982).

Certainly, in comparison to the slow and laborious copying of manuscripts, the easy availability and accessibility of printed texts and their growing centrality to society enabled and encouraged the widespread adoption of literacy, which in turn allowed for more widespread use of abstract thinking. Additionally, as Elizabeth Eisenstein (1979) argues, printing vastly increased access to data stored in texts, and to theories about the natural world, coming from different sources, all of which had been deemed authoritative. The new ease in which these sources could be placed side by side allowed for comparisons and the discovery of contradictions, thereby diminishing their authority and calling their conclusions into question. Logic was not sufficient to resolve the disagreements, making empiricism a viable alternative. The only recourse to settle these disputes was by checking things out, collecting fresh data, testing, experimentation, and observation. Moreover, printing made widespread publication possible, so that old knowledge and new discoveries could be shared and evaluated, massively improving our time-binding capabilities.

Literacy in the ancient world was associated with the first inklings of individualism, through the experience of solitary reading. Printing not only increased the legibility of texts, but was also associated with the practice of silent reading becoming commonplace; this had much to do with individualism becoming a dominant characteristic of western culture, along with the modern concept of privacy (McLuhan, 1962). This in turn weakened both tradition and community as the basis of reason. Moreover, modern science was predicated on the phenomenology of reading. Writing alone constitutes a method of encoding speech, an acoustic phenomenon, in visual form, placing unprecedented emphasis on the sense of vision. In the literate culture of ancient Greece, this gave rise to visualist tendencies heretofore unknown. This new form of visualism was limited before the advent of typography by the practice of reading out loud and in group settings, the scarcity of writing materials and written texts, and the limited levels and spread of literacy. As printing vastly amplified the visualist tendencies of western culture, reading became the model and metaphor that empiricism was based upon, so that nature came to be viewed as a text that could be read like any other text; reading represented a shift from the deductive to the inductive, from intensional contemplation to extensional observation. Again, typography amplified phenomena that were present in the literate culture of antiquity, which included the approach associated with grammarians who emphasized the study of language and literature and the interpretation of texts, paralleling and sometimes rivaling the dialectic approach of Plato and Aristotle; grammarians laid the foundation for the idea of reading writ large, reading the book of nature as well as the book of scripture (McLuhan, 2006; Strate, 2022), which is to say, modern science and the scientific method. In this way, the new visualism emerging out of the typographic media environment privileged observation, leading to the ascendancy of the empirical method.

In sum, reason is not a spontaneous, autopoietic or autochthonic phenomenon, but rather one that emerges out of a particular type of environment. Drawing on what Neil Postman (1974) referred to as general semantics writ large, aka media ecology, we can understand that the new media environment associated with the printing revolution enabled the emergence of the Enlightenment, and with it the modern idea of reason based on evidence and facts, empiricism and experimentation. Like mathematics, logic remained a tool of reason, but now in a secondary position, assisting in the interpretation of data and the formation of theories and hypotheses, but never in countermanding the evidence obtained via the senses and the instruments that serve as their extensions. This understanding suggests that the Model of the Open Society would be incomplete unless we acknowledge that literacy and typography form the basis of reason, justice, the rule of law, and democracy. For this reason, I have placed literacy and typography at the foundation of the final version of the model:

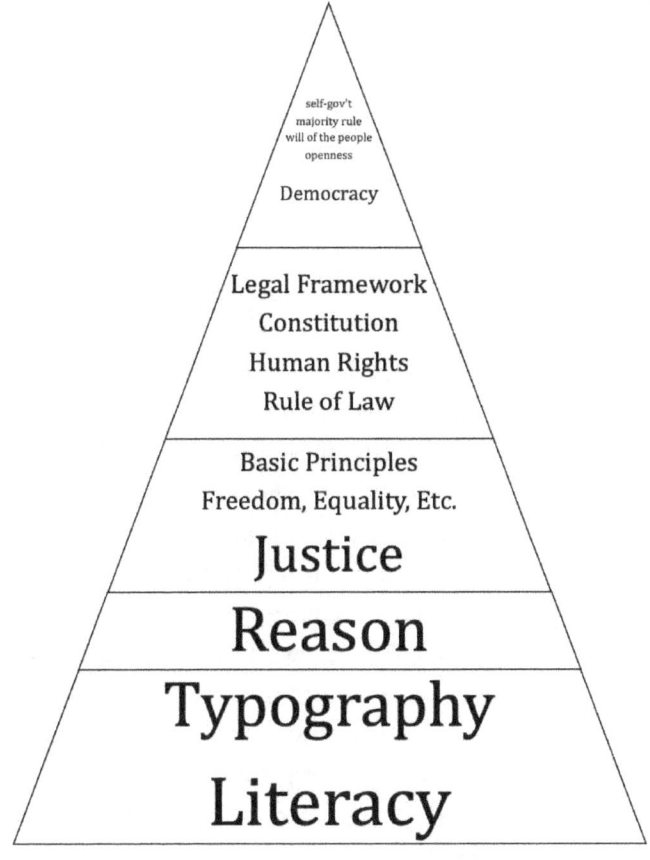

Figure 5 The Open Society Pyramid: Literacy and Typography as the Basis

Working our way back up from the foundation, we have seen how the specific concept of reason under consideration here is the product of the typographic media environment. We can also understand that basic principles such as freedom, equality, and justice are abstract concepts, and require the prevalence of abstract thinking associated with a literate society. More concretely, writing allowed for the introduction of codified law, and the printing of law books and the dissemination of legal decisions, governmental policy and legislation, and the like, as well as the resulting homogenization of legal and administrative systems across social and geographical divides that help to establish in practical terms the principle of equality before the law and the practical application of the rule of law (Eisenstein, 1979; McLuhan, 1962; Steinberg, 1996). We can see in all this the connection to the onset of modern democracy, based in part on access to information, and the spirit of experimentation, empiricism, and reliance on evidence. Further, the new concept of representative democracy, unknown to the ancients and arguably unrecognizable were any able to see it for themselves, required a good measure of abstract thinking.

Printing is also intimately connected to the rise of nationalism in the modern era and the institution of nation-states (Deibert, 1997; Eisenstein, 1979; Innis, 1951; McLuhan, 1982, 1964; Steinberg, 1996), and while democratic government was not a requirement for this shift away from feudalism, it was one of several possible answers to the need for strong central governments, while in turn requiring the innovation of representative democracy. Self-government, which is to say government by the people, requires access to information and the ability to exchange opinions, arguments and appeals, take part in debate, etc. On a local level, where *citizens* are literally *city-denizens*, this requires freedom of speech, but on a larger scale, especially a national one, access to information and the creation of a free marketplace of ideas was made possible by the invention of the printing press with movable type. Printing, McLuhan (1962) argues, led to the creation of the reading public, which is a nonlocal public, a public formed by publication. Democracy's dependence on access to information resulted in the introduction of the concept of freedom of the press (Siebert, Peterson, & Schramm, 1963), which also was linked to other freedoms, notably the right of assembly and petition. Modern democracy based on elected representatives does not necessarily require political parties, but their emergence seems all but inevitable, and their organization and campaigns depend in large part on printed materials, whether they are deemed pamphlets or propaganda, as well as, eventually, periodicals and newspapers. Government monopoly over printing would severely disadvantage whichever party is out of power, and this provides a major motive for curtailing government control and censorship of the press, particularly in regard to political content (Siebert, Peterson, & Schramm, 1963). Free and fair elections and the peaceful transfer of power are closely connected to open competition among parties or factions, and the institution of the fourth estate, all of which revolves around literacy as amplified by printing, and its concomitant form of reason.

The printing of political platforms and manifestos accounts for the origin of *ideology* in its strictest sense, as an *integrated system of ideas*, as Goody (1986, 1987) notes, and which stands in contrast to the pragmatism approach favored by Korzybski (1950) and Popper (2002). At least insofar as there are competing ideologies vying for voters' support, modern democracy deviates from the essentialism of Platonic and Aristotelian forms of dialectic, and instead works with the fuzzy logic of negotiation and compromise, avoiding the potential paradoxes that would otherwise be present. Against the idealism of Plato and Aristotle, democracy depends upon the pragmatic approach that became the hallmark of American philosophy in the 19th century, an approach Popper (2022) characterizes as piecemeal. Without a doubt, logic is still involved, and is also the basis of legal argument and interpretation, as developed within ancient Jewish culture via the Torah and Talmud, which also forms part of the basis of western culture and modern democracy. But to remain functional, logic and ideology cannot overrule facts and evidence in a democratic system. An empirical and relatively extensional orientation, along with an openness to change and evolution, would be the basis of any form of non-aristotelian politics.

Reason Undone

So far, I have distinguished between three different types of reason, associated with three different types of media environments. Employing the extensional device of indexing, and using the zero-based numbering common in computing and scientific notation, they could be identified as $reason_0$, $reason_1$, and $reason_2$. $Reason_0$ would be the type of reason associated with oral media environments (Strate, 2017) and the oral cultures that emerge within them (Goody, 1977, 1986, 1987; Havelock, 1963, 1982, 1986; Ong, 1967, 1982). With its emphasis on memory, metaphor, and musicality, as well as the concrete mindset it is associated with, $reason_0$ is easily regarded as a form of unreason from a literate perspective, reflecting the irrationality of superstition and magical thinking, as the product of a "primitive" culture and "savage mind" (Goody, 1977; Lévi-Strauss, 1966). Of course, the question of whether $reason_0$ ought to be understood as a valid alternative to other forms of reason or as fundamentally irrational comes down to a question of how we choose to define the term reason in the first place. For our purposes, what matters is that $reason_0$ does not serve as an adequate basis for democracy. $Reason_1$ on the other hand would be the kind of reason associated with chirographic media environments and the literate cultures that emerge within them. $Reason_1$, as we have seen, provides a sufficient foundation for direct democracy, the rule of law, and abstract principles such as freedom, equality, and justice. This type of reason, however, relies primarily on deductive logic, and therefore favors Aristotelian politics, the elitist politics of monarchies and empires, at least to the extent that it overcomes the tribalism associated with $reason_0$. $Reason_2$ then is the form of reason made possible by the shift from chirographic to typographic media environments, and the print cultures that emerges from them. $Reason_2$ is the type of reason associated with induction and empiricism, and with the emergence of the Enlightenment, modern science, and modern democracy. And as noted, $reason_2$ is what Popper (2002) means by reason, and the type of reason necessary for non-Aristotelian politics. It follows that if $reason_2$ is understood as a product of the typographic media environment, the transition to our contemporary electronic media environment has had a deleterious effect on much of print culture (McLuhan, 1964; Strate, 2014, 2017). Whereas $reason_2$ can be understood as an elaboration and expansion on $reason_1$, wherein $reason_2$ incorporates $reason_1$, the new form of reason that emerges within electronic culture, reason$_3$, is arguably discontinuous if not diametrically opposed to reason$_2$, quite possibly even more so than reason$_0$. Whereas reason$_0$ appears as a form of unreason from a literate perspective, reason$_3$ can be seen as being anti-reason in its actual nature.

The decline and disappearance of reason in the electronic age was a particular concern for Postman in *Amusing Ourselves to Death* (1985), where he argues that television, due to its emphasis on images and immediacy, turns serious discourse into entertainment, and favors the irrational, emotional, and visceral, over reason based on literacy and typography. Related to Postman's argument regarding American politics, his colleague Terence P. Moran (1984) suggests that democracy in the United States has been characterized by three different kinds of politics. Issue politics represents the ideal, where political debate centers on the pros and cons of genuine questions and proposals to address them. Issue politics was dominant during the early days of the republic, for example regarding the relative strength of the federal government, and have come to the fore every so often, for example regarding slavery, or whether to go to war, or more recently, over the legal status of abortion. While issues are often hotly debated, ultimately they tend to be resolved by cool reason. Early on in American history, however, issue politics gave way to party politics, in which local connection and association come to the fore, and loyalty was the main factor. While party politics have been rightly criticized for its potential for corruption and lack of transparency, Moran explains that it is still rooted in rationality, in this case having to do with enlightened self-interest. In party politics, as the saying goes, one hand washes the other, as there is a social contract in which loyalty garners rewards, favors are bestowed upon party members, and votes are repaid via services rendered, whether the service is fixing potholes or finding jobs. Reason$_2$ applies equally well to democratic decision-making based on prioritizing the greatest good for the greatest number even when it entails self-sacrifice, and when it is based on more selfish motivations such as greed and personal gain, as long as positions are coherent and choices are based on available evidence. Moreover, political parties were formed around ideological positions, as expressed by printed documents, as in party platforms and manifestos, so that even if party loyalty was based on more concrete considerations of personal reward, parties themselves coalesced around the publication of printed documents expressing rational argument and relatively consistent positions regarding issues subject to debate.

Tip O'Neill, who was Speaker of the United States House of Representatives from 1977 to 1987, is often credited with the saying that *all politics is local*, and this was certainly true for ancient Athenian society, but not so much for modern, representative democracies. In place of the ethos that was produced via personal relationships and reputation, political parties served a mediating function between voters and their elected officials. Apart from the direct person-to-person contact that parties afforded, print media played a prominent role, notably newspapers, which often boasted strong party affiliations. Electronic media offered an alternative form of communication to the media of both print and political parties in the form of broadcasting, first via radio, later via television. As McLuhan (1964) insightfully notes, totalitarian leaders such as Hitler, Mussolini, and Stalin used radio to achieve their anti-democratic aims, albeit while still working within a party structure defined by ideology. At the same time, Franklin Delano Roosevelt was especially effective at using radio to communicate to citizens in a way that provided the illusion of intimacy, via his fireside chats, allowing him to bypass the power of the newspaper press. It may be purely coincidental that his administration's establishment of social safety net initiatives such as unemployment insurance and social security severely undercut the traditional role of American political parties in providing aid and assistance to citizens in exchange for their votes. But the effect it had is undeniable.

In the postwar era, especially following the debacle surrounding Harry Truman's reelection, opinion polls further served to undermine the local expertise of party leadership, and their ability to serve as human media connecting voters to public officials. The shift away from party bosses selecting party candidates to primary elections was also a key development that undermined party politics, and this was very much related to the advent of television, and its increasingly more prominent role in political campaigns over the course of the 1960s. As television became the central medium for campaigning, especially for national and statewide campaigns, image, in the sense of appearance and personality, has come to overshadow both issues and parties. This first was noticed during the 1960 presidential campaign that saw John F. Kennedy defeat Richard Nixon, and became especially apparent in 1980 as former movie star Ronald Reagan defeated incumbent Jimmy Carter. During this period, both Postman and Moran were struck by the fact that polling indicated that the majority of voters favored Democratic candidates on the issues, but still voted for Reagan because of how they felt about him, a decided departure from the use of reason in making informed decisions. Since then, American political campaigning has arguably become ever more irrational, resulting in the election of an unqualified and unethical celebrity best known for starring on a reality TV series in 2016, and the complete abandonment of any pretense of ideology in the deliberate failure to formulate a Republican Party platform in 2020.

Postman further argues in *Technopoly* (1992) that information technology has led to information overload, handicapping our ability to engage in reflection and evaluation. In *End of Education* (1995) he points to the loss of coherent, unifying metanarratives, ideologies, or mythologies, in our culture. And in his final work, *Building a Bridge to the Eighteenth Century* (1999), he puts forth a plea for the retrieval of Enlightenment values and ideals, not to turn back the clock, but as vital resources we need to bring with us as we enter the future. Building on Postman, I have argued that print culture represented a productive balance between speech and writing, orality and literacy, one in which the word, verbal communication and expression in all of these forms, spoken, handwritten, and typographic, was primary, and that this was the fertile soil in which a culture that privileged rational discourse grew (Strate, 2011, 2014). As various forms of electronic and audiovisual media began to displace print as the dominant forms of communication over the course of the 20th century, the assault on the word came from two extremes. On one end, we have the onset of image culture starting in the 19th century due to photography and various forms of mechanical reproduction of pictures and illustrations, followed by the moving image, culminating in television, and further amplified by new media. At the other extreme, we have the growing emphasis on numbers, which places a premium on speed and efficiency, owing to technologies such as the telegraph, various forms of time-keeping technology, information processing machinery such as time clocks, tabulators, and computers, and techniques such as scientific management and the assembly line. Both the irrationality of images and the hyperrationality of numbers serve to shrink the space available for rational word-centered discourse, crowding out the cultural foundations of democracy.

This brings me now to what I have termed the double bind of democracy, by which I mean to refer to something more than the traditional paradoxes of democracy. And while I am mainly concerned with the problem of modern democracy, as a product of the typographic media environment, adjusting to a postmodern electronic media environment, I should note that there has always been a need to balance the ideal of rational discourse, aka *logos*, against the tendency to utilize irrational appeals to emotions and personal reputation, aka *pathos* and *logos* (Aristotle, 1954). In this regard, we might consider Socrates as a champion of pure logos, which is consistent with Popper's (2020) view that any anti-democratic views expressed by Socrates in the Platonic dialogues were actually expressions of Plato's own thought, and not that of his mentor. Whatever position Socrates might actually have taken, there is a distinction between open dialogue in the pursuit of truth, which is consistent with democratic values, and the manipulative dialectic that can be found in Plato's writings. Aristotle (1954) privileged logos in his treatise on rhetoric, but Aristotelian logic moved away from dialogic exchange towards purely rational and visualist thinking exemplified by the early modern educator Peter Ramus (Ong, 1958), the sort that abstracts out of debate and disputation a simple set of facts suitable for rote learning; this sort of display also tends to ignore contradictions and excludes evidence that does not fit into the predetermined system, leading to the Hegelian and Marxian version of dialectics, the basis of the totalitarian ideologies of fascism, Nazism, and Communism, according to Popper (2020).

To be fair, Aristotle did acknowledge the role of *ethos* and *pathos* in rhetoric, with the understanding that the truth needs to be expressed in as persuasive a manner as possible. *Logos*, the truth was primary, and in his view, following Plato, individuals first needed to learn what is true before learning how to dress up the truth by appeals to source credibility and the emotions. In similar fashion, it is important to recognize that reason in the modern sense, reason$_2$ and what Hannah Arendt (2006) refers to as factual truth (as opposed to logical or philosophical truth), can be more effectively conveyed when expressed within a moral frame, a narrative, and/or tied to emotional and personal appeals (Lakoff, 2002). The problem is that even with the best of intentions, *logos* tends to get lost in the shuffle, leading to purely emotional decision-making and the cult of personality. And factual truth is especially vulnerable, as Arendt explains:

> The chances of factual truth surviving the onslaught of power are very slim indeed; it is always in danger of being maneuvered out of the world not only for a time but, potentially, forever. Facts and events are infinitely more fragile things than axioms, discoveries, theories – even the mostly wildly speculative ones – produced by the human mind; they occur in the field of the ever-changing affairs of men, in whose flux there is nothing more permanent than the admittedly relative permanence of the human mind's structure. One they are lost, no rational effort will ever bring them back. Perhaps the chances that Euclidean mathematics or Einstein's theory of relativity – let alone Plato's philosophy – would have been reproduced in time if their authors had been prevented from handing

them down to posterity are not very good either, yet they are infinitely better than the chances that a fact of importance, forgotten or, more likely, lied away, will one day be rediscovered. (p. 227)

For Arendt (2006), facts and events "constitute the very texture of the political realm" (p. 277), but thereby, in contrast to opinions, are situated outside of politics, and in a sense are both apolitical and anti-political:

> Facts are beyond agreement and consent, and all talk about them – all exchanges of opinion based on correct information – will contribute nothing to their establishment. Unwelcome opinion can be argued with, rejected, or compromised upon, but unwelcome facts possess an infuriating stubbornness that nothing can move except plain lies. The trouble is that factual truth, like all other truth, peremptorily claims to be acknowledged and precludes debate, and debate constitutes the very essence of political life. The modes of thought and communication that deal with truth, if seen from the political perspective, are necessarily domineering; they don't take into account other people's opinions, and taking these into account is the hallmark of all strictly political thinking. (pp. 236–237)

Insofar as they form the texture of politics, to use Arendt's metaphor, facts along with reason occupy a meta level as the basis of democratic politics, as well as the rule of law. And their fragility mirrors the fragility of literacy itself, factual truth being associated with literate culture and the typographic media environment. Unlike speech, which is arguably universal to all human societies and cultures, and comes about naturally through typical early childhood development, literacy has been a relatively rare and recent phenomena in the history of our species, and is decidedly unnatural in that it requires schooling and a significant amount to hard work to attain.

Modern democracy, emerging out of the typographic media environment, and closely associated with Enlightenment rationalism and modern science, is based on an educated, informed, and above all *literate* citizenry capable of engaging in and evaluating rational discourse. This of course leaves open the question of who is considered a citizen and who is not, and what are the requirements for being able to vote; factors that have been used to define and limit voting rights include socioeconomic status and land ownership, location, age, gender, race and ethnicity, disability, criminal conviction, etc. In absolute terms, full political participation would require that there be no restrictions whatsoever, and the progressive extension of voting rights that we have witnessed during the modern era has brought us closer to that possibility, with the understanding that certain restrictions remain within reason (e.g., age). But this has coincided with changes in the media environment that have made rational discourse increasingly more difficult. While there is general agreement that democracy requires freedom of the press, requiring voters to be literate is at best highly controversial, not the least because in the United States literacy tests were mainly used in extremely biased ways to disenfranchise African-Americans. Naturalized citizens must pass a civics exam to earn their citizenship, but we have no similar requirement for those of us born in the USA. Neither is education of any sort required, although the easy availability of free public education is very much a part of American society, and arguably one of the pillars of the republic (Postman, 1985; Strate, 2014). There are no requirements for being well informed, and there are no tests for rationality, or for sanity for that matter, apart from the loss of voting rights due to felony convictions.

In the absence of an ideally well-informed and rational electorate, government control by political, economic, and/or technical elites, becomes a seeming necessity. Whereas political parties once functioned as a medium connecting leadership to the electorate, with some expectation of concrete benefits on the part of voters, as the size and complexity of society grew, and advances in communication technologies introduced new possibilities, public opinion became a paramount concern. Hence, in the early 20th century, we have Walter Lippman

(1922) arguing for the need to manipulate public opinion in order to garner popular support for policies. This depended on the manufacture of what Daniel Boorstin (1978) termed pseudo-events, events manufactured specifically as content for the press, and newer forms of news media, i.e., broadcasting. And as Jacques Ellul (1964, 1965) explains, while the appearance of democratic decision-making and popular support is necessary for any modern government's claim to legitimacy, the requirements of modern, technological societies cannot depend upon the vagaries of irrational opinion, so that internal propaganda is required to manufacture consent, to use the famous phrase associated with Noam Chomsky. This amounts to a reversal of the ideal order in which democratic decision making is supposed to take place, so that the outcome is decided beforehand, and voting is manipulated to give the outcome the veneer of popular support. For this reason, politics increasingly becomes a technical operation run by technical experts specializing in manipulating public opinion, while actual policy decisions are left to technical experts compartmentalized into separate areas of specialization (Ellul, 1964, 1965). Further technical manipulation of the electorate can involve various forms of voter restrictions targeted against specific groups deemed problematic (e.g., racial or economic groups), and related techniques such as gerrymandering.

Voter manipulation also involves frequent appeals to passions and emotions, especially as amplified by image-based discourse (Postman, 1985; Strate, 2014). This is where television has made a major impact, further exacerbated by online communications, especially social media. Images can serve as evidence, but facts need to be expressed as statements; images can be altered and faked, but lies can only be expressed through words (Langer, 1957; Postman, 1985). And by amplifying emotions and downplaying or eliminating propositional statements, the electronic media have made lies, which, as Arendt (2006) acknowledges, have always been a part of political discourse, almost as ubiquitous in postmodern democratic politics as they have been in authoritarian societies. This further promotes the decay of reason, or the substitution of reason$_3$ in place of reason$_2$. As Arendt (2006) observes:

> It has frequently been noticed that the surest long-term result of brainwashing is a peculiar kind of cynicism – an absolute refusal to believe in the truth of anything, no matter how well this truth may be established. In other words, the result of a consistent and total substitution of lies for factual truth is not that lies will now be accepted as truth, and the truth be defamed as lies, but that the sense by which we take our bearings in the real world – and the category of truth vs. falsehood is among the mental means to this end – is being destroyed.
>
> And for this trouble there is no remedy. It is but the other side of the disturbing contingency of all factual reality. Since everything that has actually happened in the realm of human affairs could just as well have been otherwise, the possibilities for lying are boundless, and this boundlessness makes for self-defeat. (pp. 252–253)

This sets up the double bind of democracy for citizens, candidates, and officials who favor rational discourse, as they find the kind of messaging they want to engage in to be ineffective, placing them at a significant disadvantage. In order to win elections, then, they must engage in the kind of discourse that is most effective on the audiovisual media. But the victory that such tactics may afford them ultimately contributes to the decline and decay of democracy itself. This catch-22 seems to allow for no way out of the present conundrum, no way to preserve, restore, or create true democracy, and perhaps no way even to prevent the eventual dissolution of the kind of democracy that was first envisioned by Enlightenment intellectuals.

Whereas the enemies of the open society that Popper (2002) was concerned with were committed to certain ideologies that had to be supported by argumentation, and thereby justified by reason (no matter how unreasonable they may actually have been), and therefore open to criticism through reason, today's enemies have more or less abandoned logos altogether. In this sense, while it may be convenient to use labels such as fascism, Nazism, religious nationalism, and communism, the more fitting term would be authoritarianism, autocracy, and Popper's preferred designation, totalitarianism. In the same vein, a phrase such as *illiberal democracy* is paralogical, essentially oxymoronic. And while some may see a solution in a libertarian alternative, often associated with conservativism, it would prove to be unworkable given the size and complexity of modern societies and the speed and scale at which they are obligated to function, in contrast to the agrarian society that gave birth to the American nation; moreover, if implemented inevitably it would lead into anarchy that reverses into calls for law and order and a shift into autocratic and authoritarian structures. It is no accident, then, that right wing populism combines the two opposite extremes, as both lead to the same end. Further, given the global reach and interdependence of our technological milieu and the international order, a dismantling of central government would leave a nation open to be dominated by its competitors, who would then impose authoritarian control from without.

What we are left with, then, is Postman's (1992) technopoly full blown and Ellul's (1964, 1965) Orwellian technological society, governed via propaganda, maintaining the illusion of political freedom, but in essence a totalitarian society. It is easy enough to imagine a future where we put artificial intelligence in charge of all governmental decision-making. In fact, science fiction writers have been putting forth such scenarios for decades. Notably, Alphaville, the 1965 film by Jean-Luc Godard, imagines a dystopian future society run by a computer housed in a fictional Institute of General Semantics! Holding aside fears of this sort, and of the kinds of futures depicted in films like *The Terminator* and *The Matrix*, where the AIs seek to dominate or eradicate humanity, there are more down-to-earth human concerns about the design of technologies and the coding of algorithms. Simply put, they can never be neutral, and the ways in which they are constructed will amount to another type of political decision making, albeit one less transparent than before. And one in which any sense of actual responsibility for decision-making is completely abrogated.

Here, Korzybski's (1921, 1950) less extreme notion of technocracy seems the least objectionable, but it was predicated on the general acceptance of the legitimacy and ascendancy of science, which was undermined drastically over the course of the late 20th century. As Postman (1995) argues in *The End of Education*, and Jean-François Lyotard makes a similar argument in *The Postmodern Condition* (1984), science is no longer accepted universally as the metanarrative, ideology, or mythology that is generally agreed upon, and no alternate has come to take its place. Lyotard significantly attributes this to computer technology, but I would maintain that more generally it can be considered an outgrowth of the electronic media environment. While Korzybski (1921) was responding to the same kinds of conditions that Lippman (1922) was, those conditions are no longer in effect.

A Change Is Gonna Come

Echoing the civil rights era song by Sam Cooke, it may be a long time coming, but sooner or later a change is going to come. Or as Heraclitus explained over two and half millennia ago, *change is the only constant in life*. A double bind may seem to be insoluble and inescapable, and therefore a permanent trap, but it is ultimately unsustainable (Bateson, 1972, 1979: Watzlawick et al, 1967). Of course, one reason for its persistence may well be that the alternatives are even less desirable than living within a paradoxical bind. It would certainly appear to be the lesser of two evils when considering the forces that might lead to complete systemic collapse, e.g., environmental factors such as climate change or nuclear armageddon that makes the planet uninhabitable, or results in the extinction of our species, or reduces us to survival mode and barbarism. Indeed, our popular culture is rife with apocalyptic and post-apocalyptic narratives, almost as if we are psychologically preparing ourselves for an inevitable breakdown of civilization.

Other common speculative scenarios in our popular media posit a dystopian future based on totalitarian government, and this too represents another undesirable form of systemic change, the collapse of democracy and the rule of law that the enemies of the open society predict will be inevitable, and labor to bring about. Indeed, from a Marxian perspective, the build-up of a society's internal contradictions will ultimately lead to revolution, and the contradictions inherent in a double bind are a source of extreme pressure that may well explode if not alleviated. On a more hopeful note, one possibility would be the introduction of a new, yet unforeseen technology that restores balance to the media environment, and is conducive to the kind of reason associated with the Enlightenment, or to a further elaboration of that sort of reason. Alternately, there might be some type of spontaneous evolution of human consciousness, some sort of awakening or broader form of enlightenment, that results in the establishment of a new, more healthy kind of culture, and perhaps even the creation of a truly utopian society. Of course, various religious and spiritual traditions have long maintained that at some point in the future divine intervention will lead to systemic change, often in a positive vein. But speculation concerning the supernatural lies beyond the scope of this study.

Change will come no matter what we do or do not do, but this does not absolve us of the ethical responsibility to act in ways that serve to preserve and expand the open society and liberal democracy. To this end, in the face of the clear and present danger of a slide into autocratic rule, the immediate response to the double bind of rational discourse from a utilitarian stance is to go with the flow, in this case the flow of electrons – in other words, to embrace irrational means to achieve rational ends. The negative example of the trial of Socrates looms large here, as he resisted the temptation to employ the persuasive techniques associated with rhetoric, and instead confined himself to logical argument, his philosophical conviction resulting in his judicial conviction, leading to his death. Consequently, Plato (1971, 1973) rejected rhetoric as a legitimate form of knowledge, and condemned the Sophists, his contemporaries who taught the art of oratory and persuasion without regard for "the truth" that he was confident he could determine; of course, the Sophists recognized beliefs about what constitutes the truth differed from one locale to another, and therefore anticipated the contemporary position of cultural relativism. Aristotle (1954) retrieved rhetoric from the philosophical dustbin, admitting to its importance but insisting on its subordination to logic and dialectic – in other words, rhetoric should only be used in service of promotion "the truth" and therefore only taught to those who have first learned what "the truth" actually is.

A non-aristotelian rhetoric, therefore, would require the open exchange of different "truths" expressed as clearly and persuasively as possible, along the lines of the free marketplace of ideas, the goal being the objective evaluation of completing claims based on available evidence and logical coherence. This requires a different approach to argumentation than currently seems to dominate postmodern electronic culture. The original understanding underlining the idea of freedom of speech and the press was that allowing people to express their opinions would constitute the beginning of dialogue, and through the exchange of views, they would eventually come to some form of resolution. Currently, expressing an opinion often serves to shut down any further exchange, as it leads to declarations like, *that's your opinion, this is my opinion*, the underlying sense being that all opinions are equally valid, no form of evaluation is possible, and at best all that we can do is to *agree to disagree*. That expressing an opinion represents the end of dialogue rather than its commencement, the closing of minds rather than an opening, is a reflection of the decay and disappearance of rational discourse based on factual truth. United States Senator Daniel Patrick Moynihan once said, "everyone is entitled to his own opinion, but not his own facts." But now, everything that ought to be understood as facts are all too often disparaged as opinions, and in this sense facts are no longer on a meta level, but rather reduced to mere opinion, which is to say politicized, as Arendt (2006) would put it. Logic is also lost as images replace words as the dominant form of discourse. The decline of *logos* in the context of electronic culture leaves us only with *pathos*, the appeal to emotions, and *ethos*, in contemporary parlance, source credibility. And while *pathos* and *ethos* have a place in rational discourse, the absence of *logos* represents not a non-aristotelian rhetoric, but an anti-aristotelian rhetoric.

Faced with authoritarian alternatives, the urgent need to employ whatever forms of voter persuasion and manipulation are needed to protect liberal democracy certainly seem like the lesser of two evils – and may well be so. But at best, irrational discourse can only serve as a temporary, stop gap measure, not a permanent solution. The more techniques based solely on image, personality, and emotion are employed, the more that political discourse is reduced to pure propaganda, the more powerless we become to escape the double bind. And the greater the probability that those same techniques will lead to the end of democracy and the rule of law. As Aldous Huxley (2012) put it, "the ends cannot justify the means, for the simple and obvious reason that the means employed determine the nature of the ends produced" (p. 10). It follows that the current state of affairs is simply unsustainable as far as democracy's survival is concerned and will eventually lead to the disappearance of democracy altogether. Admittedly, an argument could be made based on systems theory that the amplification of irrationality cannot continue indefinitely, and could eventually result in a reversal, and thereby the restoration of at least a measure of rational discourse, or perhaps in Hegelian fashion, a new synthesis of the rational and the irrational. Assuming that such as eventuality would occur, the means would not justify the ends, nor be consistent with them, just as suffering the consequences of war in order to establish peace is not preferable to avoiding war and promoting peace in the first place.

The goal then has to be to restore rational discourse to its rightful role in politics, so that policy deliberations and political campaigns are based on facts and evidence. This requires some means of overcoming what Barack Obama and others have referred to as our current epistemological crisis, which has significant portions of the citizenry calling into question all of our fact-based professions, including science and medicine, as well as law enforcement and the military. To make decisions, there must be a way to resolve differences of opinion, which requires mutually agreed upon facts that can be determined, so that evidence can be used to support positions in debates, and through observation and experimentation we can assess results and determine the best course of action. Popper (2002) referred to this sort of inductive and empirical approach as *piecemeal social engineering*, in contrast to the deductive, romantic and idealistic social engineering associated with totalitarianism. And this seems entirely consistent with Korzybski's (1921, 1950) call for human engineering, and the requirements of a non-aristotelian politics. Whereas Korzybski originally called for government agencies run by engineers to determine the best course of action, we might instead look for public institutions devoted to impartial evaluation of facts to provide the basis of policy debates and decision-making. Admittedly, there will always be outliers who will continue to deny factual reports and statements of description, and in the current political climate it would be difficult to achieve the kind of agreement necessary to establish such agencies, but universal agreement is not a requirement nor an expectation in a democracy – a supermajority would be sufficient to establish the legitimacy of such an institution. In this regard, artificial intelligence might be helpful, but not a panacea as it would still be dependent of its algorithms and the data it is trained on. What is needed is an institution, perhaps along the lines of the *fair witness* depicted in Robert Heinlein's general semantics-influenced science fiction novel, *Stranger in a Strange Land*; a fair witness is an individual trained to never make an inference, so that when observing a house from a distance and asked what color is it, the fair witness would respond, *it is white… on this side*. If a nonpolitical body could be established, the piecemeal approach could be used as the basis for evidence-based policy decisions.

In *Technopoly* (1992), Postman noted that the last bastion of humanistic procedure not entirely engulfed by the technical imperative is the legal system. That is why almost all disputes are now resolved by the courts, rather than by clergy, for example. When we think about the standard for trials, it includes the rule of law, which provides the framework for evaluation of cases, including the determination of what counts as evidence and what does not, as well as what arguments can be made and what arguments are out of bounds. In the United States and elsewhere, judicial decisions typically involve a jury, and the jury embodies the democratic ideal, and the basic standard of reason. And we also have the judge, who interprets the law and guides the conduct of the participants based on specific expertise. The legal system is deeply rooted in the concept of reason, in logic and evidence, deduction and induction, argumentation and empiricism. This, I would suggest, represents the best hope for preserving democracy and breaking out of our current double bind, because the rule of law is more essential than even the will of the people, and because it serves as a model for conduct based on reason. While the American judicial system is not immune from the current challenges to democracy, as can be seen by the politicizing of the judiciary and the poor conduct of certain members of the United States Supreme Court, justice remains part of the foundation of the open society, and the courts remain the last best option for resolving political disputes. Judges are expected to be well educated, especially when it comes to the law, and adding general semantics training would certainly improve their standing. But above all, the function of the judge is what our system needs going forward, someone able to make the call as to what constitutes evidence and what does not, what kinds of arguments can be made and what cannot, etc. For critics of the administrative state, this would not amount to investing even more power in the executive branch of government, but rather establishing a parallel decision-making body within the judicial system.

For traditionalists seeking a rationale based on Judeo-Christian values, there is ample biblical precedent for both the supremacy of law and the authority of judges. This is not to invest such power in a single individual, but in an institution, so that voters can then make decisions based on reason, understanding the full implications of their choices. Moreover, juries could be empaneled to serve alongside judges, to add checks and balances to the determination of facts. In this way, a system similar to the legal system, one charged with evaluating facts and evidence rather than guilt and innocence, would provide the basis for rational deliberation regarding policy. Debate over policy itself, that is, over what action to take in response to the facts that have been established, would remain open to argument and democratic decision-making, rather than being an automatic response based on technical criteria of the sort that Ellul (1964) decried, and that AI threatens to usurp. In this way, while efficiency may remain an important criterion, it would not be the only one, ethical and moral concerns could be voiced and addressed as well. Importantly, in the context of a democratic government, there would be a clear sense of human responsibility, and availability of human response. Further, policy decisions could then be evaluated based on factual evidence, so that additional decisions could be made based on their results, allowing for reality testing based on empirical methods.

As previously discussed, democracy and the rule of law is based on principles such as freedom, equality, and justice. And while these values are generally shared within American society, they tend to be invoked on a very high level of abstraction. Additional efforts at values education and civics education are sorely needed, with special attention given to operationalizing those principles. Apart from schooling and adult-oriented courses, direct experience would go a long way towards enhanced understanding. Such opportunities already exist in the form of jury service, and the addition of a court-based system to evaluate facts and evidence would provide many more opportunities. While at present, being selected for jury duty is viewed by many as an inconvenience rather than a civic duty, with some ignoring the summons, others finding ways to be excused, and still others never being selected to actually serve, the new judicial system coupled with the existing one could be paired with a new universal requirement for public service (with exceptions for genuine hardship, sickness, disability, etc.). One model might be that of reserve military service, wherein individuals are required to spend two weeks each year in active duty. With that expectation as the norm, and the period of service established well in advance so proper arrangements could be made, the bulk of the citizenry could have direct experience with justice and reason operationalized.

Recalling that reason$_3$, the kind of reason that emerges out of the electronic media environment, would be otherwise considered irrational and a form of anti-reason from the standpoint of reason$_2$, and therefore incompatible with if not antithetical to modern democracy, more and better educational efforts are sorely needed. In addition to the values and civics education noted above, science education is essential, for youth and adults alike. The emphasis, however, should not be on science as unquestioned authority, or on the teaching of science as a body of knowledge, although key facts and theories should not be ignored. But more importantly what is needed is the teaching of scientific method, the basics of induction and empiricism, observation and experimentation, reality-testing and fact-checking, the relationship between data and the formation of theories and hypotheses, replicability and reproducibility, falsifiability and probability, as well as the appropriate applications of statistics and calculation, and deductive logic. With this in mind, the teaching of general semantics principles and techniques, and related approaches concerning language and symbolic communication, epistemology and methodology, systems theory and media ecology, could be transformative in allowing for real progress in human affairs, just as Korzybski (1950, 2023) envisioned. Even if we cannot entirely retrieve reason$_2$ and restore it to its rightful place in our culture, we certainly can move beyond reason$_3$, and make progress towards a reason$_4$ that is consistent with reason$_2$, and maybe even improves upon it.

Just as we cannot return to reason$_2$, it is not within our power to reestablish the typographic media environment, even if such a return were possible. But we can continue the practice of reading, and writing, with pen, paper, and in print, for ourselves, and encouraging the same for others. In turn this requires setting aside our devices, turning them off for a time, unplugging, and turning away from the screens that surround us. Support for schooling is a must, and schools themselves must emphasize all that literacy requires, including patience, delayed gratification, reflection, analysis and criticism, and abstract thought – while avoiding what Johnson (1946) termed dead level abstracting, i.e., only remaining on a high or low level of abstracting exclusively. Education itself, both formal and informal, must be viewed as a lifelong activity, not one that ends with graduation and a diploma (or a drop out). Opportunities for adult learning need to be made easily available, and emphatically encouraged. And while reading alone is a vital activity, the goal is not simply a nation of auto-didacts. Schooling very much involves oral discussion, often based on written texts, and more generally involving the kind of discourse and thought influenced and shaped by literacy. For adults, formal situations such as continuing education classes provide opportunities for discourse that is structured but relatively open, and models for civil discussion, debate, and disputation, and perhaps even the resolution of differences. Informal opportunities such as book clubs and other kinds of discussion groups are easy enough to organize. Religious organizations, houses of worship and spiritual centers, can serve similar functions, as can other local groups such as clubs, fraternal and sororal organizations, service organizations, lineage societies, etc. Local gatherings need not be political in nature to serve a positive function in strengthening community ties, the respectful exchange of ideas, and similar practices, and can serve as models for larger community events, school board and town council meetings, etc. Of course, this is no guarantee against the injection of irrational discourse by individuals and groups, but it can mitigate or minimize the potential for disruption.

While local gatherings can be hosted by individuals in their private homes, a media environment conducive to literacy and rational discourse also requires third places, spaces outside of home and work such as cafes and bars, parks and community centers, recreational facilities, etc. (Oldenburg, 1989; Putnam, 2000). This is essential for what Jürgen Habermas (1989) refers to as the public sphere, places where citizens in a democracy can gather to discuss the issues of the day, which in turn require access to information that was traditionally afforded by newspapers and other print media, aided by the ability to engage in rational dialogue. Such places need to serve as spaces where customer turnover is not the priority, so as to encourage conversation, and also as places where newspapers and periodicals are made accessible, with a vested interest in maintaining subscriptions and subsidies for print media. This includes bookstores, which have often led the way in trying to function as cafes and gathering places, albeit with limited effect, in part because of the tendency for large chains to crowd out locally-owned, independent shops; to the extent that independent neighborhood bookstores remain, they need to be supported. Libraries too require support and patronage, and perhaps encouragement to shift their priorities from transforming themselves into media centers to making space available for readings, lectures, and discussion groups.

There is much that can be done to shore up and fortify all of the institutions and practices associated with reading and writing. This would include celebrating calligraphy as an art form, and more generally good handwriting (in this regard, it is encouraging to see recent efforts to restore the teaching of cursive in American schools). Even more important would be the encouragement of letter writing, which would also benefit from reforms to the postal system, finding means to curb the abuses that lead to the preponderance of junk mail, making the delivery of personal letters free of charge, as well as restoring the status of the post office as a vital form of public service. The need to make voting by mail available during the COVID-19 pandemic brought home the awareness of the importance of the postal system to American democracy, and the negative implications of its privatization, as the Trump administration tried to disrupt and obstruct the distribution and collection of mail-in ballots during the 2020 election to gain a political advantage. Postal service is also significant for the distribution of printed newspapers and periodicals, which can be bolstered via policy incentives, and individual subscriptions. We would do well to recall that the position of Postmaster General once was a Cabinet-level office in the United States, first filled by Benjamin Franklin. David Brin's post-apocalyptic science fiction novel, *The Postman*, and the Kevin Costner film adapted from it, help to convey the importance of letter writing and mail delivery to our sense of community.

Recognizing that we are in a double bind is an important first step, along with the understanding that finding our way out will not be easy. At the same time, we must remain hopeful and committed, for no better reason than that there is no alternative. To give up is to ensure the end of democracy, the end of rule of law, the end of justice, the end of reason. Or at best to rely on others to save the day, retreating to an infantile state that favors authoritarian impulses rather than an egalitarian ethos. And while there have been many instances throughout history where retreat was a viable option, running away is no guarantee of escape when we are living in a *global village*, to invoke McLuhan's (1962) evocative phrase. Living within our electronically mediated global village, the only good option is to *think globally but act locally*, as the saying goes. Democracy is rooted in a sense of community and communication, the rule of law requires the cooperation and commitment of citizens, principles and values can only be shared and operationalized through group interaction, reason needs to be reinforced through public discourse, and literacy is little more than a vocational skill absent a social context and a media environment that provides balance between the spoken and written word. All of the levels of the pyramid model of the open society are mutually reinforcing; each level in isolation cannot guarantee liberal democracy, and indeed has been associated with illiberal, authoritarian, and totalitarian forms of rule. As I have stated previously, based on the political philosophy of Hannah Arendt (1958), *we create the conditions that condition us* (Strate, 2017). It is within our collective power to create the kind of conditions that are conducive to the survival of the open society, liberal democracy, and progress in regard to political affairs and the human condition. Whether or not we can succeed, and even if our efforts only advance the situation in modest, piecemeal fashion, local and temporary as it may be, is it not incumbent on us, in whatever way we can, to try?

References

Anton, C., Logan, R.K., & Strate, L. (2017). *Taking up McLuhan's cause: Perspectives on formal causality and media ecology*. Intellect.
Arendt, H. (1958). *The human condition* (2nd ed.). University of Chicago Press.
Arendt, H. (2006). *Between past and future*. Penguin.
Aristotle (1954). *Rhetoric* (W. Rhys Roberts, Trans.). The Modern Library.
Aristotle. (1998). *The metaphysics* (H. Lawson-Tancred, Trans.). Penguin.
Baron-Cohen, S. (1995). *Mindblindness: An essay on autism and theory of mind*. MIT Press.
Bateson, G. (1972). *Steps to an ecology of mind: Collected essays in anthropology, psychiatry, evolution, and epistemology*. Bantam Books.
Bateson, G. (1979). *Mind and nature: A necessary unity*. Bantam Books.
Boorstin, D. J. (1978). *The image: A guide to pseudo-events in America*. Atheneum.
Burke, K. (1950). *A rhetoric of motives*. University of California Press.
Campbell, J. (1982). *Grammatical man: Information, entropy, language, and life*. Simon & Schuster.
Chase, S. (1932a, July 6). A new deal for America. *The New Republic*, pp. 199–201.
Chase, S. (1932b). *A new deal*. Macmillan.
Chase, S. (1938). *The tyranny of words*. New York: Harcourt, Brace.
Deacon, T. W. (2012). *Incomplete nature: How mind emerged from matter*. W. W. Norton.
Deibert, R. J. (1997). *Parchment, printing, and hypermedia*. Columbia University Press.
Dunbar, R. (1996). *Grooming, gossip, and the evolution of language*. Harvard University Press.
Duncan, H. D. (1962). *Communication and social order*. Bedminster Press.
Duncan, H. D. (1968). *Symbols in society*. Oxford University Press.

Eisenstein, E. L. (1979). *The printing press as an agent of change: Communications and cultural transformations in early modern Europe* (2 vols.). Cambridge University Press.
Ellul, J. (1964). *The technological society* (J. Wilkinson, Trans.). Knopf.
Ellul, J. (1965). *Propaganda: The formation of men's attitudes* (K. Kellen & J. Lerner, Trans.). Knopf.
Frith, U. (1989). *Autism: Explaining the enigma*. Blackwell.
Fukuyama, F. (1992). *The end of history and the last man*. Free Press.
Gershberg, Z., & Illing, S. (2022). *The paradox of democracy: Free speech, open media, and perilous persuasion*. University of Chicago Press.
Goody, J. (1977). *The domestication of the savage mind*. Cambridge University Press.
Goody, J. (1986). *The logic of writing and the organization of society*. Cambridge University Press.
Goody, J. (1987). *The interface between the written and the oral*. Cambridge University Press.
Habermas, J. (1989). *The structural transformation of the public sphere: An inquiry into a category of bourgeois society* (T. Burger & F.k Lawrence, Trans.). MIT Press.
Havelock, E. A. (1963). *Preface to Plato*. The Belknap Press of Harvard University Press.
Havelock, E. A. (1982). *The literate revolution in Greece and its cultural consequences*. Princeton University Press.
Havelock, E. A. (1986). *The muse learns to write: Reflections on orality and literacy from antiquity to the present*. Yale University Press.
Herman, E. S., & Chomsky, N. (1988). *Manufacturing consent: The political economy of the mass media*. Pantheon.
Hobart, M. E., & Schiffman, Z. S. (1998). *Information ages: Literacy, numeracy, and the computer revolution*. John Hopkins University Press.
Huxley, A. (2012). *Ends and means*. Transaction. (Original work published 1937)
Innis, H. A. (1951). *The bias of communication*. University of Toronto Press.
Innis, H. A. (1972). *Empire and communication* (rev. ed.). University of Toronto Press.
Johnson, W. (1946). *People in quandaries: The semantics of personal adjustment*. Harper & Row.
Klapp, O. E. (1978). *Opening and closing: Strategies of information adaptation in society*. Cambridge University Press.

Korzybski, A. (1921). *Manhood of humanity: The science and art of human engineering.* E. P. Dutton.

Korzybski, A. (1950). *Manhood of humanity: An introduction to non-aristotelian systems and general semantics* (2nd ed.). Institute of General Semantics.

Korzybski, A. (2023*).* *Science and sanity: An introduction to non-Aristotelian systems and general semantics* (6th ed.). Institute of General Semantics. (Original work published 1933)

Lakoff, G. (2002). *Moral politics: How liberals and conservatives think* (2nd ed.). University of Chicago Press.

Langer, S. K. (1957). *Philosophy in a new key: A study in the symbolism of reason, rite and art* (3rd ed.). Harvard University Press.

Lévi-Strauss, C. (1966). *The savage mind.* University of Chicago Press.

Lévi-Strauss, C. (1969). *The raw and the cooked* (J. Weightman & D. Weightman, Trans.). Harper & Row.

Lippmann, W. (1922). *Public opinion.* Harcourt, Brace.

Logan, R. K. (2004). *The alphabet effect: A media ecology understanding of the making of western civilization.* Hampton Press.

Luhmann, N. (1982). *The differentiation of society* (S. Holmes & C. Larmore, Trans.). Columbia University Press.

Luhmann, N. (1989). *Ecological communication* (J. Bednarz, Jr., Trans.). University of Chicago Press.

Luhmann, N. (1990). *Essays on self-reference.* Columbia University Press.

Luhmann, N. (1995). *Social systems* (J. Bednarz, Jr. with D. Baecker, Trans.). Stanford University Press.

Lyotard, J.-F. (1984). *The postmodern condition: A report on knowledge* (G. Bennington & B. Massumi, Trans.). University of Minnesota Press. (Original work published 1979)

Maturana, H. R. & Varela, F. J. (1980). *Autopoiesis and cognition: The realization of the living.* D. Reidel.

Maturana, H. R., & Varela, F. J. (1992). *The tree of knowledge: The biological roots of human understanding* (rev, ed., R. Paolucci, Trans.). Shambhala.

McLuhan, M. (1962). *The Gutenberg galaxy: The making of typographic man.* University of Toronto Press.

McLuhan, M. (1964). *Understanding media: The extensions of man.* McGraw Hill.

McLuhan, M. (2006). *The classical trivium: The place of Thomas Nashe in the learning of his time* (W. T. Gordon, Ed.). Gingko Press.

McLuhan, M., & McLuhan, E. (2011). *Media and formal cause*. NeoPoiesis Press.

Mead, G. H. (1934). *Mind, self and society from the standpoint of a social behaviorist* (C. W. Morris, Ed.). University of Chicago Press.

Moran, T. P. (1984). Politics 1984: That's entertainment. *ETC: A Review of General Semantics, 41*(2), 117–129.

Oldenburg, R. (1989). *The great good place: Cafes, coffee shops, bookstores, bars, hair salons, and other hangouts at the heart of a community*. Paragon House.

Ong, W. J. (1958). *Ramus, method, and the decay of dialogue*. Harvard University Press.

Ong, W. J. (1967). *The presence of the word: Some prolegomena for cultural and religious history*. Yale University Press.

Ong, W. J. (1982). *Orality and literacy: The technologizing of the word*. Methuen.

Plato. (1971). *Gorgias* (W. Hamilton, Trans.). Penguin.

Plato. (1973). *Phaedrus and letters VII and VIII* (W. Hamilton, Trans.). Penguin.

Popper, K. (2002). *The logic of scientific discovery*. Routledge.

Popper, K. (2020). *The open society and its enemies*. Princeton University Press. (Original work published 1945)

Postman, N. (1974). Media ecology: General semantics in the third millennium. *General Semantics Bulletin* 41–43, 74–78.

Postman, N. (1976). *Crazy talk, stupid talk*. Delacorte.

Postman, N. (1985). *Amusing ourselves to death: Public discourse in the age of show business*. Viking.

Postman, N. (1992). *Technopoly: The surrender of culture to technology*. Alfred A. Knopf.

Postman, N. (1995). *The end of education: Redefining the value of school*. Alfred A. Knopf.

Postman, N. (1999). *Building a bridge to the eighteenth century: How the past can improve our future*. Alfred A. Knopf.

Postman, N., Weingartner, C., & Moran, T. P. (Eds.). (1969). *Language in America*. Pegasus.

Putnam, R. D. (2000). *Bowling alone: The collapse and revival of American community*. Simon & Schuster.

Schmandt-Besserat, D. (1996). *How writing came about*. University of Texas Press.

Siebert, F. S., Peterson, T., & Schramm, W. (1963). *Four theories of the press.* University of Illinois Press.
Steinberg, S. H. (1996). *Five hundred years of printing* (rev. ed., J. Trevitt). Oak Knoll Press.
Strate, L. (2011). *On the binding biases of time and other essays on general semantics and media ecology.* Institute of General Semantics.
Strate, L. (2014). *Amazing ourselves to death: Neil Postman's brave new world revisited.* Peter Lang.
Strate, L. (2016). The effects that give cause and the pattern that directs. In C. Anton, R.K. Logan, & L. Strate (Eds.), *Taking up McLuhan's cause: Perspectives on formal causality and media ecology* (pp. 93–121). Intellect.
Strate, L. (2017). *Media ecology: An approach to understanding the human condition.* Peter Lang.
Strate, L. (2018). The medium is the membrane. *ETC: A Review of General Semantics* 75(3-4), 307–316.
Strate, L. (2022a). Science, progress, and Korzybski's progressive vision. *Anekaant: A Journal of Polysemic Thought* 14, 39–52.
Strate, L. (2022b). Science, progress, and Korzybski's progressive vision. *ETC: A Review of General Semantics* 79(3-4), 228–249.
Strate, L. (2022c). *Concerning communication: Epic quests and lyric excursions within the human lifeworld.* Institute of General Semantics.
Strauss, L. (1967, June). Jerusalem and Athens: Some introductory reflections. *Commentary,* 45–57.
Trujillo Liñán, L. (2022). *Formal cause in Marshall McLuhan's thinking.* Institute of General Semantics.
Veblen, T. (1921). *The engineers and the price system.* B. W. Huebsch.
Watzlawick, P. (1976). *How real is real?* Vintage.
Watzlawick, P., Bavelas, J. B., & Jackson, D. D. (1967). *Pragmatics of human communication: A study of interactional patterns, pathologies, and paradoxes.* Norton.
Whitehead, A.N., & Russell, B. (1925–1927). *Principia mathematica* (2nd ed., 3 vols.). The University Press.

CHAPTER 3

MODERN TOTEMS OF OUR IMAGINATION: THE ECONOMY, INFLATION AND MONEY
CHRIS MAYER

"The ability to deconstruct and analyze and criticize what's being said about the economy and the deficit and inflation... would certainly be something that would mean a lot today."
— Lance Strate, "Semantic Reactions," Episode 2

"If an old idea or a system of ideas be false and therefore harmful, it is a genuine service to attack it and destroy it even if nothing be offered to take its place, just as it is a good to destroy a rattlesnake lurking by a human pathway, even if one does not offer a substitute to take its place."
— Alfred Korzybski, *Manhood of Humanity*

On a recent abnormally warm January morning in the year 2023, the U.S. government released data on the job market. As Bloomberg reported: "Hiring at U.S. companies far exceeded expectations and applications for jobless benefits fell to a three-month low."

Great news for the economy, right? We should be happy more people are working and don't need to apply for jobless benefits.

But... The stock market dropped as the report was widely regarded as "bad news" by investors. Why?

This is one question I will sort through using general semantics. But as you'll see, the way in which we work to answer the above question has wide application – as we sort through the economy, to money, and even the idea of wealth itself.

What Is The "Economy" Anyway?

I'd like to start with what may be Korzybski's most important message: to be conscious of abstracting. Or to put it another way: to be aware of our abstractions. Abstracting, in general semantics, is a rich concept. Robert Pula takes three pages to define abstracting in his glossary of general semantics. (See his *A General-Semantics Glossary: Pula's Guide for the Perplexed*.)

For our purposes, let's say that abstracting is the process of putting what we experience or think into words (or symbols, to speak more broadly). Abstractions are those words and symbols. These words and symbols are not the thing they aim to represent or describe. As Korzybski famously put it, "the map is not the territory."

In general semantics, a first step is to be aware of the abstractions that surround us. We live in a world soaked through with abstractions. Importantly, there is no way to get around this, nor should we try to avoid using abstractions. The world we live in is an ever-changing complex of things, experiences, ideas, etc. In order to get a handle on all this "stuff" and communicate with each other, we have to boil it down somehow.

So how do we talk about the world of work? All over the United States people go to work every day. We have a vocabulary to talk about this world – we talk about "businesses" and "profits" and "losses." We have things called "prices" and we keep track of "transactions." And on and on it goes.

We have a word for all that activity in total. We call it the "economy." Giant abstraction. Because what is the "economy?" It's not really a thing is it? It's not something we can go out and point to, like a house or a dog.

Of course, you'll say, this is obvious. It *is* obvious on reflection. But the way people use the word makes me wonder. When people talk about something as being "good for the economy" they are falling prey to their own abstraction. A tax cut is not "good for the economy." It helps certain people but not everyone equally. Higher interest rates are not "bad for the economy." It may be good for some people – think people who have money in savings accounts. But it's not so good for other people – think people who borrow money.

Politicians talk about the economy being "strong" or "weak." But times are never "good" or "bad" for everyone. There are some who are doing well and others who struggle. To blot out the details and say "economy" might be convenient, even a necessity in certain discourses – but Korzybski would have you be mindful of these abstractions and to treat them with the utmost care.

In fact, Korzybski proposed a neat little trick, which I use all the time – though not so far in this paper – to help remind you of a problematic abstraction: put single quotation marks around the word. So it's always the 'economy' for me. The single quotation marks flag the term as one to use with care and reminds me to pause over the word and reflect. The single quotation marks tells me that 'economy' refers to a whole swirl of activity – of people working (or not working), making money, getting on financially, etc.

Using single quotations marks in this way should prevent you from saying something dogmatic, such as: "I think X will be good for the 'economy.'" Further, and just as important, anytime anybody says it – a politician or central banker or pundit – you'll know they're abstracting – and you'll take what they say with a good degree of the proverbial salt.

Now that you know about single quotation marks, I will use them henceforth, but judiciously. In theory, you could put a single quotation mark around everything, but then it would quickly lose its power. Korzybski's devices gain power with judicious use.

What About 'Inflation'?

Now that we have an idea of abstractions, let's tackle the idea I mentioned at the start... Why is it that more people working caused the market to go down? Why was it viewed as "bad news?" The answer is because 'the market' viewed the release as giving the Fed the green light to raise interest rates in their effort to bring 'inflation' down. Let me give you more context so that explanation makes sense. Let's start with 'inflation.'

'Inflation' is a term meant to capture the idea of a 'general rise in prices.' 'Inflation' deserves single quotation marks because it is a hard idea to measure in the world out there. The commonly used metric is the Consumer Price Index, or CPI. (A 'general rise in prices' also deserves a single quotation mark, but I'll get to why below...)

The CPI is a closely watched index. But what is it? It represents a lot of assumptions and decisions made by people about what to include in the index, what weight to give each item, how to measure change and so on. It's complicated. And people in the business debate all the time about whether or not it captures the 'true inflation rate.'

For example, there is a line item called 'gasoline.' You may have noticed that 'gasoline' prices are not the same everywhere you go. So which 'gasoline' price do you use? And on what day? There's another line item called 'new vehicles.' Well, there are a lot of 'new vehicles' and the prices are all over the place. How do you sort that out?

The list of such questions is long. And economists have come up with ideas and workarounds to try and address the kinds of questions I've asked above. I just want to get across the idea that the CPI involves many assumptions. It reflects choices people have made in creating and maintaining the index. It's not an exact science. And yet, the CPI is reported with ludicrous precision, such as 7.1%. The decimal point is unintentional comedy, if you ask me.

To complicate things even further: Over time, the way the index is computed has changed. Sometimes the changes have a meaningful impact on the reported number. I use another Korzybskian device to help keep this straight: flagging abstractions with a date.

So, for example, the CPI_{1983} is not the CPI_{2023}. Since 1983, the CPI excludes housing prices. Instead, it uses something called "owners' equivalent rent." As one estimate found, "including home prices and interest rates instead of rent would have pushed the inflation rate to 11.5 percent in February [2022], the latest date available, up 3.6 percentage points from the official figure that month." That's a 45% increase in CPI – and we've only covered one change. There are more.

Korzybski's dating device forces you to think about what you are comparing. Are you comparing "like" things? How are they different? Much of the wisdom of general semantics lies in finding differences where others see similarities, and similarities where others see differences.

And just because we have a number doesn't mean we have anything resembling what we experience. It matters a great deal what you spend your money on and how much you make. Everyone experiences 'inflation' differently. Someone who struggles to meet rent and pay for groceries and gasoline is going to feel the pinch a lot more than someone who spends only a small portion of their income on such items.

There are more complications. Goods and services available in 1983 are not exactly what's available in 2023. Smartphones didn't exist in 1983. There was also a time when people bought taped music. So the mix of products to consider in the CPI also changes – not only in kind, but also quality-wise. The typical smartphone today is way more powerful than most personal computers even 20 years ago. The typical car is much safer. And so on.

Defenders of the Fed will say the Fed knows this and they use more than just the CPI to gauge 'inflation'. There are other indexes and such. None of that matters. There are deeper philosophical issues at stake. And they raise big questions to ask yourself.

Can we speak in a meaningful way of a 'general price level?' It seems over a long period of time that we do experience a rise in the 'general price level' - which we call 'inflation.' After all, a haircut is more expensive today in dollar terms than it was 50 years ago. So is a can of Coke, an orange, a pair of jeans, a movie ticket, etc.

Can we measure it with precision, though? Or is it like the wind, dependent on where (and when) you happen to be standing? The "when" is important, too. There are billions of transactions in any year; CPI is always looking back, trying to capture what has already happened.

Perhaps most important: Can we manage it or control it? Should we? To what degree? Who decides?

Fighting Nebulous Abstractions

'Inflation,' as you can see, is a rather nebulous abstraction. Should we let such an abstraction guide public policy? The Federal Reserve thinks so. And they have jacked up interest rates under the (questionable) theory that doing so will break inflation. (The Fed doesn't actually raise interest rates. It has control over one key rate – but let such technicalities pass for purposes of our discussion here.)

The market doesn't like higher interest rates because higher interest rates mean the cost of money is higher. And that means businesses (stocks) will be worth less at a higher level of interest rates – *ceteris paribus*, as economists like to say – than they would be if rates were lower. (The problem is the *ceteris paribus* assumption never holds as things never stay the same. As any reader of Korzybski knows, the world is always changing, nothing stays still...)

Financial theory supports the idea that businesses are not worth as much with higher rates. The theory doesn't translate in the real world exactly because of many other factors. (Those things that are supposed to stay the same don't cooperate). But I'd rather gloss over that for now. It's not important to the main point.

Back to the Fed, who wants to fight 'inflation.' They want that CPI number to be lower. And one indicator that it might go lower is if more people are unemployed. It's weird, but you might think of inflation like a rubber band with a stretched rubber band representing 'higher inflation' and a loose one meaning 'lower inflation.' With more people not working but looking for work, there is slack in the 'economy' – so goes the mainstream thought – and hence 'inflation' pressures ease. (The formal model of this trade-off is captured in the Phillips Curve, which you can look up if you want to learn more. As with many other things it's a contested idea).

Ergo, when the report came out stronger than expected, the market thought "Uh oh, inflation is not coming down, that rubber band is getting tighter. Which means the Fed will keep raising rates." And stocks slid.

Note all those abstractions: 'inflation' and 'economy' even words such as 'stocks' (which stocks exactly? Are they all the same?) and 'expectations' (whose expectations?). They all beg questions.

You don't have to know about economics to ask these questions. But it helps to know general semantics. Because those things scream out at you after reading Korzybski. You won't be a dupe to economists with their technical jargon. You'll see that most of what they say is noise. As Korzybski said, it's important to discriminate "between words which symbolize something and noises which symbolize nothing." You'll see most of what passes for important economic news is deeply ambiguous, at best, and nonsensical noise at worst.

Causing Pain for the Sake of Our Abstractions

Greater questions emerge as well: Is it 'right' to have a government institution whose aim is to put people out of work for the sake of such abstractions as the 'CPI'? The chairman of the Federal Reserve, Jerome

Powell openly talked about this. In a keynote address in August of 2022, he said: "While higher interest rates, slower growth, and softer labor market conditions will bring down inflation, they will also bring some pain to households and businesses."

"Bring some pain to households and businesses..." Is that what we want? Are we such servants to our own idols that we are willing to cause human suffering on their behalf? How is this not a kind of idolatry? A modern sacrifice of human welfare to a totem of our imagination?

Besides, his chain of reasoning here is debatable, notwithstanding the easy assured manner in which he presents it. Maybe higher interest rates, slower growth (what does that even mean?) and a softer labor market will bring down 'inflation.' Maybe. Maybe the Fed's actions will 'cost' more than they are worth. Maybe the Fed's actions cause widespread unemployment, misery, social unrest... and drive down the CPI 2%. Would that be a 'success?'

Or maybe 'inflation' would've gone away on its own after a time, like a viral illness, like the common cold. There is a widespread view that the current elevated run in 'inflation' was an outgrowth of the decisions made during the initial pandemic in 2020 – the shutting down of businesses and 'stimulus spending' by governments. Or maybe it wasn't.

And who gets to decide what inflation rate is okay? Given all the problems of measuring inflation, should we think of it in terms of broad bands with a margin for error instead of a specific number?

The Fed worries about inflation, as many other people do, because of historic episodes where high 'inflation' spiraled ever higher and wreaked havoc. There was the Weimar Republic in the early 1920s when people were pushing wheelbarrows full of money to buy bread. Or Zimbabwe's more recent disaster when it printed notes with "one trillion Zimbabwe dollars" in face value that were nearly worthless. Or Argentina today where estimates put 'inflation' at 90%.

These historical episodes each have their own causes and getting into them would take us too far afield here. But there is no evidence any of that is happening in the U.S. The U.S. dollar just had one of its strongest years in decades during 2022, appreciating against nearly every other major currency in the world. U.S. dollars are still in high demand. The 10-year bond rate remains under 4%, which shows the bond market is not particularly concerned that inflation will persist. U.S. businesses are still going strong – as those hiring figures at the top of this piece seem to indicate. Maybe – just maybe – inflation fears are overblown.

I'm not arguing for one policy or another, necessarily. I am asking questions that seem not to get asked. (The conceit of Fed governors and economists always astounds me…) These terms and concepts – the 'economy,' 'inflation,' 'CPI,' etc. – have been around a long time. They are familiar and so we unthinkingly take them for granted. We start to treat these financial abstractions as real things to be managed and watched over, like livestock or tomato plants… when they are instead the work of our own minds, products of imagination and guesswork. They are treated as accurate maps when they should be treated as rough guides over uncertain terrain with built-in biases and ideologies.

Money: The Greatest Abstraction of Them All

The above questions bring an even more fundamental question to mind. The 'economy' is characterized by transactions made in dollars. And 'inflation' is measured in terms of dollars. Or, more broadly, 'money.' But what *is* 'money'? The greatest abstraction of all? Let us see.

'Money' serves as a sort of measurement, akin to inches. As with inches, Korzybski tells us in his *Manhood of Humanity*, 'money' has no value in itself. As inches measure distance, 'money' measures 'wealth.'

'Wealth' is a word that describes our inventory of useful stuff and knowledge, which is created by human efforts over time. The Korzybskian formula runs: 'money' measures 'wealth,' which is "the product of time and toil." And most of the 'wealth' we have, we must admit, comes from people long dead. It is, as he put it, "a free gift of the past."

Think of a house. It is the end product of a long and deep repository of know-how accumulated over the long history of human building efforts. Not only structural know-how, but electrical, too. And think of the plumbing, heating, cooling, etc. These sub-systems consist of many parts; parts which people had to design and fashion from raw materials.

Korzybski had a name for the ability of people to build on the knowledge of past generations. Or as Korzybski put it, "the power to roll up continuously the ever increasing achievements of generation after generation endlessly." He called it time-binding.

All of this is 'wealth,' which we measure in terms of 'money.' (The Korzybskian formulation strikes me as too narrow. Surely there is 'wealth' not measurable in terms of 'money.' But let us just note the objection here and pass on by.)

So, you might see now how inflation is a problem even in the Korzybskian scheme of things. If 'money' loses value due to 'inflation' then it is akin to having the definition of an inch change over time. Yet, in all of *Manhood of Humanity*, Korzybski never mentions inflation. I find this a striking omission; one I am not sure what to make of.

In any event, I think the chief virtue of Korzybski's formulation is that it forces you to look past the veil of 'money' to 'wealth' "rightly understood" as he says. And even then, we are pushed to see that even 'wealth' is an abstraction. When we drill even further down, we get down to the core of what Korzybski is really concerned about – which is the ability of people to partake in that glorious process of time-binding. For in his view, an ideal world is one where all people are able to enjoy that free gift and contribute to it and make it grow.

By contrast, Korzybski showed little interest in the debate between 'capitalists' and 'socialists,' or the tensions between 'capital' and 'labor.' He dismisses all these distinctions over just a few pages. His main area of interest was that "treasury left by the dead" and people's "time-binding capacity for initiation, for self-direction, and self-improvement."

I suspect if Korzybski were alive today, he wouldn't care much for ideological identities. He might look at the heated political debates of our day with disappointment, though he had lived through far worse. And he would not look favorably on so much of the world's 'wealth' being tied up in the hands of so few – hardly a "free gift." But again, not so different from what he lived through in the 1920s.

More than a century after *Manhood of Humanity*, we seem no closer to Korzybski's alluring ideal. Furthermore, we still create abstractions and then fail to see these abstractions as abstractions, mistaking the map for the territory. Such challenges will likely forever be with us, but Korzybski's general semantics provides the tools to help us think critically about them.

References

Institute of General Semantics. (2022, October 23). *Episode 2 featuring an interview with Christopher Mayer and reading by Adeena Karasick* [Video]. www.youtube.com/watch?v=eyJ9xMsxv2E

Korzybski, A. (1950). *Manhood of humanity* (2nd ed). Institute of General Semantics.

Pickert, R. (2023, January 5). U.S. labor data surprise as job market runs hotter than forecast. *Bloomberg.com.* www.bloomberg.com/news/articles/2023-01-05/us-labor-data-surprise-as-job-market-runs-hotter-than-forecast.

Pula, R. (2000). A general semantics glossary: Pula's guide for the perplexed. International Society for General Semantics.

Thompson, S. A., & Smialek, J. (2022, May 24). Why has the inflation calculation changed over time? *The New York Times.* www.nytimes.com/2022/05/24/technology/inflation-measure-cpi-accuracy.html

White, M. C. (2022, August 26). Fed Chair Jerome Powell warns fight against inflation will bring "some pain." *CNN.* www.cnn.com/2022/08/26/economy/federal-reserve-jerome-powell-jackson-hole-2022/index.html

CHAPTER 4

MEDIA BIAS, TWO-PARTY POLITICS, AND THE TWO-VALUED ORIENTATION: WHY THE UNITED STATES FINDS ITSELF ON THE VERGE OF A SECOND CIVIL WAR

THOM GENCARELLI

I do not think I am going out on a limb here if I begin here by stating the following: that general semantics scholars and practitioners cannot ignore nor understate the significance of the present-day trajectory of our global political-economic situation as one of the two most pressing issues of our times. (The other, of course, is climate change.) Likewise, those of us in the United States cannot ignore our own country's precipitously polarized politics, nor understate the fact that it is incumbent upon us to at least consider the pursuit of work and contributions that might help us rescue ourselves from the depths to which our political discourse, our political decision-making, and our political processes have sunk.

Despite my title, however, the crux of this article is not so much about politics in the United States as it is about the *context* of our politics – a context that has led to, and which is very much responsible for our present state. To be clear, I do not, by "context," mean the context that is the maelstrom within which we presently find ourselves, stunned and aghast as witnesses to some of the most bizarre, most trying and difficult, and even most precarious circumstances that voting-age citizens have ever been party to in the time we have been politically aware and involved. No, the context to which I refer is our political and political-economic system itself in the U.S.

This essay is, then, about the semantic environment in which political discourse takes place in the U.S., and what has led us to our present state of affairs. It is my intention to offer two things. The first is the attempt to make some sense of our political system as it has evolved at the federal, state, and local levels and to do so by addressing the existence of our political parties and what is – despite the "greens," the libertarians, the right-to-lifers, the "working family" party, and other smaller, rising-and-falling independent parties and movements – a *two-party* system. The second is to examine the transactional relationship between citizens and their representative government and how this relationship is conducted; how communication between the two has evolved over time. I offer these two intertwined analyses in service of the following question: How and why have we arrived at this place of hyper-polarization, and our endangered democracy, given our semantic environment?

Needless to say, the present system is not what has always been. There is no mention of political parties in the U.S. Constitution. Our first President, George Washington, was not affiliated with any party at the time he was elected, nor during the time he served. No, our original two-party system arose from his contemporaries and advisers: Alexander Hamilton, who authored the *Federalist Papers* and thus became the leader of the Federalists, and – get this – the "Democratic-Republicans," led by James Madison and Thomas Jefferson. This start was quickly followed by the collapse of the Federalist Party in 1816 and, during the early- to mid-19th Century, by the splitting of the Democratic-Republicans into the Democratic Party and the relatively short-lived "Whigs." The third phase of our political parties is then characterized by the reintroduction of the name "Republican," as the Republican Party of Abraham Lincoln arose in opposition to slavery in the middle of 19th Century. And it is at this time that the history of the Democratic and Republican parties, as the parties that remain predominant to this day in U.S. politics, begins.

Of course, that is a great deal of political history in one fell swoop. I will also add to it five additional points. The first is that all parties included in this brief history are characterized by their opposition to one another. The second is that these oppositions are from the beginning characterized mainly by opposing notions about federal versus state power, about the power of wealth, and about elitism and the question of whether all men, now all *people*, are created equal. The third point is that while such oppositions remain, we must add to them the oppositions of *social* conservatism and social liberalism as essential components of the two parties' platforms beginning during the middle of the 20th Century. The fourth point is that because the Civil War did not dispel belief in white supremacy but merely disenfranchised it and left it to fester among a resentful racist citizenry, an important shift took place with the passing of the Civil Rights Act of 1964, when the "Dixiecrats" within the southern states repudiated their party's leadership and its support of civil rights for blacks and African-Americans and, in one of the more bizarre shifts in the history of U.S. politics, became Republicans. I say "bizarre" because the Republican Party's economic platform does not otherwise represent the interests of citizens in what are effectively eight of the ten poorest states in the union as measured by per capita income, per capita state spending, poverty rate, per capita individual consumption expenditures (How Rich is Each State?), per pupil expenditures in education, etc. Fifth and finally, the abortion issue came to the forefront with respect to social conservatism when, according to North:

> During his 1972 presidential campaign, Republican Richard Nixon began staking out anti-abortion positions as part of a strategy to appeal to Catholic voters and other social conservatives. After Nixon won the election and a majority of Catholic votes, Republican strategists [then] began using the same tactics in Congress, as well as forging coalitions with evangelical groups around opposition to abortion. (2019)

The question in the face of all of this is simply this: *Why* a two-party system – a system of binary oppositions? Why does the U.S., in both of our houses of Congress, have a single aisle that separates two sides and not a system of multiple competing parties? (In asking this, I realize that not only did we not write political parties into our Constitution – the blueprint for representative governments throughout the world – but that we did not envision a parliamentary-style system either.) In other words, why do we have, and what do we *do with* a political system that situates its citizens within a perpetual semantic environment of a two-valued orientation, of "either/or" politics and the consideration and deliberation of issues? Or to use the recent, common parlance, why do we have such extreme and vehement *polarization*?

As all general semanticists know, the problem with either/or thinking is that it forces us into ways of knowing and relating that are by definition limited, limiting, and therefore insufficient; that not only is our human experience in the world fluid, multifaceted, and contradictory, but our language in thought and action needs also to be expanded in ways that allow for "both/and" thinking as well as for the consideration of all the possible shades of gray – all the gradations of color – that exist between what is otherwise rendered in black and/or white.

Of course, to be clear and fair, the two parties' platforms are themselves not always black and white. A platform is constructed based upon frameworks and statements *about*, and responses *to* all manner of civic, economic, and social issues. These are, within the parties themselves, oftentimes disputed; contentious and contended. For instance, immigration policy continues to be a matter of great urgency. To say, however, that the Democratic or Republican Party has an agreed-upon stance with respect to immigration is not true. It is, rather, something that must be hammered out within each party as compromise before they can move forward and attempt to bring a bipartisan compromise to law. In the meantime, those from outside the U.S. have, of course, a basic understanding of the defining features, the basic tenets and philosophies of our two parties. These range from matters as simple as who is a conservative versus who is a progressive to who is the party of business and industry versus who is the party of those in need. On this last point I must also acknowledge centrist Democrats who have come to be regarded as *neo*liberals – which is to say, as representatives of commerce and industry *at the same time* they purport to speak to and represent those in need.

Given all I have said thus far, however, I will add this: that while the semantic environment within which political life is enacted in the United States has changed over the course of the country's history, it has, in relatively recent years, changed in an exceptionally unsettling and, I would argue, all but debilitating way.

It is, then, the purpose of this essay to try to discern what has changed, why, and with what effect. To do so, however, requires a framing of our political-economic system of democratic-capitalism in light of how people learn about *what is going on* and thereby participate in their political life as citizens. I will, as a result, frame the either/or context of political thought and action in the U.S. in accordance with the student of our media of human communication, and in particular the student of language that I am.

To do this requires a grounding in the either/or-ness of Shannon and Weaver's (1949) transmission model of communication – their "sender and receiver" model – even *with* the addition of Wiener's (1950) "feedback." But given r/evolutions in media, it also requires an examination and understanding of the transition to the Internet and social media, as we citizens, who traditionally were mainly receivers (except to the extent that some of us wrote to and spoke now and then with our representatives) are now also senders in ubiquitous, direct and immediate, and oftentimes pseudo-active ways given our user-generated content.

To begin in earnest, then, requires *more* context: context that is about our media of communication. Because U.S. government and politics begin, and our Declaration of Independence and Constitution were written, in an age of print media and print-influenced thought, and the rise of newspapers. Newspapers are, of course, a development that came as the result of Johannes Gutenberg's invention of the printing press in Mainz, Germany in 1455 – the obvious root of the term "the press" as metaphor for journalism – and first arise in Europe in the 17th Century. Their original intent was to benefit people of means and power who needed access to information that directly and indirectly affected them and helped them to maintain their wealth, land ownership, and power. By the time the U.S. Constitution is written, however, the U.S. had already established a *daily* newspaper: *The Philadelphia Evening Post*, founded in 1783. Thus, in the face of the system of checks and balances written into the design of our government, as well as the First Amendment of our Constitution's Bill of Rights, two things become clear: (a) that citizens can only speak their voice to power, ensure their representation, and ensure that their will is enacted if they have knowledge of their elected and appointed officials' acts and actions. The work of journalists – the unofficial *fourth estate* within this system of checks and balances – is the mechanism by which an active, engaged citizenry acquires such knowledge. (b) Journalists, and the entire enterprise of journalism itself, must therefore be allowed to operate in unfettered ways – free from government interference and/or attempts at control.

This media environment, imperfect and subjective as it is, like all human endeavors, lasted through the Civil War – the battle for the soul of a "united states" – and until the introduction of the original electric/electronic medium of mass communication: radio "broadcasting," in the 1920s. The rise of radio in fact set off what came to be known as the Press-Radio War, as publishers of newspapers became rightly concerned that people would no longer take the time to read the news when they could simply listen to someone read it to them. (Reading is, after all, unnatural and difficult – a matter of doing the wholly active, focused, and uninterrupted mind work that is turning black marks on the page or screen into meaning. But we cannot close our ears to sound.) Meanwhile, McLuhan (1964) reminds us, with his adage "the medium is the message," that media shape, influence, and even dictate the things we can know and how we can and will think about them. Thus, at the time of radio's introduction, citizens' knowledge of the workings of their government via their news and information media will be differently arrived at based upon the act of listening to ephemeral voices versus reading and re-reading. The new information media ecology will be comprised of citizens who read newspapers, citizens who listen to radio news, and citizens who do both.

This hybrid press/radio environment for news lasts, however, for a much briefer time than the print-literate environment in which the American experiment in democracy was birthed and came to maturity. Because by the 1950s, a vastly powerful competitor in news media comes to the forefront: television. As scholars such as Boorstin (1962) and Moran (2010) point out, this portends the transition from a print-literate to a *post*-literate media culture – to a culture in which *images* and moving images become preeminent as the means of communicating the most important stories of the day. This has an obvious impact as, as Moran (1984; 2017) points out elsewhere, it represents what, up until that time, is a shift from the politics of issues, to a politics of party, and finally to a politics of images. And, of course, this elicits questions: What *is* the semantic environment of visual images? What ideas can images convey? What information do they convey and what knowledge and understanding can be derived from this information? And what is the consequence of image-based media with respect to the needs of an engaged citizenry who try to make informed decisions and act upon them? I will add here that the audio content of an audio-visual message is often overlooked *and overwhelmed* by the message's visual content. We say, after all, that we *watch* television rather than watch *and listen* to it. And this is not just short-hand or short-speak. However, while the audio portion of a program indeed communicates a great deal of information, what can be said is contained within the "time-based" media content of a television program rather than the "space-based" content of the newspaper page. The result is that much less verbiage can be spoken in the course of a half-hour program with commercial interruptions than can be included within the pages of a broadsheet-format newspaper.

The next important step in this history is not the invention of a media technology but rather an innovation in media practice. Historically, the electromagnetic frequency spectrum that enabled the broadcasting media of radio and television was considered a limited, and thus scarce natural resource. As a result, during the Great Depression, the New Deal government of Franklin Delano Roosevelt penned and enacted the Communications Act of 1934, which regulated the use of the spectrum by granting ownership of the airwaves as a public trust, and awarding licenses to use the limited available airwaves to a limited number of companies that could then exploit them for profit. These companies maintain and have their licenses renewed by broadcasting programs that demonstrably serve the "public interest, convenience, and necessity."

However, by the mid- to late-1970s (beginning during the administration of then Democratic President Jimmy Carter), regulatory philosophy began to shift in favor of *de*regulation and a free-market approach. This also coincided with the transition from broadcast television toward the pay/cable television industry. Chief among the deregulatory decisions that impacted news and information-based radio and television was the repeal of what was known as the "Fairness Doctrine," established in 1949. This doctrine had previously ensured a two-valued approach to the presentation of broadcast news: to wit, if a station/licensee presented one side of a controversial issue, that station's owners and its news division would be required to allocate sufficient airtime to the presentation of the opposing view. The Fairness Doctrine was repealed in 1987, during the administration of then Republican President Ronald Reagan.

The immediate upshot of the repeal of the Fairness Doctrine was the rise of conservative talk radio as a viable, and extraordinarily successful radio format. This development can be said to reach its pinnacle with talk show host Rush Limbaugh, whose program went into syndication almost immediately, in 1988, and at its peak was broadcast via over 650 stations nationwide (McFadden & Grynbaum, 2021). During this time, beginning with Limbaugh and then rapidly expanding across the rest of conservative infotainment programming, the trope of a "liberal, elite media bias" comes to the forefront in our political discourse: a trope which, notably, represents a coded reference to Jewish control of the media, and especially control of the news and information branch of the media business.

Importantly, then, in 1992, Limbaugh launched a television program based upon the success of his radio show. The producer for this program was a television producer turned Republican/conservative media adviser and consultant, Roger Ailes (Carlson, 2021). Ailes was subsequently hired, in 1996, by Rupert Murdoch, the owner of the News Corporation, to run his company's new 24/7 pay television news network, the Fox News Channel. In the face of (a) the repeal of the Fairness Doctrine, (b) the general lack of FCC jurisdiction over, and regulation of the cable (and, by then, satellite) television business, and (c) the existence of CNN as the only other 24/7 pay television news network – and thus the sole representative of supposed "liberal" news on the pay television platform – Fox News becomes the conservative opinion channel and foil during prime-time.

It is at this point, then, that the table is fully set for a two-valued political-economic system at the most base and simplistic.

Let me, though, step back for a moment from this media history and back to politics directly, while also reintroducing Shannon and Weaver and the sender side of their model. I would make the case that a significant shift also took place during the years of Democratic (and neoliberal) President Bill Clinton's administration in the 1990s: a shift that gave birth to the "Tea Party" movement. It is a straight line from the Tea Party to the present-day "Freedom Caucus" in the U.S. House of Representatives. This straight line represents the transition to a philosophy and approach to governance that rejects the kind of compromise required of a democratic system – that replaces a system that represents and respects the differing points-of-view and values of constituents and their elected officials with intransigence and an insistence on adherence to the principles of one side. Which is to say, to an insistence on *winning*. We have recently witnessed the unfortunate result of this in, for instance, Republican Senator Tommy Tuberville's refusal to support military promotions in response to a Department of Defense policy that allows members of the military to recoup travel expenses if they seek an abortion while stationed in a state that has banned or restricts the procedure.

This is a new message: an either-or message that adamantly and emphatically states that either we get our way – and win – or we refuse to play the game; that we pick up the ball and go and sit on the sidelines in protest; that we ignore the rules.

On the receiver side, this has emboldened the stance and the values of those who side with the senders. A simplistic view of how our political system works is this: A citizenry elects its officials in order that we will be represented and our will enacted. Of course, and in practice, democracies are not so neat and tidy. As has often been said, they are, in fact, downright messy. When we have differing points-of-view and values to be represented, and when we look for and demand decision-making and action that is what *we* want and what *we* think is best, where does this lead? Clearly it leads to the need for compromise. And a two-party system ostensibly makes it relatively easy to compromise, right? Forget alliances or the forming of governments in a parliamentary-type system. Let us simply find a middle ground between two extremes.

Now, however, we have in elected office people who will not compromise. As a result, those who represent *us*, represent *us getting what we want*. This is representation in accordance with a "winner-takes-all" model rather than one that is oriented to the good of the polity. In line with this distorted view of representative democracy, citizens who consider only themselves and their ilk, and who do not see or concern themselves with the bigger picture, end up believing that everything is fine. They get what they want. All is good in their world.

Yet this still does not fully explain how the present day's two-valued media and semantic environment has shifted to one side prevailing over the other on the citizen/receiver side. For this, we need to add to the equation the developments in media since the 1990s and the Clinton administration. I am, of course, talking about the introduction of the Internet and mobile Internet, of blogs, vlogs, and micro-blogs, of social media, and of user-generated content.

In a context of social media and user-generated content, we who formerly were mainly receivers of media become senders, too. We are produ*s*ers; *pro*sumers. Rather than give our attentions over to media that are primarily one-directional and one-to-many, as citizens-as-audiences did prior to this age, we now spend inordinate amounts of time immersed in and involved with media that are two-way – and not merely in the sense of Wiener's addition of feedback to the Shannon and Weaver model. We engage with these new-ish media in so-called "interactive" ways. But what does it mean to be *interactive*?

We interact, via social media, mainly in small networks of people with strong ties – which is to say that we interact with people who we know to some extent and in some way, and who are thus somehow like us. However, we also interact via social media in an interconnected web of other networks, wherein we are exposed to the views and messages of people with whom we do not have strong ties; whose views are different than ours. And it is in our willingness to connect with people outside of our small networks – *or* our inability to avoid such people and their presence and participation – that we encounter the ways and extent to which social media have altered political discourse. Prior to this age, we were exposed to different points-of-view in small doses: your uncle at Thanksgiving dinner, someone who has too much to drink at a bar and who begins to talk a bit too loudly, etc. Now, this discourse comes to us through the façade of empowerment, the pseudo-political participation that is espousing one's views on Facebook or X. Moreover, because so many citizens are swept up in this social media environment – wherein *to post is to be* – political messages are no longer handed down to us from elected and appointed officials, and then only *after* being interpreted and disseminated by news and information media professionals and their organizations. Today, such messages are spread and shared all around us, all the time, by anyone and everyone who has an opinion: no matter what their agenda, no matter how informed they are or are not, no matter how well or how carefully constructed their thoughts are. So much for Lazarsfeld et al.'s (1944) two-step flow of information.

In other words, we now read and hear the views of the polity to an extent, and with repercussions we have never known before. And it is unsettling to say the least. It is the mob's views – and not Howard Rheingold's (2003) "smart mobs," mind you. Within this new semantic environment, we find blatant, virulent, and unapologetic racism, sexism, misogyny, homophobia, xenophobia, anti-Semitism, et cetera. Not to mention what is blatantly wrong; what are "alternative facts."

Many readers have accounts on what was formerly Twitter and is now X since Elon Musk took it over and took it private – with all of the sideshow his takeover has engendered. An article in *Fortune* magazine explained why, while the company had been in play for a number of years before Musk bought it, all other potential deals for the company fell apart:

> Anyone who spends time on Twitter quickly becomes aware that there are hordes of trolls who will swarm anyone who expresses an opinion on a controversial topic. This has been a thorn in the company's side for some time, but it may also have turned away potential buyers.

Disney and Salesforce.com both backed away from bidding for Twitter in part because of the service's problem with offensive content, according to recent reports based on interviews with anonymous sources at both companies. (Ingram, 2016)

As an example, the *New York Times* reported on a study, carried out by the Anti-Defamation League, about anti-Semitic attacks on Twitter – leading up to, and after the 2016 Presidential election:

> During its investigation, the organization found that 2.6 million anti-Semitic messages were posted on Twitter from August 2015 to July 2016. Of those, 19,253 were directed at journalists.
> There was a significant uptick starting early this year (2016), when the presidential campaign began to intensify, the organization said in its report... More than 800 journalists have been the subject of anti-Semitic attacks on Twitter, with 10 of them receiving 83 percent of the total attacks.
> The words appearing most frequently in the Twitter biographies of the attackers were "Trump," "nationalist," "conservative" and "white." (Mahler, 2016)

Since Musk took over the company – with his attention-mongering and ill-formed and ill-advised First Amendment views and tendencies, and in exercising his newfound control over the company's product/service – things have only taken a turn for the worse. Or the uglier. As of this writing, Musk himself was recently accused of anti-Semitism. To wit:

> Billionaire Elon Musk told advertisers that have fled his social media platform X over antisemitic content to "Go fuck yourself" in a fiery Wednesday interview.
> His profanity-laced remarks followed a moment of contrition in a *New York Times* DealBook Summit interview. Musk said repeatedly he was sorry for publishing a tweet on Nov. 15 that agreed with an anti-Jewish post.
> Musk has faced a torrent of criticism ever since he agreed with a user who falsely claimed Jewish people were stoking hatred against white people. Musk in his post said the user, who refer-

enced the "Great Replacement" conspiracy theory, was speaking "the actual truth."

… Musk said he had "handed a loaded gun" to both detractors and antisemitic people, describing his post as possibly the worst he had made during a history of messages that included many "foolish" ones. (Dang, 2023)

Musk's original tweet, his outburst in reaction to the resulting exodus from X by its advertisers, and the larger context of this story bring to light two interrelated consequences with respect to the role of social media in politics. First, let us ask – and not in a flip or sarcastic way: Who exactly *is* Elon Musk? Yes, he is a billionaire and presently the richest person in the world (LaFranco, Chung & Peterson-Withorn). Yes, he is a wildly successful entrepreneur, and the CEO of both Tesla and SpaceX. And yes, he owns the social media platform on which this recent firestorm began, and can use it as his own personal platform and for his benefit – personal, political, business. But how are his tweets any different than anyone else's on X? They are not. He simply has a larger-than-life public profile and, just like anyone who is rich and famous, his pronouncements are therefore accorded greater weight and importance. But his fame and wealth are the *only* reason his pronouncements are accorded such weight and importance. In other words, when he tweets something ill-advised, uninformed, or simply stupid he is in effect no different than any other user on his platform: fallible and human.

Second, this speaks to a larger point that, among others, Vaidhyanathan highlights in his book, *Antisocial Media: How Facebook Disconnects Us and Undermines Democracy* (2018). That is to say, while we might think the late Roger Ailes, or publisher of the *New York Times* A. G. Sulzberger know exactly they are doing, and with what consequence, Vaidhyanathan exposes how Facebook, and now Meta CEO Mark Zuckerberg created, with his platform, a Frankenstein monster that he does not understand and can no longer control. While Zuckerberg's mantra as a salesperson has always spoken to how Facebook's purpose is "helping people share and helping people stay connected with their friends and family and the community around them" (Huddleston, 2019), the fact is that the platform has long been used by nefarious actors, including state actors, for the purpose of propaganda: distortion, deception, and disinformation. And for data collection, or data "hoovering."

Thus, to believe that Musk, Zuckerberg, and others of their ilk like Open AI's Sam Altman, understand the media platforms they own and run, much less the real-world implications these have and will continue to have in the future, is a great and risky assumption. Add to this the addition, extensions, and potentials – along the lines I have argued here – of recent developments in AI, generative AI, and LLMs (Large Language Models) like ChatGPT, and the possibilities of AGI (Artificial General Intelligence), and concerns about political life and democracy in our new media/semantic environment will only continue to grow. In the meantime, these plutocrats who have used *us* to build their corporate empires are themselves being used by others in power or with plans for power. Thus, while they may believe they are building their bunkers to protect themselves from what will happen to our natural environment as the result of human-induced climate change, they may in reality be saving themselves from the consequences of the media environment they are responsible for creating. They may be complicit in what it is that will force them underground and into hiding.

To return, in the end here and in the face of all of this, to the two-valued orientation of our political-economic system in the U.S. is to come face-to-face with the cynical view of our representative democracy – one which suggests that we citizens are not engaged and informed enough to govern ourselves. At the same time, it is to come face-to-face with the pragmatics of power, as Postman (1985), in an age before the Internet and social media, pointed to with respect to the distractions of our media environment, and as Strate (2014) revisited in updating Postman's argument for our current media age. From this perspective, our media and semantic environment can be regarded as a distraction from the real and hard job of being citizens, while allowing those with wealth and power to sustain and increase their wealth and power while – and because – we are busy doing other, relatively meaningless things.

Yet another thought is this: that the two-valued orientation of two-party politics creates a façade of democracy, a play-acting, in which relatively uninformed citizens (and consumers) can participate based not upon their thoughtfulness and degree of informed-ness, but based upon values and feelings. And wherein those who attain and sustain power benefit from this pretense; from the charade.

If any of this rings true, or is true, our only course of action is the following.

In their seminal work, *The Pragmatics of Human Communication* (1967), Watzlawick, Beavin Bavelas, and Jackson wrote about the two "levels" of human communication. The first, more obvious of these is the "content" level of communication: the thoughts and ideas we speak and put to action; the level of facts. The second is what they term the "relationship" level of communication: what our messages to one another, and how we conceive and construct these messages and put them to action, communicate about *us*; about our core values, attitudes, and beliefs.

To bring this second, relationship level of our communication to the surface is to *meta-communicate*: to communicate about our communication. However, people – other than general semanticists, because this is what we are all about – do not tend to do this. They do not know *to* do this. And even if they did, they do not, without a general semantics education, and/or without a communication and media education, know *how* to do it.

As a result, we expend a great deal of energy in the oversimplified, either/or semantic environment of our politics and governance preaching to the converted. Or alternatively, we spend it in attempts to convert those who are the "either" to our "or" with facts and other such constructions, even though to do so is folly. As Watzlawick and his colleagues would tell us, to do so is to ignore the fact that their "side" is based in an epistemic set, a history of evolved core values, attitudes, and beliefs that constitute the very foundation of what it is that makes up the self. Thus, when we try to persuade or convince on the level of facts and ideas, we cannot do so if those facts and ideas *threaten* that self – threaten the way we make coherent sense of ourselves and *for* ourselves, and how we make sense of things in our world.

In our political discourse, we never talk about these things. Instead, we continue to debate from the fixed and oversimplified position within which our political system, with the addition of our media – and now our new media – have placed us. And to which they have brought us. In the meantime, we do so at our collective peril. And things only seem to be getting worse.

References

Boorstin, D. (1962). *The image: A guide to pseudo-events in America.* Atheneum.

Carlson, M. (2021, February 17). Rush Limbaugh obituary. *The Guardian.* https://www.theguardian.com/media/2021/feb/17/rush-limbaugh-obituary

Dang, S. (2023, November 30). Elon Musk curses out advertisers who left X over antisemitic content. *Reuters.* https://www.reuters.com/technology/elon-musk-curses-out-advertisers-who-left-x-over-antisemitic-content-2023-11-29/

How rich is each state? (n.d.). Chamber of Commerce. https://www.chamberofcommerce.org/how-rich-is-each-us-state/

Huddleston, T., Jr. (2019, March 6). Watch 19-year-old Mark Zuckerberg explain 'The Facebook' in his first TV interview in 2004. *CNBC.* https://www.cnbc.com/2019/03/06/see-19-year-old-mark-zuckerberg-explain-the-facebook-in-2004.html

Ingram, M. (2016, October 18). Here's why Disney and Salesforce. com dropped their bids for Twitter. *Fortune.* http://fortune.com/2016/10/18/twitter-disney-salesforce/

LaFranco, R., Chung, G., & Peterson-Withorn, C. (Eds.). (n.d.). Forbes world billionaires list: The richest in 2024. *Forbes.* https://www.forbes.com/billionaires/

Lazarsfeld, P. F., Berelson, B., & Gaudet, H. (1944). *The people's choice: How the voter makes up his mind in a presidential campaign.* Duell, Sloan and Pearce.

Mahler, W. (2016, October 19). Anti-Semitic posts, many from Trump supporters, surge on Twitter. *The New York Times.* http://www.nytimes.com/2016/10/19/us/politics/anti-semitism-trump-supporters twitter.html?hp&action=click&pgtype=Homepage&clickSource=story-heading&module=first-column-region&region=top-news&WT.nav=top-news

McFadden, R. D., & Grynbaum, M. M. (2021, February 18). Rush Limbaugh dies at 70; Turned talk radio into a right-wing attack machine. *The New York Times.* https://www.nytimes.com/2021/02/17/business/media/rush-limbaugh-dead.html

McLuhan, H. M. (1964). *Understanding media: The extensions of man.* McGraw-Hill.

Moran, T. P. (1984). Politics 1984: That's entertainment. *ETC: A Review of General Semantics, 41*(2), 117–129.

Moran, T. P. (2010). *Introduction to the history of communication: Evolutions and revolutions.* Peter Lang.

Moran, T. P. (2017). *Crazy talk, stupid talk: Politics in 2017.* The Alfred Korzybski Memorial Lecture, New York, NY.

North, A. (2019, April 10). How abortion became a partisan issue in America. *Vox.* https://www.vox.com/2019/4/10/18295513/abortion-2020-roe-joe-biden-democrats-republicans

Postman, N. (1985). *Amusing ourselves to death: Public discourse in the age of show business* (Anniversary Ed.) Penguin Books.

Rheingold, H. (2003). *Smart mobs: The next social revolution.* Basic Books.

Shannon, C., & Weaver, W. (1949). *The mathematical theory of communication.* University of Illinois Press.

Strate, L. (2014). *Amazing ourselves to death: Neil Postman's brave new world revisited.* Peter Lang.

Vaidhyanathan, S. (2018). *Antisocial media: How Facebook disconnects us and undermines democracy.* Oxford University Press.

Watzalwick, P., Beavin Bavelas, J., & Jackson, D. D. (1967). *The pragmatics of human communication: A study of interactional patterns, pathologies, and paradoxes.* W. W. Norton & Company.

Wiener, N. (1950). *The human use of human beings: Cybernetics and society.* Avon Books.

CHAPTER 5

GENERAL SEMANTICS AND CONSTRUCTIVE POLITICAL DISCOURSE

MARTIN H. LEVINSON

These days hostility and frustration are rampant in political discussions, as people try to persuade others of the rightness of their views and the wrongness of opinions held by those they are speaking with. Typically they do not succeed in their efforts and end up feeling angry and discouraged. Better to not talk about politics, they surmise, than to engage in fruitless dialogue that will only result in ill will and perhaps indigestion or a rise in blood pressure.

The aforementioned scenario may be true for people not versed in general semantics. But for those in the GS know such doom and gloom, and the desire to gain the upper hand in political exchanges, can largely be avoided. To that end, this chapter offers the following general semantics ideas and formulations to use when having political discussions.

Alfred Korzybski's Happiness Formula

One way to beat the political-discussion blues is to acquaint yourself with Alfred Korzybski's "happiness formula": maximum effort + minimum expectations = best results. Maximum effort means understanding that listening is as important, and probably even more important, than speaking in discussions. If a person feels their ideas are truly being heard, they may be inclined to give some heed to the views of the person they are talking with. Therefore, it makes sense to put lots of effort into listening to what the other person is saying.

The second part of the formula, "minimum expectations," is as crucial to having constructive political discussions as the first part. The odds are close to zero that you will sway someone from their entrenched positions in a political discussion. Getting people to even consider viewpoints differing from their own may be a heavy lift. But you may be able to have a civil conversation by replying calmly to arguments being presented to you and by taking those arguments seriously. Sarcasm and self-righteousness tend to put people off, so it is probably best not to employ these communicative forms. Approaching a conversation with a genuine interest and openness to others' perspectives is in most instances a far better way to achieve a true exchange of opinions and ideas.

The Value of Delayed Evaluation

Alfred Korzybski was fond of pointing out that a key difference between human beings and other animals is the ability we have to engage our higher brain functions and delay long enough to evaluate circumstances before reacting to them. Using this technique tends to produce better outcomes in situations than reacting quickly or impulsively. In the context of political discussions, rather than copy the rapid-fire, in-your-face style of cable TV news hosts in speaking with people, one can pause to think about what the other person is saying and respond in a mindful manner.

Will delaying your reactions win you kudos from a partisan on the opposite side of issues you feel strongly about? It might because, generally, people believe what they are saying is worthy of consideration. But even if you are not commended for your courtesy, not going hell for leather in an argument over politics may spare you and your fellow conversationalist from bodily upset and uttering words you may regret later.

The Limitations of Either-Or Thinking

The law of the excluded middle, one of Aristotle's "laws of thought," encourages us to believe that every question can be answered in terms of "either-or." The English language pushes us in a similar direction. Its many polarizing terms—good/bad, hot/cold, tall/short, thin/fat—pushes us to think in extremes rather than gradations.

Most things we encounter are more accurately mapped by a statistical distribution rather than by either-or terms. This idea can be seen on a bell-curve of normal distribution. If you plot instances from daily life, like days above and below 100 degrees F., I.Q., height, weight, etc., on a graph, it is the middle range that has the most distribution. Either-or comparisons show up at the two extreme ends of the graph.

To get past either-or thinking, general semantics recommends using a *multi-valued approach*. This approach involves examining more than just two alternatives. Rather than arguing immigration is good/immigration is bad, affirmative action is good/affirmative action is bad, defense spending is good/defense spending is bad, a multi-valued approach might involve examining pluses and minuses of various policies regarding immigration, affirmative action, and defense spending. Such analysis may surface ideas one had not reflected on and, at the very least, shed more light than heat on the topic under discussion.

Overcoming *Allness Attitudes*

No one can know *all* about anything. That statement may seem obvious, but everyday people say or imply they do know it all. Individuals who speak in this manner are demonstrating *allness attitudes*. They think they know what it is impossible to know—everything about a specific topic.

It is hard to talk with people who claim to know everything. They resist any new information you bring to a discussion, so why bother trying to have one. Individuals with allness attitudes do not want to exchange ideas and opinions. They want to pontificate.

Indexing, a GS tool that involves examining individual cases within a larger category, can be useful in overcoming allness attitudes. For example, John says, "I don't like Arabs, Jews, Blacks, and Hispanics." Does John know every Arab, Jew, Black, and Hispanic? $Arab_1$ is not $Arab_2$ is not $Arab_3$; Jew_1 is not Jew_2 is not Jew_3; $Black_1$ is not $Black_2$ is not $Black_3$; $Hispanic_1$ is not $Hispanic_2$ is not $Hispanic_3$. Every human being is unique and the categories we place them in are artificial constructions that do not contain the entirety and distinctiveness of the person inhabiting that category. Indexing can be a good way to get beyond stereotyping and focus on differences that might make a difference in understanding how particular individuals behave.

Employing qualifying terms like "to me," "I think," and "in my view," when making statements is another general semantics approach for defeating allness attitudes. Such expressions – "To me, X is a great candidate," "I think the Y party is the best one to move America forward," "In my view, the government needs to provide more (or less) student aid," – make it clear that our observations and opinions have definite limits.

Thinking in a "non-elementalistic" manner can reduce allness inclinations. Elementalism is involved when we seek *the* cause, cure, or way to handle something, unconsciously assuming there is only one cause, cure, or way, to wit: *the* cause of juvenile delinquency, *the* cure for bad government, *the* way to handle homelessness. Most problems in life cannot be dealt with so simply, as the circumstances that surround most problems, and their solutions, tend to be multi-faceted. As such, thinking in terms of "plurals" – e.g., the causes of juvenile delinquency, the cures for bad government, the ways to handle homelessness – may offer a better approach in coming up with effective solutions to problems.

Finally, we can follow Korzybski's suggestion to add a silent "etc." to our thinking to remind us there is always more that can be learned and more that can be said. When I am engaged in political discussions I try to remind myself, and those I am speaking with, that when it comes to politics there is more to heaven and earth that can be contained in any person's particular political philosophy.

Beware the "Is of identity"

If we employ the word "is" (or its variants) we can say, "John is a Republican" or "Mary is a Democrat." But is that all they are? Of course not! People have multiple identities. They may also be lawyers, parents, volunteer workers, military reservists, Scrabble players, computer nerds, etc. When having a political conversation with a member of a political party different than yours, you may want to keep in mind that the Republican or Democrat you are talking to has manifold identities, and interests, and if the conversation looks like it is getting out of hand you may want to engage those other identities and interests and talk about things other than politics. Getting bent out of shape and even cancelling people who vehemently disagree with your political views is not your only option. We are more than the narrow political identities that are placed on us or that we place on ourselves. Don't let the "is of identity" fool you into thinking that is not the case.

Differentiating Facts from Inferences

One reason political discussions go off the rail is that the people having those discussions are operating from separate sets of "facts." Can one have a reasonable discussion if the very basis of that discussion is in dispute? Probably not. Does that mean one should walk away from the conversation? Not necessarily.

People often mistake statements of inference for statements of fact. To avoid fact/inference mix-ups Irving J. Lee, the author of *Language Habits in Human Affairs* and other books on general semantics, offers these distinctions (Johnson, 2004, p. 13):

Statement of fact

- Made *after* observation or experience
- Is confined to what one observes or experiences
- Only a *limited* number can be made
- Represents a high degree of probability, is close to certainty

Statement of inference

- Made anytime—before, during, or after observation
- Goes beyond what one observes or experiences
- Can make an *unlimited number* in any situation
- Represents some degree of probability

It may be worthwhile to introduce Lee's distinctions in political discussions and see if everyone can get to agree on the "facts" of the matter. If such agreement is not forthcoming there will likely be difficulty in dialoging, as one party will be talking about apples while the other is speaking about oranges. There can be value in introducing Lee's fact/inference distinctions to those not familiar with them, as they may induce reflection on matters taken for granted. If that's not the case in the near term, they may spur reflection down the road.

We Live in a Process World

Individuals change over time as new facts present themselves and new circumstances emerge. Are you the same person today that you were a year ago, five years ago, ten years ago? Do you look exactly identical?

Has your behavior stayed the same? It is comforting to think the world and the people in it are invariable from day to day. It makes for easy predictability. But life is process so change must occur.

Dating, a GS tool that involves attaching dates to our evaluations, can help us stay attuned to the fact that we live in a changing world: Afghanistan$^{\text{a decade ago}}$ is not Afghanistan^{now}, the ethnic population in the United States^{1960} is not the ethnic population in the United States^{2025}, America's dependence on oil imports$^{\text{during the Carter Administration}}$ is not America's dependence on oil imports$^{\text{during the Biden Administration}}$. Dating shows that ours is a restless universe, where everything mutates over time, and that includes politics.

Some people yearn for "the good old days" in America. They say if we could only get back to that time things would be just "perfect." But nothing stays perfect and that includes the idea of "the good old days," which is a highly subjective descriptor.

You can freeze vegetables but as far as can be scientifically determined you can't freeze time. Change is ongoing and that is most certainly true when it comes to politics.

Searching for Meaning in the Right Places

What is the difference between a "freedom fighter" and a "terrorist?" Were the victims at the Abu Ghraib prison in Iraq subjected to "abuse" or "torture?" Are organizations that comment on news reporting "media watchdog groups" or are they "pressure groups?" Do not look to the dictionary for the answers to these questions. Their answers depend on how individuals interpret events.

It is an axiom in general semantics that, strictly speaking, words don't "mean," people "mean." The physicist P.W. Bridgman put it this way, "Never ask 'What does word X mean?' but ask instead, 'What do I mean when I say word X?' or 'What do you mean when you say word X?'" (Johnson, 2004, p. 21). The fact is words do not have "one true meaning"—for the 500 most used words in the English language, the *Oxford Dictionary* lists 14,070 meanings (Johnson, 2004, p. 21).

Words mean different things to different people. The field of law is based on this principle.

Words mean different things at different times. In 1896, the nine men on the U.S. Supreme Court said separate but equal facilities for Blacks and whites are constitutional. In 1954, a set of nine different men said, in effect, *separate* and *equal* are opposites.

Words mean different things in different contexts: He beat (hit) the drum with a stick. Beats me (I don't know). The reporter has the mayor on his beat (area to cover). He beat (defeated) Joe at chess.

We use words to categorize and label people and events. But the categories we formulate are not "out there," in the "real world." They are created in our heads and expressed in language.

How we label or categorize a person or a situation will depend upon our purpose, our projections, and our evaluations. For example: North Korea labels itself the "Democratic People's Republic of Korea." Vladimir Putin claims that Russia and Ukraine are "one people." The current lifetime office holder Ali Khamenei is Iran's "Supreme Leader." Whose purposes, projections, and evaluations do you think these labels serve?

Putting people into categories is commonplace in political discourse on talk radio ("You believe that because you're a 'liberal'!" "That's what I thought a 'conservative' would say!" "What do you expect from a 'reactionary'!"). Such pigeonholing does not advance political dialogue. Rather it leads to a malady quite common in politics, "hardening of the categories." Is there a remedy for that condition? Yes, in political matters focus on issues not labels.

Conclusion

Many people advise not talking politics in polite company. But at this time in America's history, with the country so divided and the political stakes possibly existential, there are sound reasons not to follow that advice. If you choose not to follow it, and want to engage with others over politics in a civil and respectful manner, try putting the ideas discussed in this chapter into practice. I wish you good luck and good chatting.

Reference

Johnson, K. G. (2004). *General semantics: An outline survey* (3rd ed). Institute of General Semantics.

CHAPTER 6

HASHTAGTHIS: #FREEPALESTINE, POLITICAL POSITIONS, AND SOCIAL MEDIA TRENDS
ETAI ESHET and EVA BERGER

Years of demonstrating, volunteering, and supporting peace initiatives have led, in the wake of the horrors of October 7th, to an unexpected discovery: that people we thought shared our values, do not. People we believed shared our humanism, our steadfast belief in human rights, women's rights, LGBTQ+ rights, have turned a blind eye to the atrocities committed by Hamas.

In an almost automatic manner at first, we insisted on distinguishing between legitimate criticism of policies of the government of Israel and antisemitism. We got into fights with family for daring to say what we still deeply believe: that despite the horror and the instinct for revenge, Israel should strive to resolve and not manage the conflict. But the inability or refusal of many in the world to condemn the Hamas massacre and the wave of antisemitism that ensued, sent us to reconsider our beliefs, to recalibrate the narratives of our lives.

How could people who were supposed to be our allies in the global fight against violence, not see our suffering? How is it possible that the global left has sided with the fundamentalist right? We have at least a partial answer. We may be wrong but if nothing else, the answer provides us (and we hope others) with something to hold onto when everything is moving: In the world of social media, there are no ideologies or opinions. Only trends. On Instagram and TikTok, #Free Palestine is a trend - a hashtag - not a real political position.

In the digital age patience for long texts has decreased and skim reading is the norm. Relatively longer texts are still written on various platforms and then shared on Twitter or Facebook. But they are read less and less. Like the one by Barack Obama who presents the dangers of the reality in which Hamas seems to intentionally hide among civilians, and the Israeli government cuts off food, water and electricity to a captive civilian population. And he acknowledges that in an age of misinformation on social media, it is hard to expect respectful dialogue. But explains that if we want to keep open the possibility of peace, security and dignity for future generations, we should try to model, in our own words and actions, the kind of world we want them to inherit.

There is no room on social media for such nuanced texts. There, short texts, photos, and video clips are posted, reshared, and responded to by people, often without having watched or read them, adding their own title to them. AOC quote-tweeted someone else's quote-tweet of Obama's piece adding her own "lift the blockade." Had she read Obama's piece more carefully, she probably would have chosen someone else's article – more fit in content and tone – to stick her demand on top of. And she is not alone. Thirty-four student groups signed the Harvard letter supporting Palestinians and blaming Israel for the Hamas attacks. The groups that rescinded what they signed admitted they didn't read the letter closely. Like in the children's game of broken telephone, the more the original message is shared, the more distorted it gets.

After the October 7th massacre, #FreePalestine is a trend – almost a fashion – based on ignorance. When asked to explain their positions, many of those chanting "free Palestine" or "from the river to the sea," either stutter in embarrassment, explain they are actually not there to talk politics, or they simply leave.

Like every other issue on TikTok, millennials and GenZ experience the Israeli-Palestinian conflict in black and white – with no shades or complexity. They rush to judge, they panic, and have no capacity for real discussions of complex situations. They are a simplistic version of a real progressive left. As Nissan Shor (2023) says "they drape themselves in the Palestinian flag out of an aesthetic position and racist fetishization of the Oriental subject." They also make sure their selfie fits the aesthetics of social media. Porn star turned influencer Mia Khalifa even urged members of Hamas to flip their phones and film their atrocities "horizontal."

The TikTok left's radical positions are status symbols. Clueless young people hang on to terms like "decolonization" out of an empty sense of guilt. They find it easy to reject their own colonialism on the back of this war. They don't call upon British museums to return most of their exhibits to their owners. They ignore grave suffering in other countries in the same region of the world because they can't categorize it as a racial-environmental-gender conflict. If they only applied the same mental gymnastics to the war in Syria and framed Bashar Assad as a cis-Alawite-male, they'd be on the streets for the past 12 years.

Some of these woke influencers use the word "context" to justify their views – or at least the signs they carry – and in their intersectionality-gone-haywire, they reveal how blind they are to context. Once in a while someone will point out how misguided they are in connecting LGBTQ+ rights with Palestinians' struggle, in insisting that Black people should automatically blame Jews, or why Israel does not automatically equal white privilege. Not all social-justice causes fit neatly together, as Helen Lewis (2023) explains in her *Atlantic* article: "The Progressives Who Flunked the Hamas Test."

When you claim to use the occupation as context for the October 7th atrocities and don't know the history of Israeli occupation, you are context blind (2022). The word context loses its meaning. It becomes a mantra. A hashtag....

> As Anshil Pfeffer (2023) puts it:
> Israel's many misguided and vicious actions and policies towards Gaza and the Palestinians over the past 75 years are all context. But not the only context... If the only context to the killings of Simchat Torah is Gaza and Israel's conflict with the Palestinians, why are synagogues and Jewish schools around the world now being required to take extra security measures... How are they part of the context? Why did supporters of Hamas in Sydney... rally this week crying "Gas the Jews" – what's the context there?

How's this for Context? Hashtag this:

#BritishMandate_BalfourDeclaration_FleeingNaziRule_Holocaust_ WarofIndependence/Naqba_SixDayWar_Occupation_YomKippur-War_Intifadah_OsloAccords_RabinAssasination__AnotherIntifadah_DisengagementPlan_HamasTakeoverOfGaza...

We have been fighting for the end of occupation for years. We are working hard to remain human. As human rights lawyer Michael Sfard (2023) put it

> ... being human is hard work. Staying human in the face of inhuman cruelty is even harder... We went through terrible trauma at the hands of human beings who lost their humanity, and now we are shelling and killing and starving and hardening our own hearts to stone. Moral corruption is no less dangerous to our existence than Hamas.

The degeneration of the sympathy for Palestinians' plight into full-fledged anti-Semitism is morally corrupt, too. The framing of Hamas' murderous attack on Israel as a legitimate Palestinian civil uprising is evil. The "enlightened" TikTok left can specify who-knows-how-many pronouns for every self-determination but not what river and which sea they are chanting about; everything is a trigger for them, but not decapitation and rape. They are acutely aware of microaggressions but are blind to murder and baby kidnappings. They are ignorant about the conflict generally and about the occupation specifically, and repugnantly self-righteous regarding the events of October 7th.

We – Israelis and Palestinians – are living the complex reality **here**. Not on TikTok. There are two peoples from the Jordan River to the Mediterranean Sea. The reasoned and argumented call to end occupation, and the right of both peoples to a homeland is a position. Hashtag-FreePalestine is not.

*Note: It has been over a year since the writing of this article. We are still on the streets calling for the end of the war in Gaza, the return of the hostages still in Hamas captivity, and the end of occupation.

References

Berger, E. (2022). *Context blindness: Digital technology and the next stage of human evolution*. Peter Lang.

Lewis, H. (2023, October 13). The progressives who flunked the Hamas test. *The Atlantic*.

Pfeffer, A. (2023, October 13). The Inconvenient Context: Palestinians Massacred Jews for Being Jews. *Haaretz*.

Shor, N. (2023, October 26). I'm not angry at Hamas or Bibi. I'm angry at those who I believed were just like me. *Haaretz*.

Sfard, M. [@sfardm]. (2023, October 22). Being human is hard work. Staying human in the face of inhuman cruelty is even harder [Tweet]. X. https://x.com/sfardm/status/1716142370079551794

CHAPTER 7

INCITEMENT AND THE FLASH MOB

SUSAN J. DRUCKER and GARY GUMPERT

Sabadell, Catalonia Spain

It's 6:00 p.m. at a public square in Sabadell, Catalonia Spain. Shopping families cross back and forth along with some children crossing the square on scooters. The café is full this late afternoon. Toward one side of the square a classical bass player wearing a tuxedo begins to play the "Ode to Joy" theme from Beethoven's Ninth Symphony. A young girl stares at the musician and places a coin into the top hat in front of the players when suddenly a woman with a chair and cello joins the bass player. The spectators grow in number and from the increasing crowd a bassoon player steps out of a doorway. From one of several doorways' violinists emerge followed by violists. Unexpectedly a young man wearing a yellow striped polo shirt begins to conduct the growing ensemble. The audience nods, claps, and mimes the conductor, in rhythm, as the increasing number of performers join the ensemble: brass players, tympanists, and kettle drummers join the increasing number of musicians – the performers have grown to about 50. The growing crowd stares, conducts, and nods in time. Some children are dancing. And suddenly many members of the audience join in singing, in Catalan, the refrain from "Ode to Joy." They are clearly members of an organized chorus. The performers are probably 100 in number and the audience by now double or triple the size. And suddenly the event is over. It has taken five minutes and forty seconds. The performers, the infectious occasion and its participants disperse, disappear, into the crowd, buildings, and adjoining streets. The diminishing crowd continues their strolling, shopping, and talking. All is as before. The joyful assembly, now known as a *flash mob*, had left, and the excitement of planned spontaneity dissipated into the normal activities of the place and the moment.

Washington, D.C.

It's noon on January 6, 2021, a cold blustery day in Washington, D.C. and a crowd is slowly gathering in the ellipse in front of the White House. They began assembling early in the morning to participate in the defeated president's "Save America Rally." They are his crowd – cheering and yelling. Ten thousand people, perhaps more, some waving banners, others dressed in home-created patriotic costumes, yelling and cheering. They have come to hear the defeated Donald Trump argue against the validity of the election, exhorting his audience "to fight like hell, never give up, never concede!" He speaks for one hour and eleven minutes finally urging the crowd to walk down Pennsylvania Avenue to demonstrate in front of the Capitol. The joint session of Congress convenes at 1:00 p.m. to count the Electoral ballots certifying the election of Joseph Biden as the 46th President of the United States. By 10:30 a.m. hundreds of Proud Boys were headed to the Capitol complex. At 1:49 p.m. part of the crowd breaks down the barriers, entering the Capitol, injuring defending police, breaking into offices, smashing windows, wreaking havoc. By 5:40 p.m. the police had cleared the rioters from the capital and a curfew goes into effect. At 8:06 the Senate reconvenes to continue their task confirming the election of the President. All is not what was before. While the mob has vacated the Capitol premises, there is no joy.

Clearly there are significant differences between the two mobs, but they are united by the attempt to energize and coordinate a spectacle in a selected public venue and to produce an ensuing act. One act was benevolent and modest while the other was malicious, designed for political purposes on a grand scale. Yet they both reveal the effectiveness of online coordination of a seemingly extemporaneous public event. Both rely on the technologies of secrecy to communicate and orchestrate.

Language Crimes and the Political Landscape

The political landscape of the United States characterized by deep persistent division can be said to have culminated in the charges that Donald J. Trump incited an insurrection, increasingly identified as seditious conspiracy, against the Constitution he swore to preserve, protect, and defend. The allegation has been rooted in the former president's speech seen as merely the final act of provocation in a campaign spanning months to delegitimize the election in the public mind and provoke resistance to acceptance and confirmation. The "Stop the Steal" campaign was a multi-mediated transmission of a Big Lie.

The two events, previously described, are quite different yet related. The joy of Spain consists of two groups of participants. The first are the conspiratorial players – the musicians organized to surprise—while the second group of participants is the gathering audience, entertained by a group of supposedly "accidental" performers. The power of the January 6 gathering also had two groups of participants, the first are the conspiratorial players – the Proud Boys, the Oath Keepers and, perhaps, the Trump campaign—while the second group of participants is the gathering audience stirred by a group on stage and in the crowd among those around the Ellipse.

According to the House select committee investigating the January 6 insurrection at the Capitol, some of those in the second group became essential in providing the manpower needed to imminently breach the Capitol. The success of each event requires both surprise and planning. Incitement and seditious conspiracy can be characterized as language crimes in which the criminal act is, itself, performed by using language.

Language crimes are about illegal communication acts. Crimes involve wrongful acts, and the wrongful act may be committed by the word. There are a host of these crimes which include solicitation, perjury, threatening, bribery, and conspiracy. All language crimes concern themselves with the actor's intent "with some concerned with the intent of the actor (referred to as the act's illocutionary force), others by the effect that the act has on the hearer (referred to as the act's perlocutionary effect)" (Tiersma & Solan, 2012). They are classic examples of language in action. The words don't simply make assertions about the situation but create the situation.

Conspiracy is associated with agreement to commit a crime which may be explicit or implied. Some jurisdictions require that the agreement be followed by an overt act in furtherance of the conspiracy. Language crimes are committed directly and indirectly so that one need not state "we agree" in order to be found conspiratorial. Linguistic cues are used by a jury to infer that there was an agreement, such as the use of the pronoun "we" (Tiersma & Solan, 2012). Seditious conspiracy ratches the criminality of conspiracy up a notch in that it suggests the "conduct strikes at the heart of American democracy and falls within the same conceptual category as the most serious political crimes, such as rebellion, insurrection and treason" (Anderson et al., 2022).

A question looming in the background of the events of January 6 has been whether the violence at the Capitol was spontaneous or the result of sinister planning, whether people or the result of incitement and intentional provocation. Over 750 have been arrested nationwide for the assault on the U.S. Capitol on January 6, 2021. Some were charged with violent entry and disorderly conduct, some charged with acts of physical violence on restricted grounds, some charged with civil disorder. Other charges for incitement have been contemplated while indictments have been handed down for a very different crime, that of seditious conspiracy.

Coordinating the Flash Mob Insurrection

Analyzing the Donald Trump podium speech for potential liability for incitement does not yield a definitive determination. The highly mediated events of the day bring to mind a mediated coordinated mob, perhaps akin to a flash mob. Mobs are not new. Political mobs in American history are not new. So too, mediated mobs have been around and used for so-called e-incitement.

The role of media in organizing mobs for all sorts of purposes has grown over time. A particular variation of the mediated mob has been referred to by the name "flash mob" originally meant to describe a phenomenon in which a group of people assembles in a public space, perform a seemingly random act, then quickly disperse.

The flash mob dates to June of 2003, when Bill Wasik, then deputy editor of the *New York Times Magazine*, used email in an attempt to organize a gathering in New York City for 10 minutes in what was a MOB project. The initial effort failed when police learned of the plan and barred the doors of the store identified as the location of the gathering. The next social experiment took place at the home furnishing department of Macy's in Manhattan (Nicholson, 2005). That public performance was meant to poke fun at the hipster community and to be pointless with no strategy and no intent. They asked a Macy's salesperson about a $10,000 "love rug" before leaving. Approximately 150–200 people were amassed for 10 minutes before disbanding (Tan & Abu Bakar, 2015). This phenomenon quickly became known as a "flash mob" by participants and the local media. This name stems from an analogy to a "flash flood," where all participants arrive at once, then disperse within minutes "just like water from a sudden storm" (Wasik,

2011). The flash mob phenomenon became widespread and by July of 2004 "flash mob" was added to the Oxford English Dictionary (Wasik, 2006). Conceptually, the flash mob has been appropriated by various disciplines concerned with mustering an assemblage of people in virtual and/or physical spaces (Al-khateeb & Agarwal, 2021).

The phenomenon grew quickly around the world. During the summer of 2003, flash mobs occurred in Europe and from the United States to Asia and Australia. By July of that year, 200 people in Rome gathered in a bookstore to request a non-existent book, then scattered. Later that same month, 70 people in Berlin suddenly met to exercise then quickly scattered. In August, flash mobs arrived St. Petersburg, Moscow, and Australia, with the first flash mob taking place on a beach in Sydney where people gathered, put a foot in the water and laughed before disbanding.

The "smart mob" is a related term introduced by Howard Rheingold, in his book, *Smart Mobs: The Next Social Revolution* (2002). Rheingold, making note of the phenomenon the year before Wasik's initial endeavor, referred to mobs which form for diverse reasons ranging from the political to the commercial. This was Rheingold's name for "what another researcher has called 'mobile ad hoc social networks' – groups of people who use their mobile 'phones' and 'texting' to organize themselves 'on the move'. Sometimes the purpose is social, like fixing a gathering point for a party, sometimes it is subversive, like the organization of the public demonstrations." Since flash mobs have moved from entertainment and advertising purposes to political protest, this is the umbrella term applied in this work (Wilson, 2002).

While classical flash mobs were seen as apolitical, political flash mobs "politmobs" have taken place around the globe. Myriad examples exist (e.g., flash mob rallies coordinated in 180 cities to raise awareness of violence against woman, a pro-independence rally in Barcelona and a rally held in, Syria against Syrian President Bashar Assad's regime). Political flash mobs have been identified in protests in Hong Kong to support democracy, in Myanmar to protest against military rule, and even in the protests of the Arab Spring in 2010, including those associated with the revolutions in Tunisia and Egypt. All of these are variations on a theme of flash mobs. The United States too has not been exempt from political flash mobs (e.g., San Francisco's BART transit system protest: an Anti-Trump flash mob outside of the White House on July 4, 2017). Another involved 200 demonstrators united to spell out the word "RESIST!" in 30-foot-high letters to express their view of the policies of Donald Trump's administration (ABC News, 2017). Pro-Trump flash mobs have been organized as evidenced by those taking place in support of the then-2016 candidate that includes "flash mobs" in 25 places across Michigan (Gray, 2016). It has even been argued that the politmob can be seen as a "special form of political activity of citizens" which is distinct from the classical flash mob and represents a "new form of political participation and transforming activity of civil society" (Fedorchenko, 2011).

The illusion of spontaneity and the element of surprise are at the heart of the phenomenon. Surprise is an essential element of a flash mob. Whose surprise? Clearly the audience or spectators experience the unexpected. In some situations, participants and organizers themselves experience an element of surprise. Perhaps the surprise is the size of the audience, perhaps their reactions, perhaps the unforeseen number of participants who heeded the mediated call. Surprise is a variable for all involved.

Another dimension of some flash mobs is that they transform people in public spaces into an audience or spectator. In some cases, they are conscripted into participants and the flash mob grows. Who is the mob in the flash mob? The mob is created through the interaction of the audience and performers—many, if not all, there as a result of mediated planning.

There is a performative nature to each flash mob. The degree of coordination of each mob ranges from very loosely organized to carefully choreographed. The level of synchronization and management is related to the intended goal.

Mobs predate flash mobs. Traditionally, mobs were associated with disorder, but flash mobs, on the contrary, can be extremely organized as exemplified by performances in which specific parts have been predetermined, instruments have been assembled, and musical arrangements prepared. When does the soprano join in? When do the percussion instruments dominate? Rehearsals are arranged, and performances are synched as much as possible. Orchestration is evident moving further down the organizational continuum of flash mobs.

In a comprehensive University of Cincinnati law review article entitled "Incitement to Riot in the Age of Flash Mobs," Margot Kaminski, on the faculty at the University of Colorado Law School, looked at crowd psychology, which, she argues, should be a factor in any government regulation of crowd behavior. In her examination, she notes the work of convergence theorists who see mobs as being made of likeminded individuals who could be held responsible for their own acts as distinct from a crowd mentality. "Convergence theorists believe crowds are not innately bad but may give rise to bad behavior under certain conditions" (Kaminski, 2012, p. 77). This is contrasted with network theory suggesting that under certain circumstances crowds can behave differently than individuals. Kaminski notes that there has been a significant amount of research into "the assembly and dispersal process" of crowds (p. 75). Certain crowd conditions lead to mob violence. Two factors have been identified in leading to mob violence, legitimacy and perception of power. Legitimacy is associated with "the extent to which the crowd feels that the police and the whole social order still deserve to be obeyed" (Wasik, 2012) but the shared identity formed in the crowd can change this. In mobs formed online prior to the in-person assembly, the creation of the identity can develop prior to the event itself," thereby frontloading what Clifford Stott, professor of social psychology who studies crowds, has called the "complex process of norm construction." The second factor in crowd violence, perception of power, according to Stott is "the perception within a crowd that it has the ability to do what it wants, to take to the streets without fear of punishment," often associated with crowd size, which, can multiply significantly in the case of flash mobs (Wasik, 2012).

Seditious Conspiracy

The seditious conspiracy charges are rarely applied but Stewart Rhodes, a founder of the Oath Keepers, was convicted "for what prosecutors say was not a suddenly ignited riot but a coordinated plot to stop the transfer of presidential power" (Richer & Whitehurst, 2022). Seditious conspiracy is generally viewed as a less serious counterpart to treason. Case law (United States v. Lee, 1993) suggests that key to proving such a case is unity of purpose, the intent to achieve a common goal. The pre-January 6 planning and the resultant flash-like mob become central to these charges.

The word conspiracy is steeped in intrigue and history. One can easily envision the whispered plotting well before March 1544 BCE, when, at a senate meeting, 60 conspirators surrounded Caesar, uncovering daggers from beneath their togas and stabbing him from all sides. According to the *Online Etymology dictionary*, conspiracy is "a plotting of evil, unlawful design; a combination of persons for an evil purpose," from the Anglo-French *conspiracie*, Old French *conspiracie* "conspiracy, plot," from Latin *conspirationem* (nominative *conspiratio*) "agreement, union, unanimity," noun of action from past-participle stem of *conspirare* "to agree, unite, plot," literally "to breathe together."

In U.S. law seditious conspiracy was codified into law after the Civil War to arrest Southerners who might keep fighting the U.S. government. In order to win a seditious conspiracy case, prosecutors have to prove that two or more people conspired to "overthrow, put down or to destroy by force" the U.S. government or bring war against it, or that they plotted to use force to oppose the authority of the government or to block the execution of a law. In this light, are we seeing a trial of a flash mob as a conspiracy?

"According to the indictment, Rhodes began to plan for a rebellion just two days after the 2020 presidential election, when he told Oath

Keepers members to reject Biden's victory. 'We aren't getting through this without a civil war,' he said on an encrypted Signal chat. Over the following weeks, Rhodes called on other Oath Keepers in open letters and private chats to use violence to stop Biden from assuming office. In one instance, he said that if Biden were to assume the presidency, 'We will have to do a bloody, massively bloody revolution against them'" (Anderson et al., 2022). On the basis of these statements and other similar communications, 11 of the defendants were charged under 18 U.S.C. § 2384 with seditious conspiracy among other crimes. Originally Rhodes was charged with the more common crime of criminal conspiracy, but a superseding indictment upped this to seditious conspiracy (Title 18 U.S. § 2384).

While the flash mob is generally associated with the provocation of joyful interaction, can it not be used to provoke and organize insurrection, bodily harm, fear and the threat of death? "Conspiracy," "persuasion," "advocacy," "incitement," and "medium" are inexorably connected. The circumstance of interpretation and the quest for the truth provides us with a link to the concept of the medium as an intermediary between one perception of reality and another. It is the "medium" that is at the heart of the relationship between message and trusted source. Trust has become an increasingly studied phenomenon.

Mobs haven't generally carried connotations of scheming or treachery. Political mobs in American history are not new. Yet, there is something new in contrasting *this* conspiracy and *this* mob which brings the two together differently than mobs of old. This, after all, was not a conspiracy which took shape in a movie-worthy smoke-filled backroom, nor was the resulting mob a chaotic band of uncoordinated fellow travelers swept up in the moment. This was a conspiracy planned online, a heavily social media-based conspiracy resulting in a mediated mob.

One facet of the successful flash mob is the illusion of spontaneity. There is an element of surprise when a nearby unnoticed person suddenly joins the action. The participants in the flash mob are embedded in the crowd. There is a conspiratorial quality of the flash mob easily neglected in the produced experience of the impromptu spectacle.

Flash mobs rely on the overlapping of electronic connection and physical space. These spaces co-exist and come together in the use of mobile media in public mass gatherings such as the mob or flash mob which stormed the U.S. Capitol. Members of the Oath Keepers paramilitary group moved up the steps to the U.S. Capitol using an encrypted messaging app to transmit, "Arrest this assembly, we have probable cause for acts of treason, election fraud" (Hsu, Jackman, & Barrett, 2021). Allegedly, the Proud Boys used specific frequencies on Baofeng radios (Chinese-made devices) that can be programmed for use on hundreds of frequencies, making it difficult for outsiders to eavesdrop (Richer & Kunzelman, 2021). The use of Signal, an app for an end-to-end encrypted messaging, was strategically used. The plethora of social media posts reveal coordination and a feedback loop between participants, organizers and even the sitting president. Much social media-facilitated planning operated in closed, unmoderated groups with potential violence openly discussed.

Incitement

Significantly, the indictments and convictions to date have not included political leaders. Incitement suggests that the legal system has penalized the utterance of words which relate to the commission of a crime. Both incitement and conspiracy are considered inchoate crimes, an unfinished or incomplete offense (*Legal Dictionary*, n.d.). The crime has been committed when the words are uttered regardless of any response. "The most salient characteristic of incitement, in comparison with the other forms of inchoate crime, is the existence of a communication that is made with a view to persuading the addressee(s) to commit an offence" (Jaconelli, 2017). It is a crime of instigation, of words expressed regardless of the response (if any) that the words arouse. The language of the crime of incitement can also be characterized by such terms as "counsel," "promote," "induce," "encourage," and "solicit." The call to action may be direct or indirect. Direct incitement explicitly urges another person to commit the predicate offence. "Indirect incitement is more circumspect, consisting of such forms as to state that committing a particular crime is morally justified or to be applauded, the message possibly being communicated even by the use of metaphor" (Jaconelli, 2017, p. 248). The provocation communicated involves a "predicate offence" or the criminal act, whether committed or not.

In the United States, for words to be punished by the government there must be implied provocation, the seeking of action, some deed, which the government may prohibit. The speech act, words alone, are not punishable, but words used to produce action produce criminal liability. The seminal case on what is looked to currently as the clear and present danger doctrine, Brandenburg v. Ohio (1969), saw the U.S. Supreme Court refine the Schenck v. U.S. test (falsely shouting fire in a crowded theater case) by establishing that speech advocating illegal conduct is protected under the First Amendment unless the speech is *likely* to incite "lawless *imminent* action."

Therefore, incitement to imminent lawless action is considered unprotected by the First Amendment, allowing for government punishment. This so-called *Brandenburg* test or "Imminent lawless action" test is seen as a three-part test as to how courts should evaluate the probability that an inciting speech act will cause imminent wrongdoing. The nature of "the media of incitement" is the key to understanding the events of January 6, 2021. The mob was not a spontaneous event, but rather the amalgam of instigation and medium.

Flash Mobs and Protected Speech

While flash mobs may conger up images of seemingly spontaneous musical or dance events, they have also been used to coordinate crimes, some resulting in violence. Robberies, or "flash robs", have been reported. What began as a peaceful gathering, "flash mobs have – taken a darker twist as criminals exploit the anonymity of crowds, using social networking to coordinate everything from robberies to fights to general chaos" (Abrams, 2011). The resulting criminal conduct clearly falls within existing criminal codes, but whether the online communication used to plan and execute those violent criminal acts are punishable has raised novel legal questions. Noted First Amendment lawyer Floyd Abrams has argued planning to meet is not illegal (Abrams, 2011). It has been argued that "content-based laws designed to punish organizers of criminal flash mobs will best serve the compelling goals of state and local governments to deter crime and violence" (Steinblatt, 2012, p. 757). Some jurisdictions have attempted to address these questions so that, following a flash mob that became violent, the city of Cleveland passed a law that prohibits acts that incite riots listing "electronic media devices" such as computers and cell phones as criminal tools (Galbincea, 2011). Constitutional experts, such as Lyle Denniston, National Constitution Center advisor, have noted how explicit and direct the call to action must be to meet the *Brandenburg* standard within the social media context.

The *Brandenburg* test and the issue of incitement itself can be better understood through the examination of the medium used to advocate as well as the media environment in general. The current media environment includes social media, access on demand, echo chambers, confirmation bias, and political polarization. Further, the digitalization of a medium transforms a message.

This takes one back to how the relationship of language, messages, posts, texts, and effect can be assumed when considering the flash mob. The incitement embedded within the online announcement can easily be interpreted as a call to action, which may or may not be imminent and or lawless.

If the mob of January 6th is considered a form of flash mob given the degree of coordination online, the *Brandenburg* test could be interpreted as imminent with the degree of predictability associated with the commitment of the organized groups communicating via social media. The language certainly directed a gathering at a concrete, predictable time, and suggested mayhem. While not directly advocating violence, Trump did frame the moment as a last stand, needing to stop once Congress from accepting the results of the electors that afternoon, thereby shutting the door to more legal challenges. Finding implied provocation within the meaning of the clear and present danger doctrine is a reasonable conclusion.

Other Incitement: Other Speech Liability?

January 6th was not unique in the annals of Donald Trump's call to arms. In the weeks leading up to the first criminal indictment of a former president, Trump repeatedly called on supporters to protest. Online chat warning of protests and violence if Trump was arrested followed. "Threats varying in specificity and credibility" were posted including "calls for armed protesters to block enforcement officers and attempt to stop any arrest" (Tucker & Kunzelman, 2023). Further, in anticipation of an indictment by a Manhattan grand jury, in April 2023, Trump called District Attorney Alvin Bragg an "animal" who "doesn't care about right or wrong." While no widespread protest actually materialized, these exhortations, threats, and conversations were monitored by authorities and taken seriously leading to preparations by the New York City police and security forces. No widespread or violent protests ensued, perhaps deterred by the fate of so many who faced federal prosecution after the attack on the Capitol. It has been suggested that these protests did not occur, since no specific instructions were given as they were in the call to march on the Capitol. The call to action lacked the specificity of time, place, and manner so clear on January 6th.

During his arraignment on 34 felony counts related to falsifying business records associated with a pre-election hush-money payment made to a porn star, the judge, Juan M. Merchan, warned both defense and prosecution to "refrain from making statements that are likely to incite violence and civil unrest." The judge warned counsel not to make remarks that could jeopardize the safety of others. "Please refrain from making comments or engaging in conduct that has the potential to incite violence, create civil unrest, or jeopardize the safety or well-being of any individuals," Merchan admonished against "incendiary rhetoric" (Bromwich et al., 2023). Commentators noted that the judge "has the rare power to constrain the former president's speech" and can hold violators in contempt of court including a sentence of up to 30 days in jail (2023). The judge issued this warning to both sides, asking prosecutors to remind their witnesses not to make inflammatory public statements. Merchan told Trump's defense team to do the same with Trump and "anybody else you need to."

But on the very day of the arraignment, Trump held a rally at Mar-a-Lago later. While he railed against the Judge, District Attorney, and the charges, Trump did not explicitly call for violence or widespread protests. Following this, his lawyer, Joe Tacopina, took to talk shows to publicly dismiss the notion that Trump was inciting violence against the judge, or anyone, during his speech in Mar-a-Lago on the evening of the day of his arraignment ("Donald Trump demands defunding of FBI and Justice Department," 2023). In social media posts on his Truth Social site, the former president called for Republicans in Congress to defund the Department of Justice (DOJ) and the Federal Bureau of Investigation (FBI). He argued: "The Democrats have totally weaponized law enforcement in our country and are viciously using this abuse of power to interfere with our elections!" (Wagner, 2023). This led to much contemplation as to whether this behavior could actually lead to a court-imposed gag order. The judge however noted, "Certainly, the court would not impose a gag order at this time even if it were requested… Such restraints are the most serious and least tolerable on First Amendment rights…" (Bromwich et al., 2023).

Conclusion

The made-for-television spectacle of January 6th, like the Flash Mob, represents not one isolated event but the culmination of mediated planning and provocation. The specific media environment is essential to establishing the elements of incitement and seditious conspiracy. For instance, conspiracies are secretive, an agreement to commit an illegal act. The *technologies of secrecy* have grown exponentially. Each medium offers different degrees or increments of secrecy.

The opportunities to communicate anonymously, in closed, unmoderated online environments, via encrypted channels are all components of the digital media landscape. When is the apparently spontaneous, concealed plotting? How can law enforcement and laws adapt to a need to assume a hybrid reality lived at the intersection of electronic connection and physical space? To understand mobs and prove conspiracy requires acknowledgment of *the inner workings* of the technologies of secrecy.

Flash mobs are marked by the element of surprise, a mustering of people who briefly gather to perform an unexpected act, and then disperse. These events, at least in part, feel extemporaneous and fleeting taking place in public space. One aspect of the successful flash mob is the illusion of spontaneity. There is the element of surprise when the unnoticed person nearby suddenly joins the action. Some participants in the flash mob are embedded in the crowd. Flash mobs rely on the overlap of the world of electronic connection and physical space, the interstice between the two is key. These spaces co-exist and come together in the use of mobile media in public mass gatherings such as the mob or political flash mob which stormed the U.S. Capitol on January 6, 2021. While much attention has been paid to vivid overt violent crimes against people, property, and obstruction of governmental process, the significance of language crimes within the mediated context must not be overlooked.

References

ABC News. (2017, May 14). *Flash mob of 200 spells out 'RESIST!' at Trump golf club near Los Angeles*. https://abcnews.go.com/Politics/flash-mob-200-spells-resisttrump-golf-club/story?id=47399265

Abrams, F. (2011, September 7). Flash mob violence and the Constitution. *Wall Street Journal*. https://www.wsj.com/articles/SB10001424053111904583204576544531039409522

Al-khateeb, S., & Agarwal, N. (2021). Flash mob: A multidisciplinary review. *Social Network Analysis and Mining, 11*(97). https://doi.org/10.1007/s13278-021-00810-7

Anderson, S. R., Jurecic, Q., Kurup, R., Orpett, N. K., & Rozenshtein, A. Z. (2022, January 14). Seditious conspiracy: What to make of the latest OathKeepers indictment. *Lawfare*. https://www.lawfareblog.com/seditious-conspiracy-what-make-latest-oathkeepers-indictment

Brandenburg v. Ohio, 395 U.S.C 444 § et seq. (1969).

Bromwich, J. E., Rashblaum, W. K., & Christobek, K. (2023, April 7). Dilemma for judge in Trump case: Whether to muzzle the former president. *New York Times*, p. 13A.

Donald Trump demands defunding of FBI and Justice department. (2023, April 13). *The Telegraph*. https://www.telegraph.co.uk/world-news/2023/04/05/donald-trump-newsindictment-arrest-charges-latest/

Fedorchenko, S. (2011). Political flashmob – A sign of a new society? Problem analysis and public administrative design. https://www.researchgate.net/publication/259182530_POLITICAL_FLASHMOB_-_A_SIGN_OF_A_NEW_SOCIETY

Galbincea, P. (2011, December 13). Flash mob ordinances become law in Cleveland minus Mayor Frank Jackson's signature. *Cleveland.com*. https://www.cleveland.com/metro/2011/12/flash_mob_ordinances_become_la.html

Gray, K. (2016, August 30). Donald Trump flash mob gets honks — and the finger. *Detroit Free Press*. https://www.freep.com/story/news/politics/2016/08/30/donaldtrump-flash-mob-gets-honks-and-finger/89586406/

Hsu, S. S., Jackman, T., & Barrett, D. (2021, January 19). Self-styled militia members planned on storming the U.S. Capitol days in advance of Jan. 6 attack, court documents say. *The Washington Post*. https://www.washingtonpost.com/local/legalissues/conspiracy-oath-keeper-arrest-

capitol-riot/2021/01/19/fb84877a-5a4f-11eb-8bcf-3877871c819d_story.html
Jaconelli, J. (2017). Incitement: A study in language crime. *Criminal Law and Philosophy, 12,* 245. https://doi.org/10.1007/s11572-017-9427-8
Kaminiski, M. E. (2012). Incitement to Riot in the Age of Flash Mobs. *University of Cincinnati Law Review, 81*(1). https://scholar.law.colorado.edu/articles/1351
Legal Dictionary (n.d.). https://dictionary.law.com/Default.aspx?selected=918#:~:text=inchoate,some%20object%20which%20is%20incomplete
Nicholson, J. A. (2005). Flash! Mobs in the age of mobile connectivity, *The Fibreculture Journal, 6.* https://www.researchgate.net/publication/26490729_Flash_Mobs_in_the_Age_of_Mobile_Connectivity
Online Etymology Dictionary. https://www.etymonline.com/search?q=conspiracy.
Rheingold, H. (2002). *Smart mobs: The next social revolution.* Perseus Publishing.
Richer, A. D., & Kunzelman, M. (2021, March 10). U.S. narrows in on organized extremists in Capitol siege probe. *AP.* https://apnews.com/article/organizedextremists-capitol-riot-probe-8e6ddb336b23d1813b18e8932f321e40
Richer, A. D., & Whitehurst, L. (2022, September 28). EXPLAINER: Rare sedition charge at center of Jan. 6 trial. *AP.* https://apnews.com/article/what-does-seditioncharge-mean-3aa820dda5f501dd874c4dd6d60ca1ce
Schenck v. United States, 249 U.S.C. 47 § *et seq.* (1919).
Steinblatt, H. (2012). *E-Incitement: A framework for regulating the incitement of criminal flash mobs,* 22 Fordham Intell. Prop. Media & Ent. L.J. https://ir.lawnet.fordham.edu/iplj/vol22/iss3/4
Tan, E., & Abu Bakar, B. (2015, May 20–22). *Experiencing the flash mob: Meanings and experiences in an unplanned event in Singapore.* [Conference session]. World Convention on Hospitality, Tourism & Event Research and International Convention & Expo Summit, Seoul, Korea. http://researchrepository.murdoch.edu.au/id/eprint/40386
Tiersma, P. M., & Solan, L. M. (2012). *The language of crime.* Brooklyn Law School Legal Studies. https://doi.org/10.1093/oxfordhb/9780199572120.013.0025

Title 18 U.S. § 2384. https://codes.findlaw.com/us/title-18-crimes-and-criminal-procedure/18-usc-sect-2384/

Treisman. R. (2021, March 2). Prosecutors: Proud Boys gave leader 'war powers,' planned ahead for capitol riot. *NPR*. https://www.npr.org/2021/03/02/972895521/prosecutors-proud-boys-gave-leader-war-powers-planned-ahead-for-capitol-riot

Tucker, E., & Kunzelman, M. (2023 March 20). Trump's calls for protests fail to gain traction ahead of anticipated indictment. *PBS News Hour*. https://www.pbs.org/newshour/politics/trumps-calls-for-protests-fail-to-gain-traction-ahead-ofanticipated-indictment

United States v. Lee, 455 U.S.C. 252 § et seq. (1993).

Wagner, J. (2023, April 5). Trump says Republicans in Congress should 'defund' Justice Department, FBI. *The Washington Post*. https://www.washingtonpost.com/politics/2023/04/05/trump-defund-fbi-justice-department/

Wasik, B. (2006, March). My crowd. *Harper's Magazine*. https://harpers.org/archive/2006/03/my-crowd/

Wasik, B. (2011, December 16). #Riot: Self-organized, hyper-networked revolts coming to a city near you. *Wired*. https://www.wired.com/2011/12/ff-riots/

Wasik, B. (2012, January 27). Crowd control: How today's protests, revolts and riots are self-organising. *Wired*. https://www.wired.co.uk/article/crowd-control?page=4

Wilson, T. (2002). Review of Rheingold, Howard. Smart mobs: The next social revolution. *Information Research*, 8(3), review no. R086, Perseus Publishing, http://informationr.net/ir/reviews/revs086.html

CHAPTER 8

AN OUNCE OF PREVENTION: GENERAL SEMANTICS AND CONSPIRACY THEORIES
JOSHUA CLEMENTS

"The history of learning is an adventure in overcoming our errors. There is no sin in being wrong. The sin is in our unwillingness to examine our own beliefs, and in believing that our authorities cannot be wrong. Far from creating cynics, such a story is likely to foster a healthy and creative skepticism..."
— Neil Postman, *The End of Education*

Introduction

Various research on conspiracy theories (CTs) and conspiratorial thinking illustrate a connection between CTs and democracy (Moore, 2016; Uscinski & Parent, 2014). CTs such as Pizzagate and QAnon have led some believers to act violently in attempts to uphold their erroneous beliefs, often with political motives (Amarasingam & Argentino, 2020). Other CTs, such as Watergate, have been less violent but no less politically motivated. However, to lump all CTs and theorists into a pathology, as some research has attempted (Sunstein

& Vermeule, 2009), is erroneous (Coady, 2018) and potentially dangerous to democracy (Smallpage, 2019; Uscinski, 2019). In several instances, CTs turn out to be correct, such as the U.S. government perpetrating unethical medical practices on African Americans on more than one occasion (Vernon, 2020).

Moore (2016) noted that CTs may be problematic for democratic governments. He stated, "in the context of a largely stable and transparent democratic order, conspiracy theory seems to represent a threat to the proper functioning of democracy itself" (Moore, 2016, p. 6). Still, other researchers see CTs as a check on power in a democratic society (Keeley, 2019; Uscinski, 2019). Following this second line of thought, it may be prudent to understand CTs and conspiratorial thinking better and investigate ways to increase critical thinking while maintaining a healthy skepticism.

Conspiracy theory research has diversified in recent years from its emphasis on pathologizing people who believe in CTs. Still, much of the research is primarily conducted in Western, English-speaking countries (Mahl et al., 2022). However, several scholars have expanded CT research into other areas, such as Russia (Yablokov, 2019), Turkey (Nefes, 2019), and Argentina (Filer, 2019). The number of research studies on CTs has also grown exponentially, largely due to the rise in online environments that allow (or even encourage) the easy spread of information and opinions (Mahl et al., 2022). The ability of CTs to spread so easily has also exposed them to criticism.

Often, the knee-jerk reaction when we hear something that sounds outlandish, as many CTs may seem, is to want to argue with the person espousing the conspiracy theory, thinking our argument and contrary evidence will somehow change the theorist's mind. However, this attempt can lead to theorists holding tighter to their theories, what some researchers have labeled the *backfire effect* (Nyhan et al., 2013). Subsequent research showed that even when new evidence increases the conspiracy theorists more accurate beliefs, the effect decays within a short period from the exposure (Nyhan, 2021).

Krekó (2020) suggested that there may not be an express need to argue about, debunk, or regulate CTs, as doing so may be a form of political suppression. Given the reality that some CTs have proven to be correct, an issue with attempting to completely "cure" conspiracy thinking would inevitably lead some people away from sometimes accurate information, instead of toward it (Uscinski, 2018). Another tactic that may be a more helpful approach in the long run is the prevention of entrenched viewpoints (Krekó, 2020). In this regard, an under-explored area of CT research is how to discourage or prevent radical conspiratorial thinking and find constructive methods to encourage critical thinking while maintaining a healthy skepticism.

One system with a history of teaching people to think critically is Alfred Korzybski's general semantics (GS). Also within this tradition is the concept that our ideas could be wrong or need more information, tenets generally associated with scientific thinking (Feynman, 2009; Sagan, 2011). In this essay, I will suggest that GS can help conspiracy thinking by providing a framework for people to analyze information more rationally. Additionally, this essay includes concepts from conspiracy theory curator and provocateur Robert Anton Wilson, whom Korzybski and GS influenced.

The purpose of this essay will be to illustrate how GS as a form of prevention can benefit people who may have conspiratorial worldviews or conspiratorial thinking. Using GS principles, a person may prevent the dogmatic thinking typically associated with CTs. By applying GS principles to conspiratorial thinking and worldviews early enough, conspiracy theorists may see that they do not have all the information needed to make their claims. This recognition may encourage conspiratorial thinkers to revise their theory to align with a more accurate picture of the world. This suggestion also acknowledges the negative stigma surrounding CTs in many societies and how applying GS principles may lessen the negative perceptions. Tempering skepticism with critical or scientific thinking may be the combination needed to protect our democracy and our individual freedom.

Definitions

As a way of illustrating the importance of how CTs are defined, Bost (2019) offers this example of two individuals with differing explanations of what took place on September 11, 2001:

> [O]ne who attributes those events to secret, coordinated action among members of a terrorist organization, and another who attributes the same events to secret, coordinated action among members of the United States government. Both believe that a conspiracy has occurred, but only the second is a "conspiracy theorist" whose belief is subject to public ridicule as well as scrutiny by research psychologists. The point is obvious but important: Until we establish the boundaries that distinguish conspiracy theories from other types of beliefs, it is unclear what beliefs and believers researchers should be studying. (p. 271)

Several important terms in this essay warrant definition, including conspiracy, conspiracy theory, and conspiracy thinking. Uscinski (2019) defined conspiracy as "a secret arrangement between two or more actors to usurp political or economic power, violate established rights, hoard vital secrets, or unlawfully alter government institutions to benefit themselves at the expense of the common good" (p. 48).

Following this, a *conspiracy theory* may be defined as "an explanation of past, ongoing, or future events or circumstances that cites as a main causal factor a small group of powerful persons, the conspirators, acting in secret for their own benefit and against the common good" (Uscinski, 2019, p. 48). In this regard, CTs are fundamentally about who has power and what they do with it unaware to the public. Conspiracies are usually tied to an event or set of events later accepted as true by various authorities. CTs are accusations that often conflict with the authoritative narrative and may or may not be true. Lastly, conspiracy thinking, sometimes called conspiratorial thinking, refers to "an underlying worldview or disposition, similar to political ideology, toward viewing events and circumstances as the product of conspiracies" (Uscinski, 2019, p. 50).

In synthesizing published works on CTs and corroborating Uscinski's (2019) definitions, Bost (2019) described several typical components. These include multiple coordinated actors working in secret, who often accuse elite individuals or groups of abusing their power, operating clandestinely with nefarious intentions. Another element sometimes associated with CTs in the literature is the tendency of CTs to dispute official narratives of events, and what some have called epistemologically broken or crippled, which follows Vermeule and Sunstein's (2009) critique.

Enders and Smallpage (2019) suggest several key points about CTs in America, namely that they are pervasive, believed by people across the political spectrum, and often disruptive to politics. Though most Americans believe in at least one CT (Oliver & Wood, 2014), they are not all equal in their implications. While believing in UFOs, for example, may be harmless in most cases, at the opposite end of the spectrum, some CTs can lead to such events as the storming of the Capitol on January 6, 2021. Now we turn to how CTs affect democracy.

CTs and Democracy

While the events that occurred on January 6, 2021, may appear as a danger to democracy, America has a history of radical action and conspiratorial thinking. In their book *American Conspiracy Theories*, Uscinski and Parent (2014) called the Declaration of Independence "the original conspiracy theory" (p. 1), illustrating the founding of our nation as birthed out of conspiracy. Several researchers of CTs see them as, in many ways, protective of democracy. Uscinski and Parent (2014) noted, "Paradoxically, democracy is both a salve for, and a source of, CTs… A skeptical eye toward power is therefore not only sensible but also desirable, and CTs are the culmination of this attitude" (p. 162). Consequently, if democracy relies on an informed electorate with free, independent thought, encouraging healthy skepticism may be prudent (Smallpage, 2019).

Uscinski (2019) considered CTs as a form of antagonism with mainstream narratives and institutions. Conspiracy theorists offer explanations that question mainstream institutions. They question and often "undermine the establishment by providing alternative facts, realities, and ways of knowing" (Uscinski, 2019, p. 15). However, in many ways, these activities encourage the public to be skeptical and offer a balancing mechanism to those in power. CTs are tools used by those who typically lack positions of power to disrupt and instill fear in powerful entities (Atkinson & Dewitt, 2019). They act like alarm systems for groups weaker in society (Uscinski, 2018). When suggesting ways to curb conspiratorial thinking or to safeguard against the harmful elements of CTs, one must be careful not to completely squelch those ideals because to do so would leave some believers "without an important tool for thwarting potential abuse" (Uscinski, 2019, p. 20).

Vermeule and Sunstein (2009) claimed that CTs are plagued by a crippled epistemology, meaning the knowledge environments surrounding conspiracy theorists are limited by various forces, or the individuals themselves shut off access to opposing information. They suggested CTs should be cured, such as through governmental action. However, Bjerg and Presskorn-Thygesen (2016) argued that the "cures" Vermeule and Sunstein suggest "are in fact that the government should do precisely what conspiracy theorists are claiming that it is already doing" (p. 17). Applying both early and later Wittgenstein's concepts of language illustrates that the problem with the perception of CTs is not in their proposition (early Wittgenstein), but in their current usage (later Wittgenstein) (Bjerg & Presskorn-Thygesen, 2016). Research such as Vermeule and Sunstein's (2009) relegate some of the legitimate concerns of CTs to fringe pathologies, dismissing them from any meaningful dialogue. There is a better way to work with CTs.

GS as a Way Forward

GS has been, since its inception, connected to the American experiment of democracy. As a World War I veteran and spectator of the coming World War II, Korzybski understood the importance of free thought and an informed electorate. He believed in democracy over despotic dictatorships, but this came with a caveat. Korzybski (2005) wrote, "We argue so much today about 'democracy' versus 'totalitarianism.' Democracy presupposes intelligence of the masses; totalitarianism does not in the same degree. But a 'democracy' without intelligence of the masses under modern conditions can be a worse human mess than any dictatorship could be" (p. lxxvii). His system, GS, encourages a more intelligent electorate and a balanced understanding of social interaction.

Despite the need for balance, one of the major issues surrounding conspiratorial thinking is mistaking the map for the territory. Borrowing from Karl Popper, Moore (2016) noted the conspiracy theory problem of reducing societal wholes to individual psychologies, such as giving individual agency to "the working class" or conversely to the "one percent." This is similar to what H. S. Jennings called the "fallacy of attributing to one cause what is due to many" (quoted in Korzybski, 2005, p. 5). The likelihood of mass collusion is minuscule, and if there is any coordinated effort, it is often less effective than realized.

Conspiratorial thinking is often seen as "monological," meaning belief in one CT indicates a tendency to believe in other CTs, or what is often described as a conspiratorial worldview (Sutton & Douglas, 2014). The implication here is a closed mindset, but one that may develop through inculturation and conversion into an in-group (Franks et al., 2017) as opposed to an innate predisposition. Also, the mindset may be an error in what the person knows. GS advocate and human relations pioneer Bateson (2000) wrote, "Epistemological error is often reinforced and therefore self-validating. You can get along all right in spite of the fact that you entertain at rather deep levels of the mind premises which are simply false" (p. 488). If kept in check, this type of error is tolerable to a point, Bateson suggested, as long as it was not allowed to grow like a weed or parasite and choke out clear judgment. Hence, as the phrase goes, an ounce of prevention is better than a cure.

Once deeply rooted and invasive, the closed mindset can lead to intuitive thinking rather than rational. This sense of intuition is akin to pattern recognition and is the opposite of scientific or analytic thinking (Wood & Douglas, 2019). Conspiracy theorists take various bits of information strung together around a motive of how authorities use or maintain power and fabricate a compelling story of how these elements work to create the present condition. Kahneman (2011) illustrated that people often cease to look for new information when they have a coherent story about the world. In this manner, CTs are stories about how the world works according to whose purpose or to what end.

Creating a coherent narrative is "the main form of legitimating knowledge in a conspiracy theory" (Mason, 2002, p. 43). These narratives form cognitive maps of a history of events and how they lead to a certain future. However, Korzybski and GS suggest that the map is not the territory. In this case, the cognitive map may look very little like the territory and, therefore, should not be viewed dogmatically as such. Korzybski (2005) stated, "[t]o know that we know, to have conviction of conviction, ignorance of ignorance, shows the mechanism of dogmatism" (p. 440). Korzybski's project was, in many ways, an attempt to lessen this entrenched style of belief.

Another area where GS offers clarity is in the "loaded language" often seen in CTs. Klein and Hendler (2022) described several forms of this loaded language, including *thought-terminating clichés* or "semantic stop-signs." These are "a form of loaded language commonly used to quell cognitive dissonance" (Klein & Hendler, 2022, p. 2672). These clichés are similar to Kahneman's concept that *what you see is all there is* (WYSIATI), or coherent stories the mind uses for intuition. These clichés include such phrases as "it's God's will," "agree to disagree," and "it is what it is." GS practitioners have explicitly addressed this last cliché, including Strate (2021), who articulated that when someone says, "it is what it is," one can be assured that "it is what it isn't" (n.p.). For example, when someone says, "This is a pencil," the item is not, in fact, a pencil, but a thing, "pencil" being the label applied to the thing.

A second form of loaded language listed by Klein and Hendler (2022) is *euphemistic and dysphemistic language,* which is where a "neutral or inoffensive word/expression is substituted with one that is considered more pleasant or less derogatory" (p. 2672). Examples include such phrases as 'pass away' for die or 'between jobs' for unemployed. These euphemisms soften the emotional impact of various terms and work through ambiguity. However, one of the aims of GS is to add clarity to language. Therefore, through encouraging clarification, we may shine a light on the ambiguity of loaded language found in conspiracy theorizing and expose it to constructive criticism.

To add clarity to language use, Korzybski (2005) advocated the use of self-referential statements to lessen the emphasis on the "is" of identity. In GS, the 1st non-aristotelian principle is the principle of non-identity, usually indicated by the phrase, "the map is not the territory." Maps are useful, but when wrong, can lead to devastating results. Korzybski (2002) illustrated this point in one of his lectures, saying, "We take a map in which the towns are in the wrong order. Now such a map is not fit to travel by. We do not have predictability for traveling by such a map. Then such a map is harmful" (p. 53). The lack of predictability often leads a person to a psychological crisis or insanity. Korzybski continued, "a great deal of 'mental' illness is built up by chocks and fear due to uncertainty and unpredictability. A good many 'mental' maladjustments would be eliminated if we could predict 'something' would happen, and 'something' happened" (p. 55). The map is useful so long as it accurately represents the territory it espouses.

Following this dictum that the map is not the territory, Strate (2022) stated that "our representations and understandings of our environment should not be mistaken for the environment itself" (p. 108). Mental maps, as a form of representation and understanding, cannot accurately model an objective reality without the individual's subjective experience. People see the world as they are, not as it is. If people perceive a power imbalance in the world, they will likely believe it is due to certain factors, not their particular view of things. Then, when they describe the world, their words indicate an individual perception, not a universal reality.

The mistaken universal reality and the closed mindset often prevalent in CTs coincide with an "allness" mentality, meaning individuals who maintain an allness attitude typically resist any new information that might come to light on a topic, a phenomenon sometimes seen in conspiratorial thinking and called motivated reasoning (Uscinski, 2020). GS could influence this area of CTs, as many conspiracy theorists embrace this type of mentality. Once the theorist has a coherent story, it pervades everything. This phenomenon recalls Kahneman's (2011) WYSIATI. Conspiracy theorists can embrace the 2nd non-aristotelian principle, the principle of non-allness, which "reminds us that our perception and knowledge about any given event or object is necessarily incomplete, and all the more so our depictions and descriptions" (Strate, 2011, p. 24). Training in GS teaches us to remember that there is always more to learn about anything.

Another tactic suggested by GS as a way to combat an allness attitude is to use self-referential statements such as "to me" or "it seems" (Korzybski, 2005; Levinson, 2014). These phrases imply a localized, individual perception, not a universal, prescriptive mandate. CTs are full of this "to-me-ness," but most theorists fail to acknowledge it. Admitting this may temper the effects of conspiratorial thinking. For instance, one might say, "to me, the Republicans could do better reaching out to minority populations," or "it seems like Democrats typically want more government oversight." Strate (2011) described this as the 3rd non-aristotelian principle: the principle of self-reflexiveness. In another work, Strate (2022) noted the importance of self-reflexiveness in that "our representations and understandings can extend not only to our environment, but back towards themselves, so that we can also have representations of our representations, and representations of our representations of our representations, etc." (p. 109). Adopting this tactic may help conspiracy theorists recognize that their understanding of and statements about an event or set of events are not ultimately generalizable to everyone.

Recognizing the lack of generalizability of our statements and that our verbalizations about the world are not inherent properties of the world but representations embodies a non-aristotelian approach. Korzybski saw his system as a way of overcoming the limits of aristotelian categorical thinking, which often allows people to mistake their words for the things being described, or mistaking the map for the territory. In this regard, GS takes an extensional approach to navigating the world, rather than an intensional one.

Intension means "an aristotelian definition by properties" (Korzybski, 2002, p. 59). This type of definition will never be adequate to cover individual cases properly. An intensional orientation to the world often involves accepting or deferring the dictionary or textbook definition of a word as the *de facto* meaning of the word and cannot be undermined. A conspiratorial thinker exhibits intensional thinking by lumping all liberals into one global cabal, as many QAnon adherents have, or all vaccinations are harmful and cause autism (Quick & Larson, 2018). On the other hand, another example of an intensional definition would be to lump all CTs into one group, instead of addressing each in its own context and according to its merit. Or, perhaps lumping all conspiratorial thinkers into one category without investigating the individuals themselves would be another example.

Conversely, *extension* means a mathematical and semantic definition (Korzybski, 2002). This type of definition properly exhibits individual cases. Applying this type of view would require a conspiratorial thinker to evaluate each scenario, fact, or tidbit of information on its own merits instead of how they might automatically fit into the chosen narrative. Without merely accepting information, a thought, or a comment at face value, a person exhibiting an extensional orientation would ask such questions as "How do I know that?," How do you know that?," "Where did that thought come from?," "What evidence is there to support this claim?" etc. (Pula, 2000). One could easily see how an extensional orientation and questions such as the ones above could help not only conspiratorial thinking but embody the meaning of critical thinking in general.

To help a person apply extensional orientation, Korzybski advocated using what he called working devices, including indexing, dating, and adding, etc., to our comments and thoughts. These three methods are part of a larger set of extensional devices Korzybski put forward to give proper emphasis to differences, which largely get lost in our verbal expressions. Indexing, for instance, borrows the mathematical subscript to differentiate between entities. In this manner, X_1 is not X_2, and $Smith_1$ is not $Smith_2$. Conspiratorial thinking often involves assuming similarity across categories, such as assuming all people in a particular party think the same, or all people of a certain class believe a certain way about another class. Indexing would help alleviate this dogmatic thinking by helping a conspiratorial thinker see differences in people, things, and events.

Dating also helps abolish dogmatism (Korzybski, 2002). Dating embraces the Heraclitean notion that we are not the same person today as we were yesterday or will be tomorrow. We often see this phenomenon in writers and describe their works in early or later terms, for example early Heidegger or later Heidegger, or early Wittgenstein or later Wittgenstein. A simpler method espoused by Korzybski is to date the statement or text, such as $Wittgenstein_{1921}$ or $Wittgenstein_{1953}$. Applying this concept to CTs would require a theorist to date his or her own thoughts and comments about the world, as well as dating perceptions of events. To illustrate how dating helps visualize the changing states of individuals, Marjorie Taylor $Greene_{2023}$ may agree that much of her perceptions about the QAnon phenomenon do not represent Marjorie Taylor $Greene's_{2017}$ understanding (Miller, 2021).

Following indexing and dating, GS advocates adding a silent "etc." to our thoughts and statements to remind us that there is always more to be learned or said about a topic (Korzybski, 2005; Levinson, 2014). This tactic embodies the scientific notion that our information and what can be said about that information is limited, often by default. By adopting this tactic, a conspiracy theorist may realize that even with a coherent story and present evidence, there is much more to be learned about a given situation.

Korzybski (2005) pointed to the problem of *abstraction*, the process of our nervous systems, through sensory inputs, selecting certain characteristics about a given object or event (territory) and building a mental description (map) as a way of understanding. In other words, we build internal maps to represent external territories (Strate, 2022). The problem is not necessarily the abstraction as mentally produced, but when the person mistakes the map for the territory. This is often seen in how people describe the event or object they perceived. Accordingly, "[w]hen we use such terms, we are dealing with characteristics which are absent in the external world, and build up an anthropomorphic and delusional world non-similar in structure to the world around us" (Korzybski, 2005, p. 384). The error in this cognitive mapping process is not what is included in the map, but what gets left out. Abstracting is inherently exclusionary because we "did not *abstract 'all'* characteristics... this would be an impossibility" (Korzybski, 2005, p. 427). The unfortunate nature of abstracting is that humans can produce unlimited numbers of abstractions.

The abstracting process illustrates much of conspiratorial thinking. Any given conspiracy theory is a story about how the world works. Nevertheless, these narratives "are by necessity gross simplifications. They are not merely grand explanatory narratives; they are grand simplifying narratives that summarize and connect holistically in a way that can be made consistent with ideology" (Robertson & Dyrendal, 2019, p. 417). Through awareness of the abstracting process, conspiracy theorists could recognize their limited perception of the events they describe and edit or adjust their claims accordingly. At a minimum, they might be able to see where their theories err and take a more agnostic stance.

Robert Anton Wilson

The writer, futurist, and psychologist Robert Anton Wilson exemplifies an agnostic perspective toward everything. Wilson (2020) called his attempt to enlarge people's ability to think a "guerilla ontology" (p. 47). In this state of being, a person is constantly subverting his or her conceptions of reality in an attempt to arrive at a better understanding of the world. Wilson applied this type of thinking by questioning what he knew and adopting complete agnosticism toward every facet of knowing. Alfred Korzybski and GS also influenced Wilson. Many of his works involve elements of GS.

Due to his perpetual agnosticism, Wilson may also be seen as a hyper-conspiracy theorist or, at minimum, a fringe Libertarian. However, Wilson understood the problem of "symbol rulers" mentioned by Korzybski (2005). According to Wilson (2020), the battle for power is a battle for semantic and symbolic territories as well as physical territory. The symbolic territory may manifest as an ideology, a belief system, or a reality tunnel. A reality tunnel can be understood as a mix of ontology and epistemology, a way of being and knowing. Reality tunnels offer people ways of seeing the world that also relegate them to only seeing it one way (Wilson, 2020). In this regard, a reality tunnel is an abstraction that is taken to extremes.

Following Korzybski, Wilson (2020) believed that just as no one abstraction says all there is to say about any one object or event, "no *one* 'reality-tunnel' is adequate for the description of all human experience, although *some* reality-tunnels are better for *some* purposes than others are" (p. 21, italics in original). His point was to illustrate how people hold beliefs about things for a purpose, whether it is a way to offer hope about the future, explain why an aspect of the world is the way it is, or help us be better human beings toward others. The utility

AN OUNCE OF PREVENTION   187

of the reality tunnel does not, however, dismiss its inadequacy. Wilson (2020) noted, "any choice between reality tunnels is *always* made on the basis of insufficient data, because we have no way of knowing what new data will be discovered the next day, the next decade, or the next century" (p. 23, italics in original). This concept recalls the GS principle of non-allness.

A word Wilson (2020) suggests we should adopt to help with an allness attitude is "sombunall," meaning some-but-not-all. His point, following Korzybski (2005), is that perception always involves some level of abstraction (subtraction in some cases), and people's realities are composed of coordinated or orchestrated abstractions. The "sombunall" mentality combats an "allness" attitude, which has led to numerous atrocities throughout human history. Examples include slavery, the holocaust, various other genocides, etc. It becomes hard to utter rationally that all Canadians are bad or that all Americans are good when a person is trained to think, "sombunall Americans are good," or "sombunall" Canadians are bad, the definitions of good and bad notwithstanding. Embracing a "sombunall" reflexivity may help temper the dogmatism of conspiratorial thinking.

Wilson (2020) also adopted the self-referential style associated with GS, going so far as to suggest that our sense of truth is relative to the type of proof we need for a given scenario. This might include such truths associated with scientific, mathematical, and legal proof, all of which operate according to different rules. This means they are fundamentally different kinds of truth. To illustrate his point, Wilson (2020) stated, "Self-referential 'truths' are valid for only one person at a time, or one group of persons, and do not refer to anything but the nervous system or nervous systems of those who espouse them. This does not mean that they are 'false'" (p. 65), but they are different from another person's truth and based on the utility needed by the person at the time. To say, "to me, the sky is blue" indicates not an inherent truth of blueness in the sky, but that the individual has a purpose for the sky being blue at that moment. A conspiracy theorist saying, "it seems to me that the JFK assassination was an inside job" is different from a person saying outright, "JFK's assassination was an inside job." One is a statement of evaluation that can be questioned, amended, or redacted. The latter, however, is a statement of "truth" with little recourse other than to argue aimlessly with the individual espousing it.

The problem with arguing against CTs is that they are often statements of faith from the theorist, modes of knowing that cannot be questioned empirically. Epistemology takes trust or faith. Wilson (2020) described this issue stating, "Absolute Laws in the Platonic sense cannot be known scientifically – as Plato himself realized. They can only be 'known' (or imagined) by intuition or by some Act of Faith" (p. 76). CTs have a history of similarity with religious beliefs, often fulfilling similar cognitive functions (Franks et al., 2013; Wood & Douglas, 2018). The relatively recent meta-conspiracy theory known as QAnon was seen as similar to a new religion (LaFrance, 2020). Wilson was the Pope of Discordianism, a made-up religion meant to parody how religious beliefs fascinate and indoctrinate people into various reality tunnels (Robertson, 2012).

Wilson (2020) saw his form of guerilla ontology and agnosticism as a remedy for the type of dogmatic thinking that leads to an entrenched reality, a form that often plagues conspiratorial thinkers who hold viscerally to their beliefs. While any questioning or speculation about a belief can seem intrusive to a fundamentalist or dogmatist, no amount of speculation or skepticism will bother an open mind (Wilson, 2020).

Conclusion

CTs and their underlying modes of thinking make for an interesting case study. They are, in many ways, important to the ongoing experiment we call democracy (Uscinski & Parent, 2014; Uscinski, 2019). However, one cannot acknowledge their utility without also addressing their potential danger. The conversation does not have to be binary, however. As illustrated in this article, taking a middle-ground approach may protect the free thought needed in democracy while also encouraging a healthy skepticism of personal beliefs and perceptions.

By embracing GS principles early and following the suggestions of Robert Anton Wilson, conspiracy theorists may temper their dogmatic beliefs, adjust their claims about people or events, and realize their maps do not always reflect the territory accurately. I do not, however, believe this aspirational goal will be easy. Korzybski (2005) himself understood the difficulty of the task, going so far as to write:

> A bad habit cannot be easily eliminated except by forming a new semantic counter-reaction. All of us have some undesirable but thoroughly established linguistic habits and [semantic reactions] which have become almost automatic, overloaded with unconscious 'emotional' evaluation. This is the reason why new 'non-systems' are, in the beginning, so extremely difficult to acquire. We have to break down the old structural habits before we can acquire the new [semantic reactions]. (p. 379)

The imperative in these words indicates our need for better habits, linguistically and perceptually.

Calls for curing conspiracy thinking (Vermeule & Sunstein, 2009) dismiss the need for different modes of thinking, modes that help us question authority and often lead to new understanding. However, we can learn to think more critically and scientifically while also questioning the authority of symbol rulers (Korzybski, 2005). Perhaps Strate (2011) articulated the issue most accurately, stating, "When everyone is able to think and operate like scientists, humanity will be able to function in a mature, rational, peaceful, and fair manner" (p. 22). GS has the tools to help us get there.

References

Amarasingam, A., & Argentino, M. A. (2020). The QAnon conspiracy theory: A security threat in the making. *CTC Sentinel, 13*(7), 37–44.

Atkinson, M. D., & Dewitt, D. (2019). The politics of disruption. In J. Uscinski (Ed.), *Conspiracy theories and the people who believe them* (pp. 122–133). Oxford University Press.

Bateson, G. (2000). *Steps to an ecology of mind*. University of Chicago Press.

Bjerg, O., & Presskorn-Thygesen, T. (2017). Conspiracy theory: Truth claim or language game? *Theory, Culture & Society, 34*(1), 137–159.

Bost, P. R. (2019). The truth is around here somewhere. In J. Uscinski (Ed.), *Conspiracy theories and the people who believe them* (pp. 269–282). Oxford University Press.

Coady, D. (2018). Cass Sunstein and Adrian Vermeule on conspiracy theories. *Argumenta, 3*(2), 291–302.

Enders, A. M., & Smallpage, S. M. (2018). Polls, plots, and party politics: Conspiracy theories in contemporary America. In J. Uscinski (Ed.), *Conspiracy theories and the people who believe them* (pp. 298–318). Oxford University.

Feynman, R. P. (2009). *The meaning of it all: Thoughts of a citizen-scientist*. Basic Books.

Filer, T. (2019). The hidden and the revealed. In J. Uscinski (Ed.), *Conspiracy theories and the people who believe them* (pp. 395–407). Oxford University Press.

Franks, B., Bangerter, A., & Bauer, M. (2013). Conspiracy theories as quasi-religious mentality: An integrated account from cognitive science, social representations theory, and frame theory. *Frontiers in Psychology, 4*(424), 1–12.

Franks, B., Bangerter, A., Bauer, M. W., Hall, M., & Noort, M. C. (2017). Beyond "monologicality"? Exploring conspiracist worldviews. *Frontiers in Psychology, 8*(861), 1–16.

Kahneman, D. (2011). *Thinking, fast and slow*. Macmillan.

Keeley, B. L. (2019). The credulity of conspiracy theorists. In J. Uscinski (Ed.), *Conspiracy theories and the people who believe them* (pp. 422–431). Oxford University Press.

Klein, E., & Hendler, J. (2022). Loaded language and conspiracy theorizing. In J. Culbertson, A. Perfors, H. Rabagliati, & V. Ramenzoni (Eds.). *Proceedings of the Annual Meeting of the Cognitive Science Society, 44*(44), 2671–2679.

Korybski, A. (2002). *General semantics seminar 1937: Olivet College lectures* (3rd ed.). Institute of General Semantics.

Korzybski, A. (2005). *Science and sanity: An introduction to non-Aristotelian systems and general semantics* (3rd ed.). Institute of General Semantics.

Krekó, P. (2020). Countering conspiracy theories and misinformation. In M. Butter & P. Knight (Eds.), *Routledge handbook of conspiracy theories* (pp. 242–256). Routledge.

LaFrance, A. (2020). Nothing can stop what is coming. *Atlantic, 325*(5), 26–38.

Levinson, M. H. (2014). Ten common blocks to clear thinking with general semantics correctives. *ETC: A Review of General Semantics, 71*(1), 21–32.

Mahl, D., Schäfer, M. S., & Zeng, J. (2022). Conspiracy theories in online environments: An interdisciplinary literature review and agenda for future research. *New Media & Society*. https://doi.org/10.1177/14614448221075759

Mason, F. (2002). A poor person's cognitive mapping. In P. Knight (Ed.), *Conspiracy nation: The politics of paranoia in postwar America* (pp. 40–46). New York University Press.

Miller, R. W. (2021). What is QAnon? What to know about the baseless, far-right conspiracy theory connected to Marjorie Taylor Greene. *USA Today*. https://www.usatoday.com/story/news/nation/2021/02/04/what-qanon-marjorie-taylorgreeneand-false-conspiracy-theory/4385690001/

Moore, A. (2016). Conspiracy and conspiracy theories in democratic politics. *Critical Review, 28*(1), 1–23.

Nefes, T. S. (2019). The conspiratorial style in Turkish politics. In J. Uscinski (Ed.), *Conspiracy theories and the people who believe them* (pp. 385–394). Oxford University Press.

Nyhan, B., Reifler, J., & Ubel, P. (2013). The hazards of correcting myths about health care reform. *Medical Care, 51*(2), 127–132.

Nyhan, B. (2021). Why the backfire effect does not explain the durability of political misperceptions. *Proceedings of the National Academy of Sciences, 118*(15), 1–7.

Oliver, J. E., & Wood, T. J. (2014). Conspiracy theories and the paranoid style(s) of mass opinion. *American Journal of Political Science, 58*(4), 952–966.

Pula, R. P. (2000). *A general-semantics glossary: Pula's guide for the perplexed*. Institute of General Semantics.

Quick, J. D., & Larson, H. (2018). The vaccine-autism myth started 20 years ago: Here's why it still endures today. *TIME*. https://time.com/5175704/andrewwakefield-vaccine-autism/

Robertson, D. G. (2012). Making the donkey visible: Discordianism in the works of Robert Anton Wilson. In C. Cusack & A. Norman (Eds.). *Handbook of new religions and cultural production* (pp. 421–441). Brill.

Robert Anton Wilson. In C. Cusack & A. Norman (Eds.). *Handbook of new religions and cultural production* (pp. 421–441). Brill.

Robertson, D. G., & Dyrendal, A. (2019). Conspiracy theories and religion. In J. Uscinski (Ed.), *Conspiracy theories and the people who believe them* (pp. 411–421). Oxford University Press.

Sagan, C. (2011). *The demon-haunted world: Science as a candle in the dark*. Ballantine Books.

Smallpage, S. M. (2019). Conspiracy thinking, tolerance, and democracy. In J. Uscinski (Ed.), *Conspiracy theories and the people who believe them* (pp. 187–198). Oxford University Press.

Strate, L. (2011). *On the binding biases of time: And other essays on general semantics and media ecology*. Institute of General Semantics.

Strate, L. (2021). It is what it isn't! Copula-shun and general semantics [Video]. *YouTube*. https://www.youtube.com/watch?v=9aq1FtAF0zg

Strate, L. (2022). *Concerning communication: Epic quests and lyric excursions within the human lifeworld*. Institute of General Semantics.

Sunstein, C. R., & Vermeule, A. (2009). Conspiracy theories: Causes and cures. *Journal of Political Philosophy, 17*(2), 202–227.

Sutton, R. M., & Douglas, K. M. (2014). Examining the monological nature of conspiracy theories. In J. W. van Prooijen, & P. A. M. vanLange (Eds.), *Power, politics, and paranoia: Why people are suspicious of their leaders* (pp. 254–272). Cambridge University Press.

Uscinski, J. E. (2018). The study of conspiracy theories. *Argumenta, 3*(2), 233–245.

Uscinski, J. E. (Ed.) (2019). *Conspiracy theories and the people who believe them*. Oxford University Press.

Uscinski, J. E., & Parent, J. M. (2014). *American conspiracy theories*. Oxford University Press.

Vernon, L. F. (2020). Tuskegee syphilis study not America's only medical scandal: Chester M. Southam, MD, Henrietta Lacks, and the Sloan-Kettering research scandal. *Journal of Health Ethics, 16*(2), 3.

Wilson, R. A. (2020). *The new inquisition* (2nd ed.). Hilaritas Press.

Wood, M. J., & Douglas, K. M. (2018). Are conspiracy theories a surrogate for God? In A. Dyrendal, D. Robertson, & E. Asprem (Eds.), *Brill handbook of conspiracy theory and contemporary religion* (pp. 87–105). Brill.

Wood, M. J., & Douglas, K. M. (2019). Conspiracy theory psychology. In J. Uscinski (Ed.), *Conspiracy theories and the people who believe them* (pp. 245–256). Oxford University Press.

Yablokov, I. (2019). Anti-Jewish conspiracy theories in Putin's Russia. *Antisemitism Studies, 3*(2), 291–316.

CHAPTER 9

KORZYBSKI AND CHANTAL MOUFFE: GENERAL SEMANTICS CONTRIBUTION TO AGONISM
JERMAINE MARTINEZ

Agonism is a socio-political theory that views conflict as both positive and necessary for democratic vitality. In her book *On the Political* (2005), Chantal Mouffe argues for making a distinction between "the political" – or those perennial dimensions of antagonism constitutive of human affairs – and "politics" as referring to the historical practices and institutions citizens use to order the political. On the basis of this distinction, she suggests one way of coping with the antagonistic potential of contemporary politics is to adopt an attitude of agonistic pluralism. A number of General Semantic principles, concepts, and tenants are implicit in her argument. I will attempt to make those explicit in this chapter.

First, I review the socio-political trend of "post-politics" that prompted Mouffe to write her book. Second, I read Mouffe's argument alongside Korzybski's observations on "Infantilism" in *Science & Sanity*, surveying intersections in their diagnoses of the causes of polarizing forms of political discourse while walking through examples of how a post-political Zeitgeist manifests itself in today's socio-political semantic environment. Finally, I address how training in general semantics might contribute to Mouffe's call for an "agonistic pluralism" as a palliative for hyper-partisan times. In light of my reading of Korzybski and Mouffe, this paper demonstrates the practical relevance of general semantics to contemporary political affairs by offering an answer to the question: "how would today's political climate be different if more people understood and practiced basic principles of general semantics?"

The Post-Political Zeitgeist

Chantal Mouffe's (2005) book, *On the Political,* responds to what she calls a "post-political" Zeitgeist "which informs the 'commonsense' in the majority of Western societies…" (p. 1). The idea is that at the turn of the century societal evolution has arrived at the point where economic and political developments provide forms of modernity that allow individuals to "dedicate themselves to cultivating a diversity of lifestyles…" free from "antiquated attachments" (p. 1). The free world (or free market) has "triumphed over communism, and with the weakening of collective ties, a world without enemies is now possible" (p. 1). Given emergent forms of globalization and consensual democracy, there is a sense that a royal road has been paved towards which partisan conflicts can become things of the past as "consensus can now be obtained through dialogue" (p. 1). Those who adhere to a post-political view may often wittingly or unwittingly covet globalist aspirations for a world beyond political partisanship, beyond we/they, beyond left and right (cf. Giddens, 1994). In short, Mouffe is responding to those progressive views that idealize consensual forms of democracy-through-dialogue as invariably leading to a cosmopolitan future of peace, prosperity, and universal human rights.

Admittedly an over-the-top example of the post-political Zeitgeist is the United Nations' charter to "harmonize nations" and "achieve international co-operation in solving international problems of an economic, social, cultural, or humanitarian character, and in promoting and encouraging respect for human rights and for fundamental freedoms for all without distinction as to race, sex, language, or religion" (UN Charter, art 1., para 1). Speaking at the first annual UN's International Day of Happiness in 2012, Secretary General Ban Ki-Moon commented that the world "needs a new economic paradigm that recognizes the parity between the three pillars of sustainable development. Social, economic, and environmental well-being are indivisible. Together they define gross global happiness" (International day, 2012). Post-political aspirations often frame natural, social, economic, and personal adversities as problems to be solved through globalized collective actions of nation-statist, rational procedures. Other examples might include new global order advocates, such as the rhetoric of both Bush administrations (Bush, 1990; Bush, 2005) and Obama administrations (Obama, 2016) that often envisioned the spread of democracy world-wide as an unquestioned pathway for achieving global peace and harmony. Still other examples might be the media coverage of the "Arab Spring" and the general sentiment in some coverage that adopting Westernized forms of democracy are inevitable signs of global political progress (Krauthammer, 2005). Or finally, we can take as exemplars the ways that significant political figures see the Covid-19 pandemic as an opportunity to idealistically "build back better" a new socio-political, economic global order (Biden, 2021; Kissinger, 2020).

The Usefulness of a Non-el Approach to Post-Political Views

Mouffe (2005) observes a tendency in post-political perspectives to idealize human sociality, that is, to assume that modern societies are essentially moved by empathy and reciprocity. In light of this idealized view, adversarial tendencies within human sociality are viewed as correctable through the employment of rational procedures for clear communication (cf. Habermas, 1990). This idealized view gains traction due to a post-political faith in the "... progress of exchange and the establishment, through a social contract, of transparent communication among rational participants" (Moufee, 2005 p. 3). Moufee argues that rationalist expectations hoisted upon acts of deliberative dialogue are not only "profoundly mistaken" but also are at the "origin of many of the problems democratic institutions are currently facing" (p. 2). Rationalist interventions for addressing adversarial tendencies in political affairs – both theoretically and in practice – need to offer more than mere verbal formalisms (i.e., formalized procedures for talking about conflicts). This is because such formalisms can be full of elementalistic meanings that can cloud awareness of affective, para-rational factors that also accompany conflict between citizens. As Alfred Korzybski's (1994) work reminds us, when intervening in human affairs it is best to begin with an organism-as-a-whole view. Interventions for addressing adversarial tendencies in political affairs may benefit from *non-el* re-education and not simply a reflective, "rational" understanding of what is going at verbal levels. An organism-as-a-whole view offers a more substantive intervention by not only accounting for the logical-rational factors that contribute to conflict between citizens but also the affective and habituated semantic reactions of citizen interlocutors (Korzybski, 1994, p. 23).

When discussing the difficulty of re-training semantic reactions, Korzybski writes, "it is *more* difficult to influence the affect than to affect the rationalization" (p. 501). Both Moufee and Korzybski offer important addendums to rationalistic takes on human sociality by highlighting the ineradicable role of affects in political affairs for a time-binding, social class of life. Moufee (2005) writes

> ... 'Passions' refer to the various affective forces which are at the origin of collective forms of identifications. By putting the accent either on the rational calculation of interests (aggregative model), or on moral deliberation (deliberative model), current democratic political theory is unable to acknowledge the role of 'passions' as one of the main moving forces in the field of politics and finds itself disarmed when faced with its diverse manifestations. (p. 24)

Nationalism, extremism, and political polarization can be bewildering today because our current rationalist thinking about political affairs can beguile fuller appreciation for the role of affective relationality in the constitution of socio-political affairs. Capacities for evaluating relations and differences as we affectively dwell in human affiars and bodily sensations are extraverbal matters. As such, talk about them in a reflective, rational way is often not enough to influence them at their more objectively silent levels as lived, especially if certain affective dispositions – some way of mapping out relations-in-process – have both become habituated and given social utility within a semantic environment.

Idealized views of rational consensus-making are hard pressed to account for the affective and ambivalent nature of human sociality, including, as Moufee (2005) observes, "the fact that reciprocity and hostility cannot be dissociated" (p. 3). This is why idealized views of rational consensus-making are problematic for her, for such views provide few terms for coming to terms with conflicts – disagreements, misunderstandings, alternative viewpoints, etc. – as legitimate forms of democratic political expression. She writes,

> A central thesis of this book is that, contrary to what post-political theorists want us to believe, what we are witnessing is not the disappearance of the political in its adversarial dimension but something different. What is happening is that nowadays the political is played out in the *moral register*. In other words, it still consists in a we/they discrimination, but the we/they instead of being defined with political categories is now established in moral terms. In place of a struggle between 'right and left' we are faced with a struggle between 'right and wrong.' (2005, p. 5; cf. Lakoff, 1996)

Mouffe's observations about the moralization of politics are grounded in an important distinction she draws between "politics" and "the political." In the next section I'll review how this distinction resonates with core G.S. principles. For now, however, I want to note that Mouffe's account of the post-political Zeitgeist provides a way of diagnosing our contemporary polarized political climate. Specifically, she illuminates a hidden dialectic of consensus and antagonism. When idealized views of communication as rational and transparent talk are taken up as a royal road for achieving post-political forms of consensus, then those very same aspirations can exacerbate the antagonisms such aspirations aim to overcome. As this dialectic of over-idealization attunes political disagreements into moral, two-value oriented registers, the pursuit of consensus is keyed up to consensus-at-all-costs. Under such semantic conditions, people may find few opportunities – nor feel the necessity – for developing competencies that attune to nuanced dimensions of legitimacy in the conflicting viewpoints voiced in pluralistic political culture. For Mouffe, some kind of capacity for sensing nuance dimensions of legitimacy in conflicting viewpoints – especially in the emotional heat of disagreement – is a lifeblood competence for democracy. Thus, Mouffe's work might be understood as motivated by a concern with how this democratic competence can be overshadowed by over-idealized and overly rationalistic expectations for global consensus – expectations native to post-political worldviews. In this sense, a non-el orientation is well suited for teasing out not only the rational and conspicuous elements of conflicting viewpoints, but also the para-rational dimensions contributing to socio-political conflict that lurk in the backgrounds of semantic awareness.

The Political, Politics, & Post-Political Infantilism

Whereas general semantics encourages us to "always mind the etc..." as a reminder that it is impossible to say all there is about any subject, Chantal Mouffe would have us mind something like the *atg*, that is, the (A)n(T)a(G)onism that serves as a perennial condition for the constitution of socio-political identities. Minding the tendencies of antagonism in human affairs is a kind of extensional check on over-idealized, rationalist, and individualist post-political aspirations for global consensus. Relying on the insights of Jacques Derrida, she reminds us of the role of the 'constitutive outside' in the creation of an identity. She writes,

> The creation of an identity implies the establishment of a difference, difference which is often constructed on the basis of a hierarchy... once we have understood that every identity is relational and the affirmation of a differences is a precondition for the existence of any identity, i.e., the perception of something 'other' which constitutes its 'exterior, we are, I think, in a better position to... understand the ever present possibility of antagonism and to see how social relation can be the breeding ground for antagonism. (2005, p. 15)

For a time-binding, social class of life, antagonism is both a natural and constitutive feature of human identity and civilization more generally. And, by minding the "atg," Moufee (2005) offers a kind of system check on dominant tendencies in liberal thought "characterized by a rationalist and individualist approach [to political theorizing] which forecloses acknowledging the nature of collective identities [and passions]" (p. 10). She continues, "this kind of liberalism is unable to adequately grasp the pluralistic nature of the social world, with the conflicts that pluralism entails; conflicts for which no rational solution could ever exist" (p. 10). In an effort to explain this view of the constitutive dimensions of human social existence, Moufee draws a distinction between "politics" and "the political." This distinction contains some interconnections with G.S.

Alfred Korzybski (1994) writes that "our actual lives are lived on objective, un-speakable levels, and not on verbal levels" (p. 35). He observes that words for things at the objective level are better understood as names for relations. We live-through our relations with others, the world, and ourselves. Affective relations are neither wholly objective (i.e., just there) nor purely subjective (i.e., only representations of the mind). Thus, whereas literate language allows for talking about these contingent relations as though they are things, Korzybski emphasizes that the realm of "undefined terms" is a lived-world "overloaded with emotional values," a world of silent-yet-affective relations (p. 505). For Moufee (2005), "the political" is an ontological category that references perennial dimensions of antagonistic relations constitutive of human affairs. "Politics," on the other hand, refers to historical practices and institutions citizens use to order the conflictual territories of the political. From Korzybski's time-binding view, "the political" is perhaps how we find ourselves in socio-political territories whereas "politics" are those derivative verbal maps, social doctrines, and institutions developed for symbolically figuring those antagonistic, silent-yet-affective relations. This recalls Irving Lee's (1941) distinction between "two media": the world of words and the world of not-words in *Language Habits & Human Affairs* (p. 16). The political, I suggest, is closer to the ontological grounds of the unspeakable, objective level of social existence whereas "politics" refers to any socially instituted ways of ordering those conflictual dimensions of "the political," which is to say, those ways of symbolically expressing and comprehending "it."

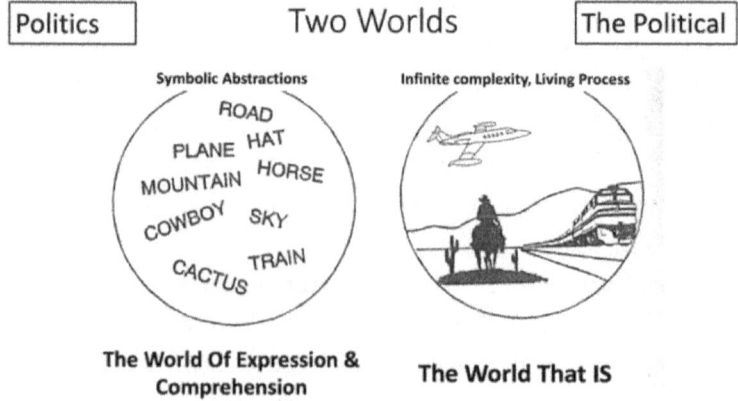

Korzybski, like Moufee, also highlights how human affairs always has ambivalent dimensions. In a section titled "Un-sanity & Sanity" in *Science & Sanity*, Korzybski (1994) outlines a rough ontogenetic view that explains how adjustment to antagonistic relations provide necessary conditions for "sane" human development. Indeed, a democratic nation's "sanity" might be measured by its citizens' facility in adjusting to socio-political conflicts and by how well its socio-political semantic environments make possible and necessary such aptitudes in adjustment. Or following Moufee (2005), we have to be willing to "elaborate the democratic project on an anthropology which acknowledges the ambivalent character of human sociability" (p. 3) and, rather than designing institutions which, "through supposedly impartial procedures, would reconcile all conflicting interests and values," be willing to "envisage the creation of a vibrant agonistic public sphere of contestation where different hegemonic political projects can be confronted" (p. 3). Whilst Moufee elaborates such an anthropology in her book via a critique of Nazi political theorist Carl Schmitt, she perhaps misses an opportunity to rely on a more humane source in Alfred Korzybski's ontogenetic view.

Korzybski's (1994) ontogenetic account of sane human development notes that once the human infant is born, "the struggle for existence" begins (p. 494). Semantic reactions are natural capacities of infants in the form of sensing, of feeling. An infant's bodily senses establish their own semantic values by way of relational encounters, that is, by way of sensual evaluations of the brute mass of energy in which the child finds itself. He calls this the "auto-erotic" stage, because – "as with animals" – it is centered on sense gratifications. Human "feels" (as the youth say, today) emerge as a possibility in relation to "coefficients of adversity" (Sartre, 1984, p. 619). Korzybski also notes that at this stage of development, the struggle for existence includes early relational encounters with "environmental impingements" of language and doctrines. He continues his ontogenetic tale by describing the next stage of development, the "narcissistic period," a period existing from about "seven to fourteen years" and characterized as "a semantic period of self-love" that is "egotistical, egoistical, self-centered and *asocial*" (1994, p. 495). Finally, Korzybski describes the "social semantic period" which leads to a normal socialized adult, involving less narcissistic tendencies in evaluation of relations. This ontogenetic view nicely explains the perennial nature of social antagonism and how relations with other people – in terms of both significant others and the generalized others of culture – can serve as life-long constitutive resistances to our existence. Indeed, this view helps bring home how hortatory thou-shall-nots of society and culture, for instance, provide dramatistic grounds for the performance of human character and identity (Burke, 1966, pp. 3–25). It helps us pause and reflect on how relations with others can serve as both forms of aesthetic consummation (i.e., others as relational sources for experiencing a full sense of selfhood) as well as forms of social alienation (i.e., others as sources of objectification of our living selfhood) (Anton, 2001, pp. 53–82). In this sense, Korzybski's ontogenetic view seems to resonate with Mouffe's use of Derrida's "constitutive outside" but in the ontogenetic form of "adjustments to struggles for existence." This provides a view of how time-binders are naturally sentenced to constitute themselves through life-long adjustments to resistances to their existence, which is to say, in life-long coping with felt affects, language as a communicative condition, and ambivalent sociality in forms of socio-political doctrines.

As if speaking of our own contemporary political climate, Korzybski (1994) writes of the socio-political tone of his own time:

> Our present commercial civilization can be characterized as of an infantile type, governed mostly by structurally primitive mythologies and language involving primitive s.r. One need but read the speeches of merchants, presidents, and kings to be thoroughly convinced of this. ... Adult infantilism becomes a usually potent wrecker of individual lives, and, when viewed from a social, national, or international point of view, accounts, also for the majority of our semantic difficulties in the social, economic, and political fields. (p. 509)

When an individual or whole nation is unable or unwilling to actively adjust to its own "struggle for existence," Korzybski refers to this state as a kind of infantilism (p. 508). Infantilism in adults is characterized by semantic symptoms that mirror the auto-erotic, organ erotic, and narcissistic stages of childhood. What Korzybski calls "primitive s.r." are the infant's narcissistic fixation on sense-gratification and the present moment. An infant has underdeveloped capacities for evaluating relations in more semantically sophisticated, socially conscious, and historical ways (i.e., the social semantic stage of development). As such, to be an infantile adult means to exhibit semantic reactions that mimic these underdeveloped capacities for evaluating relations, such as confusing orders of abstraction, ascribing objective reality to terms and symbols, or confusing conclusions and inferences with descriptions. Insofar as encountering political disagreements can trigger an awareness of the antagonistic potential of socio-political relations, infantile dispositions in such moments are bound to produce difficulties. By offering few terms for coming to terms with the antagonistic tendencies of human sociality, over-idealized post-political aspirations for global consensus can *in effect* arrest more sophisticated semantic evaluations of socio-political antagonisms. In this sense, implied in Mouffe's view of the post-political approach may be forms of what Korzybski explicitly identifies as infantilism.

Infantile-like Reactions of Demoralized Post-Political Citizens

The political polarization and extreme partisanship within our contemporary semantic environment may be seen as infantile-like reactions of a demoralized, post-political citizenry. This socio-political demoralization may be born from frustrated, over-idealized post-political aspirations. Wendell Johnson (1946) observes that some semantic maladjustments are necessary consequences of Aristotelian (rationalist) orientations that over-idealize territories of human aspirations. Moods of demoralization – or a "general loss of interest in possible opportunities for achievement" – can follow, arising logically as unrealistic ideals routinely meet against the life-facts that all human achievements are relative (pp. 3–23). Mouffe would likely agree that such rationalist attitudes are at work in post-political aspirations as well. Indeed, it may be that by offering few terms for coming to terms with antagonistic moments in socio-political relations, post-political expectations for global consensus via rational, transparent communication, contribute to infantile-like dispositions and semantic environments woefully equipped for coping with the pluralities of contemporary socio-political life. Mouffe's book only hints at how post-political aspirations influence the tenor and tone of ground-level civic life. As such, I offer some brief examples of how the post-political Zeitgeist may be playing out in current public discourse as forms of infantile reactions of a demoralized citizenry.

Eva Berger's (2022) book, *Context Blindness: Digital Technology and the Next Stage of Human Evolution,* elegantly explains the ways context technologies (e.g., mobile GPS, weather apps, social media, etc.) can dim our awareness of context and dull capacities for properly contextualizing life-facts, that is, dim capacities and sensitivities for evaluating relations. Berger identifies many symptoms of "context blindness." Three examples she identifies in particular can also be seen as symptoms of a post-politically grounded demoralization: cancel culture, identity politics, and tribalism (cf. Berger, 2022, pp. 87–97). Over-idealized post-politicized semantic environments offer citizens few terms for coming to terms with the perennial antagonistic potential of the political, that is, with the always diverse, messy viewpoints encountered in democratic socio-political relations. As such, what follows is a brief discussion of how cancel culture, identity politics, and tribalism can be understood as tactical avoidance strategies arising as a necessary consequence of post-political over-idealization of – and subsequent demoralization with – the possibilities of communication. These symptoms of context-blindness will also help further highlight interconnections between Chantal Mouffe's critique of the post-political and Alfred Korzybski's observations on infantilism.

Cancel culture aims to avoid granting legitimacy to some political views by working to silence their expression, particularly when such viewpoints are perceived as politically problematic or, in today's post-political climate, as immoral. In a *Boston Globe* op-ed, Jeff Jacoby (2022) observes the rise of student "informers" on university campuses. Reporting on a study of university student's views on free speech conducted by the Challey Institute for Global Innovation and Growth at North Dakota State University, Jacoby notes a majority of students endorse the idea that if a professor or fellow student says something perceived as offensive they should be reported. Still other examples of cancel culture include shouting down conservative speakers on university campuses (Beinart, 2017; Cross, 2019; Soave, 2018), academic articles that explicitly advocate for not conversing with viewpoints perceived as politically problematic (Tonn, 2005), and the firing of university faculty on the basis of viewpoints expressed in speech (Carter, 2022). Moreover, this is not considered to be simply a left-of-center tendency (cf. Rosenberg, 2021). The point is that cancelling tactics can have a chilling effect on open discourse and is perhaps why, according to a Cato Institute poll, 62% of Americans feel afraid to share their political views (Ekins, 2020). With few terms for coming to terms with the antagonisms found in democratic socio-political affairs, cancel culture reveals a generalized loss of interest in the possibilities that anything can be achieved by socio-political conversations. From a *non-el* view, we might thus explore how this demoralization can arise logically when over-idealized expectations for global consensus – especially when undergirded by faith in transparent, rational communication as its royal pathway – routinely come up against the messy territories of socio-political encounters.

If, as Moufee (2005) observes, many post-political views "refuse to acknowledge the antagonistic dimension of politics and the role of affects in the construction of political identities because they believe that it would endanger the realization of consensus, which they see as the aim of democracy," (p. 29) then the demoralized moods of the post-political in effect grant social utility to "cancelling" as a tactic of conversational avoidance if only because its semantic worldview simply offers few terms for coping with anything more in the face of disagreement. From this vantage point, cancelling mimics the infantile-like underdeveloped personal capacities for more nuanced evaluation of relations, as well as signaling the way contemporary socio-political environments fail to encourage more nuanced evaluation of relations. It is illuminating that Korzybski (1994) describes infantile reactions as if he is describing today's cancel culture dispositions when he writes,

> Not having the critical semantic capacity for proper evaluation, their likes and dislikes are very intense... The immediate 'sense' perception or 'emotion' unduly influences their actions... This results in weak judgements, over-suggestiveness, 'emotional' outbreaks, exaggerated sensibility... they become easily intimated and frightened, and easily influenced by others. (p. 517)

If cancelling functions to tactfully avoid, or *in effect* avoid, occasions that might demand adjusting to those salty sensations of experiencing offense at others' speech, then at one level of analysis the act of cancelling seems to mimic infantile semantic stages when "word relations have predominance over actualities" (p. 516). Indeed, ascribing objective reality to terms and symbols, "tolerance," as Korzybski (1994) observes, "is not one of their characteristics" [i.e., people who cancel]. "To them," he continues, "persons and ideas are evaluated in extremes, either good, wonderful, or bad, terrible" (p. 518). In this way, persons or whole cultures can mimic infantilism's underdeveloped capacities, exhibiting an inability or unwillingness to "comprehend anything complicated" (p. 516), seeing some elements of expressed viewpoints, but missing the relative wholes of how expressions of problematic viewpoints come to be viewed as sensible by those who express them. Korzybski's account of infantilism thus provides terms for coming to terms with some of the general conditions that make the semantic reactions of cancel culture possible at all.

Identity appeals in public arguments may be another example of infantile-like reactions of a demoralized post-political citizenry. Identity politics is a form of political advocacy that grounds the legitimacy of its claims in exclusive subject position identifiers such as one's race, class, gender, religion, or cultural identity. A common use of identity appeals is to either self-attribute or other-attribute subject position identifiers to oneself or others in the heat of argument for the purposes of claiming "epistemic privilege" and/or "epistemic qualification" for their viewpoints (Anton & Peterson, 2003). Used in this way, identity appeals employ variations of what Neil Postman and Charles Weingartner (1969) (via McLuhan) define as the "label-libel gambit," or the literate tendency to dismiss ideas by the expedience of naming them (p. 25). Other-attributing charges such as "You are just saying that because you are a White male," or self-attributed qualifications such as "... as a Black Woman, I can say..." mobilize the human tendency to label-libel so as to shift the grounds of debate from the presentation (and contestation) of conflicting viewpoints (i.e., exploring differences in degree) to a more neat and tidy presentation of grounds for claiming identity-based ethos (i.e., identifying differences in kind). When used in this way, identity appeals can *in effect* tactically avoid messier conversations on important and nuanced socio-political problems by regulating whose viewpoints are granted or not granted legitimacy when speaking about socio-political concerns. With few terms for coming to terms with the antagonisms found in democratic socio-political affairs, post-politicized forms of identity politics reveal a generalized loss of interest in the possibility that anything can be achieved by messy socio-political conversations. Let's explore how this demoralization can arise logically when over-idealized expectations for global consensus – especially when undergirded by faith in transparent, rational communication as its royal pathway – routinely come up against the messy territories where the meanings of socio-political identities are constituted.

Moufee (2005) observes, "The mistake of liberal rationalism is to ignore the affective dimension mobilized by collective identifications and to imagine that those supposedly archaic passions are bound to disappear with the advance of individualism and the progress of rationality" (p. 6). The rationalism at work in post-political worldviews tends to filter its view of human identity through a lens of a dispassionate, atomistic individualism. As such, the demoralized moods of the post-political in effect grant social utility to identity appeals as a tactic of conversational avoidance if only because its semantic worldview offers few terms for identifying more than differences in kind. This post-political outlook can't help but see the rational calculation of interests or moral deliberation between individuals or aggregates of individuals (i.e, the ordering of essential kinds) as best achieved through formalistic procedures for deliberate, reflective kinds of political communication. This helps explain how post-political outlooks can be unable or unwilling to entertain more-than-rational considerations, for instance, of how "any we/they opposition is never merely a conflict between two or more essentialist identities that somehow pre-exist the process of identification" (Moufee, 2005, p. 18). When identity appeals fall under the spell of the "'is' of identity" derivative verbal formalizations of lived through moments of socio-political relationality/difference can feel like references to objective differences in kind. As such, post-politicized identity appeals can mimic infantile-like underdeveloped personal capacities for more nuanced evaluation of relationality, especially in passionate moments of disagreement. More still, such semantic reactions might also signal how post-political semantic environments fall short of encouraging or celebrating more nuanced evaluations and talk of socio-political relationality.

Impairments in abilities or willingness to appreciate differences and relations in sophisticated, more-than-rational ways can be seen as signs of child-like infantilism. Korzybski (1994) writes,

> Children and superior idiots appreciate resemblances more readily than differences. ... Because of semantic underdevelopment, differences become a disturbing factor to them; they

want everything standardized. On national grounds, the adult infants standardize all they can and have even a kind of hostility to anything that has individual flavor. For instance, those who wear straw hats after an arbitrary date are attacked on the streets. Not wanting to think, or to bother about differences, they fancy that they can regulate life by legislation, and they keep busy manufacturing 'laws.' (p. 517)

If the favoring of resemblances over differences, and standardization over individuality, are some of the symptoms of child-like dispositions, then when people identify intensely with verbal formalizations of race, class, gender, or cultural identifiers (i.e., identities as a "said") this can *in effect* mimic infantile preferences for tidy standardized identity marker appeals and the favoring of legislative ordering. The rationalism at the heart of post-politicalized identity-based appeals can give rise to semantic environments where political conversations about cultural identities hinge on how adept the conversation celebrates verbal formalisms, or rationalistic "laws" of civic discourse (e.g., political correctness norms, death by over-qualification, etc.), rather than on how adept interlocutors can attune to nuanced dimensions of legitimacy between differing viewpoints. Relatedly, Korzybski (1994) observes, "Not being able to 'think' for themselves, they [infantile adults] leave that bothersome function to politicians, priests, newspapermen," (p. 517). Or, said in the context of this paper, being unable or unwilling to think through differences in sophisticated ways, the demoralized post-political citizen is inclined instead to tactfully employ libel labels culled from rationalistic discourses of similarly demoralized academic theorists, YouTube political partisans, late night talk show hosts, talk radio, or the darker corners of the internet. The semantic result is that political talk is judged as either legitimate or illegitimate on the mere basis of how well it expresses a reflective, rational attention to the pluralism of cultural values and extols tolerance for identity-based claims. In this sense, persons or whole cultures can mimic infantile-like underdeveloped capacities for evaluation, exhibiting instead tidier two-value maps that misorient citizen evaluations of socio-political issues embedded in messier, affective territories of socio-political identity formation. The fraught socio-political territories where identities form – though perhaps perceived as irrational from a post-political perspective – can be seen from a GS view as rife with para-rational values that nonetheless factor in problematic viewpoints *feeling* logically coherent to those who express them. The demoralized moods of the post-political grant social utility to identity-based appeals as a kind of conversational avoidance, even if only in effect, because its semantic worldview offers few terms for mobilizing anything more in the face of disagreement. Korzybski's account of infantilism thus provides terms for coming to terms with some of the general conditions that make identity appeals, as semantic reactions, possible at all.

Tribalism may be seen as another example of infantile reactions of a demoralized post-political citizenry. Eva Berger (2022) explains how tribalism arises as a logical response to human incapacities to be in touch with as many people as technology allows. That is, as people's online and offline social networks scale in size, breakdowns in consensus reality and social cohesion follow. As a result, "Tribes," Berger writes, "provide a more manageable context" (p. 88). Tribalism can tactically avoid messier conversations on important and nuanced socio-political problems by employing self-insulating discursive maneuvers that augment a group's worldview. This manifests as forms of demagogic spellbinding, or discursive appeals to popular prejudices of us/them. Some examples include the comments of Barack Obama referring to some Americans as bitter clingers to guns, religion, and anti-immigrant sentiment (Pilkington, 2008), or Hillary Clinton's description of some Americans as a "basket of deplorables" (Reilly, 2016), or Mitt Romney calling 47% of Obama supporters government-dependent victims (Cillizza, 2013). These appeals to popular prejudices occurred when speaking to sympathetic audiences of campaign fundraisers. Or consider the following case. Perceiving pro-Trump candidates as easier to beat in midterm congressional elections, a recent Democratic campaign strategy involves spending half a million dollars on GOP primary campaign ads to actually amplify the conspiratorial views of pro-Trump candidates (Ferris & Mutknick, 2022). Seemingly, with few terms for coming to terms with the antagonisms found in democratic socio-political affairs, appeals to popular prejudices signals a demoralized loss of interest that anything can be achieve by communicating one's policies or political principles openly and faithfully. And, of course, this is to say nothing of the four-year long populist demagoguery routinely decried by many as the hallmark feature of Trump administration rhetoric (Mercieca, 2020). We might thus explore how this form of socio-political demoralization can arise logically when over-idealized expectations for global consensus – especially when undergirded by faith in transparent, rational communication as its royal pathway – routinely come up against the messy territories of the political.

If, as Moufee (2005) observes, commonsense understandings of the political have failed to learn lessons from Freud and Elias Canetti, namely that "in societies which have become very individualistic, the need for collective identifications will never disappear since it is constitutive of the mode of existence of human beings," (p. 28) then the demoralized moods of the post-political in effect grant social utility to "tribalism" as a tactic of conversational avoidance if only because post-political semantic worldviews simply offer few terms for sensing dimensions of legitimacy that may be present when encountering differing viewpoints. This includes the ability and willingness to have real-time awareness of the process character of identity formation – that is, the contingent character of relationality in moments of disagreement with others. Moufee (2005) emphasizes that any we/they confrontation is never simply between two essentialist identities that pre-exist the relational process of identification. Rather, she observes, "... the constitution of a specific 'we' always depends on the type of 'they' from which it is differentiated" (p. 19). In a similar way, Korzybski (1994) observes that proper evaluation involves "assuming the minimum." This "minimum" is not some kind of nothing definable in words, or a metaphysical something. Rather, he writes that the minimum "as in mathematics" is more properly understood as an undefined "betweenness," or order (p. 154). Moments of conflict between two or more viewpoints is both a moment of differentiation and an encounter with the fecund possibilities of relationality. Though in an antagonistic tone, socio-political conflict is a kind of betweenness nonetheless. Betweenness is the minimum. Despite there being an objective character to betweenness, post-political citizens' ability or willingness to maintain awareness of the contingent and process character of relationality – especially in moments of disagreement – is often impaired by zealous aspirations for communicatively achieved global consensus to what are often group prejudices. From this vantage point, tribalistic demagogic appeals mimic underdeveloped personal capacities for more nuanced evaluation of relations, as well as signal the way contemporary socio-political environments fail to encourage more nuanced sensitivity to the live-time, process nature of relationality.

As reviewed above, infantile-like dispositions exhibit semantic inclinations that emphasize tidy similarities over messier evaluations of relations or differences and are often guided solely by narcissistic sense-gratification, or "feels." Thus, the salty feelings that arise when a post-political citizen encounters different viewpoints may not only have a rational basis, but also may signal the relative lack of resources post-political semantic environments provide for coping with difference itself. As if writing of post-political tribalists, Korzybski (1994) observes,

> The infantile individual himself cannot fail to notice that something is wrong, for life makes him quickly aware of it. But, in his self-love, exaggerated self-esteem, he overlooks his own shortcomings, and blames everybody and everything but himself. In the face of injustice, he becomes discouraged, timid, or bitter and pessimistic. (p. 512)

Like infants who are by necessity developmentally driven by narcissistic sense-gratification, but soon develop to later project these inner sensations onto outside events – thus "personifying" them (Korzybski, 1994, p. 33) – an infantile-like adult comes to *feel* their personal projections as non-personal, objective features of existence. They are seemingly absent to their non-rational complicity in bringing into existence the tenor and tone of "the political," yet all too aware of their rational justifications for their political actions and decisions. This infantile inclination is augmented by the rationalistic assumptions of post-political views. Post-politicalized citizens can often be led by their worldview to assume that their views on socio-political matters have an objective value to others just as they do for themselves. With few terms for coming to terms with difference, the post-political citizen is ill equipped to deal with communication breakdown, when other people do not share similar views on matters, or when socio-political events do not turn out as expected. Korzybski presciently observes that when a "... semantic conviction that his [sic] observations are the only, uniquely correct observations," then – "... in acute cases" – he [the infantile adult] is likely to feel that "everybody misunderstands him; nobody is fair to him; everybody is hostile to him; he will get even with them; in the name of 'justice,' he will punish them," (p. 174). The post-political citizen's infantile inclinations – though they would quickly explain their rational grounds – nonetheless, might aim to *feel* a global sense of requital from people they deem responsible for life's injustice.

Interestingly, Moufee (2005) draws on Jacques Lacan to underscore how socio-political identifications "provide the social agent with a form of jouissance (of the body)," or, perhaps in Korzybski's (1994) terms, "sense-gratification." That is, if we tentatively permit this cursory connection between Korzybski's sense-gratification and Lacan's jouissance, then we might at least consider paying attention to the affective conditions that activate tribalistic inclinations. For, as Mouffe further elaborates (this time drawing on Slavoj Zizek), "nationalist hatred emerges when another nation is perceived as threatening our enjoyment. It has its origin therefore in the way social groups deal with their lack of enjoyment by attributing it to the presence of an enemy which is 'stealing' it" (Zizek, as cited in Mouffe, 2005, p. 28). The same diagnosis might apply to contemporary antagonisms that arise amongst the pluralistic tribes and nations of U.S. citizens (Chua, 2018; Woodward, 2011). The infantile-like adult [or nation] is awash in sense-enjoyments of their tribe's worldview and are unable or unwilling to attune to the sufferings of outside others, or to evaluate the consequences of their actions for the nation in the future. "They" [the infantile-like adult], Korzybski (1994) observes, "love praise, but despise blame," and thus "shiver and shrink at disapproval" (p. 516). Today's post-political citizen thus is inclined to retreat into the warm confirming feelings of their tribe's shared worldview and to maintain anxious vigilance for threats to those warm "feels" from outside others. Tribalism is the "we/they" playing out in a moralistic post-political drama where justice is achieved only when disagreeable views are removed from public discourse, that is, when the words of "those people over there" are felt to be eternally silenced. The demoralized moods of the post-political grant social utility to tribalism as a kind of conversational avoidance, even if only in effect, because its semantic worldview offers few terms for attuning to more than potential threats to the sense-gratifying confirmations of one's own worldview. Korzybski's account of infantilism thus provides terms for coming to terms with some of the general conditions that make post-political tribalism possible at all.

In conclusion, I want to be very clear: those who employ tactical avoidances strategies of cancellation, identity politics, or tribalism more often than not have very justified and legitimate grounds for doing so, for instance, desires for equity and civil rights, resistance to authoritarian or discriminatory violence, or the gamut of historical rationales (and traumas) for social justice and civil liberty claims. The ends are unquestionably justified. I would only ask that we push against *attachment* to our justified rationalizations. Whereas Wendell Berry observes that "abstraction is the enemy whenever it is found," I'd add that semantic attitudes which favor attachment to our verbal formulations are abstraction's hidden accomplice. We must recall that "it is *more* difficult to influence the affect than to affect the rationalization" and, as such, rational, verbal formalisms, can beguile our attentiveness to the sense-gratification of cancelling, identity appeals, or tribalism at the objective, silent level of the political. Or, as Moufee (2005) notes, "the problem with our societies is not their proclaimed ideals but the fact that those ideals are not put into practice" (p. 32). At issue when examining acts of cancelling, identity politics, or tribalism from a general semantics view is not just probing how well aligned to "life-facts" are the rational arguments and historical justifications proclaimed for employing these tactics of conversational avoidance. The focus can be equally on how post-political aspirations shape a citizenry's semantic reactions, that is, on how their affective evaluations of socio-political relations are predisposed in such a way that cancelling, identity politics, and tribalism *feel* like rational and justified responses to begin with. When lacking terms for coming to terms with conflict as a legitimate feature of a democratic socio-political culture – that is, when a citizenry lacks both capacities and the will for evaluating the messy territories of socio-political encounters with a nuanced attunement to dimensions of legitimacy – then "... the we/they confrontation is visualized as a moral one between good and evil, the opponent can be perceived only as an enemy to be destroyed" (p. 32) or, in short, avoided. In this two-valued archetypical drama, there is a kind of sense-gratification, a child-like joy. A GS treatment calls on us to wrestle with how post-political tactics of conversational avoidance might be both rational and justified yet still leave infantile orientations in their wake – orientations born of demoralized views of political encounters activated by its own over-idealized, post-political aspirations for a communicatively achieved global consensus. And people wonder why shit never seems to change!

Conclusion: General Semantics Contribution to Mouffe's Call for Agonism

Korzybski (1994) writes that those interested in problems of politics should investigate their problems from the semantic point of view of infantilism (p. 521). I've tried to offer such an orientation in this paper with help from Chantal Moufee. With few terms for coming to terms with conflict, post-political aspirations can lead to frustrations that can slide into socio-political demoralization, which can then itself map messy territories of "the political" into moralistic orientations of right/wrong, or us/them. This infantile-like orientation then lends social utility to conversational avoidance strategies. Mouffe's (2005) alternative to post-political worldviews does not seek to overcome this we/they distinction, but rather to "tame" this perennial antagonism with an attitude of agonism. She writes,

> If we want to acknowledge on one side the permanence of the antagonistic dimension of the conflict, while on the other side allowing for the possibility of its 'taming', we need to envisage a third type of relation. This is the type of relation which I have proposed to call 'agonism'. While antagonism is a we/they relation in which the two sides are enemies who do not share any common ground, agonism is a we/they relation where the conflicting parties, although acknowledging that there is no rational solution to their conflict, nevertheless recognize the legitimacy of their opponents. They are 'adversaries' not enemies. (p. 20)

Moufee is not being nihilistic when she emphasizes the conflictual dimensions of politics. Rather she wants citizens to develop a consciousness of the constitutive outsides and relationality of human existence. She further explains,

> An agonistic conception of democracy acknowledges the contingent character of the hegemonic politico-economic articulations which determine the specific configuration of a society at a given moment. They are precarious and pragmatic constructions which can be disarticulated and transformed as a result of the agonistic struggle among the adversaries. (p. 33)

Mouffe's call for agonism implies a call for a thoroughgoing awareness of the relational and contingent character of time-binding existence and its ever-present potential to slide into antagonism. And rather than attempt to remove dissent and conflict from socio-political spheres by some kind of communicatively achieved global consensus, Moufee asks for commitment to consensus on the institutions constitutive of democratic life, "liberty and equality for all" (p. 31). Moufee considers the expression of conflicting views and disagreements as the "stuff of democratic politics" (p. 31). I would add that another kind of "stuff" would be a cultivated civic competence to attune to para-rational dimensions of legitimacy in disagreement. In other words, Moufee is pleading for citizens to outgrow their childish tendencies and commit to ethico-political attitudes that can keep in check over-idealizations and inappropriate uses of rationalist procedures in the realms of the political. She is pushing back against zealous forms of rationalism that fail to offer terms for coming to terms with the para-rational elements encountered in contemporary socio-political affairs. This plea for citizen attitudes that are more amenable to agonism finds supportive contributions in general semantics.

In the introduction to the book *Korzybski And...*, Corey Anton & Lance Strate (2012) write that Alfred Korzybski's non-Aristotelian system aims to

> ... enable individuals to take control of their own semantic reactions, improve their ability to evaluate statements, messages, and percepts, and thereby become better human beings. In this way, the goal was sanity for individual and society alike, and through sanity, progress, not just in science and technology, but social progress, political and economic progress, and moral progress. (p. 12)

Political progress can be measured by the degree of sane adjustment practiced by citizens and encouraged by its socio-political semantic environments. If the infantile-like adult exhibits underdeveloped capacities for evaluating relations such as confusing orders of abstraction, ascribing objective reality to terms and symbols, or confusing conclusions and inferences with descriptions, then we can see that such attitudes fall short of the attitudes necessary for agonism. Korzybski's (1994) *non-el* view of language stresses the development of a mature thoroughgoing consciousness of difference and a rejection of identity, a kind of revolt against "infantile (erotic) semantic fixations" (p. 514). General semantics extensional practices of dating, indexing, attending to silent levels, using the structural differential, and having a general consciousness of abstracting all provide terms that help tame post-political semantic reactions and encourage favorable attitudes for agonism. As Korzybski (1994) observes,

> With consciousness of abstracting, the joy of living is considerably increased. We have no more 'frights,' bewilderments, or similar undesirable semantic experiences. We grow up to full adulthood; and when the body is natured for taking up life and its responsibilities, we accomplish that, and find joy in it, as our 'mind' and 'emotions' have also matured... Joys, pleasures, and 'emotions' are not abolished... but are sublimated to higher adult semantic levels. Life becomes fuller, and the individual ceases to act as a nuisance and a danger to himself and others. (p. 527)

The infantile jouissance of narcissistic self-gratification, or joy_1, is not abolished with a well-honed consciousness of abstracting. Rather, the joy of a balanced semantic attitude is a joy that sublimates emotions to higher adult semantic levels, or joy_2. Joy_2 is a balanced semantic attitude capable of not only offering rational talk aligned with life-facts but also – with equal facility – capable of having an awareness of the affective, para-rational bases of its rational talk.

A citizen with this balanced semantic attitude might experience a daily, fuller kind of joy_2 of living that can help tame socio-political antagonism and open a space for agonism. Indeed, by offering a throughgoing awareness of not only rational arguments (i.e., politics) but also para-rational affective dimensions that ground citizens' socio-political views (i.e., the political), general semantics training provides people with extensional checks that can free them up to find nuanced points of connection in moments of disagreement. A citizenry for whom semantic reactions are under "full control, capable of being educated, influenced, transformed quickly and efficiently," (Korzybski, 1994, p. 27) would be a citizenry ready for agonism. We might imagine a citizenry whose socio-political talk reflects an ethical attunement to matters of relation that naturally accompany socio-political disagreements rather than only a narcissistic awareness of how their talk can be used for deliberate, strategic positioning (i.e., matters of power) (cf. Latour, 2004). So how would today's political climate be different if more people understood and practiced basic principles of general semantics? Consider these questions. As citizens, how would our experience of socio-political disagreement be different if instead of only reacting to conflicting verbal arguments we could in those moments equally attune ourselves toward the ever-present para-rational conditions we share as social, time-binding beings? What if we could listen past the verbal formalism of our arguments in moments of disagreement and instead feel-through to the underlying, silent levels of our fear and uncertainties? How would citizens experience of socio-political disagreement change if not a single day went by without a deeply felt and joyous$_2$ awareness of their irreducible relationship to the processes shaping socio-political life and existence more generally?

References

Anton, C. (2001). *Selfhood and authenticity.* SUNY Press.
Anton, C. & Peterson, V. (2003). Who said what: Subject positions, rhetorical strategies, and good faith. *Communication Studies, 54*(1), pp. 403–419.
Anton, C., & Strate, L. (2012). *Korzybski and....* Institute of General Semantics.
Beinart, P. (2017, March 6). A violent attack on free speech at Middlebury. *The Atlantic.* https://www.theatlantic.com/politics/archive/2017/03/middlebury-free-speech-violence/518667/

Berger, E. (2022). *Context blindness: Digital technologies and the next stage of human evolution.* Peter Lang.

Biden, J. (2021). *Remarks by President Biden announcing the framework for his build back better agenda and bipartisan infrastructure bill* [Transcript]. https://www.whitehouse.gov/briefing-room/speeches-remarks/2021/10/28/remarks-by-president-biden-announcing-the-framework-for-his-build-back-better-agenda-and-bipartisan-infrastructure-bill/

Burke, K. (1966). *Language as symbolic action.* University of California Press.

Bush, G. (1990). *Address before a joint session of congress on the Persian Gulf crisis and the federal budget deficit* [Transcript]. https://bush41library.tamu.edu/archives/public-papers/2217

Bush, G.W. (2005). *Remarks to the national endowment for democracy* [Transcript]. https://www.presidency.ucsb.edu/documents/remarks-the-national-endowment-for-democracy

Carter, S. (2022, January 6). Collin college to pay $70,000 to history professor let go amid free speech debacle. *The Dallas Observer.* https://www.dallasobserver.com/news/history-professor-fired-for-tweets-lora-burnett-to-receive-70000-from-collin-college-13285526#:~:text=On%20Tuesday%2C%20after%20more%20than,her%20%2470%2C000%20plus%20attorneys'%20fees

Chua, A. (2018). *Political tribes: Group instinct and the fate of nations.* Penguin Press.

Cillizza, C. (2013, March 4). Why Mitt Romney's 47% comment was so bad. *The Washington Post.* https://www.washingtonpost.com/news/the-fix/wp/2013/03/04/why-mitt-romneys-47-percent-comment-was-so-bad/

Cross, I. (2019, December 17). Holy Cross dean defends protestors who disrupted Heather MacDonald lecture. *The College Fix.* https://www.thecollegefix.com/holy-cross-dean-defends-protestors-who-disrupted-heather-mac-donald-lecture/

Ekins, E. (2020). Poll 62% of Americans say they have political views they are afraid to share. *Cato Institute.* https://www.cato.org/survey-reports/poll-62-americans-say-they-have-political-views-theyre-afraid-share

Ferris, S., & Mutknick, A. (2022, July 7). House dems berate campaign arm over 'very dangerous' GOP primary scheme. *Politico.* https://

www.politico.com/news/2022/07/27/meijer-dccc-trump-primaries-00048104

Giddens, A. (1994). *Beyond left and right: The future of radical politics*. Stanford University Press.

Habermas, J. (1990). *Moral consciousness and communicative action*. MIT Press.

International day of happiness. (2012, March 20). www.un.orghttps://www.un.org/development/desa/dspd/international-days/international-day-of-happiness.html

Jacoby, J. (2022, July 13). Informers on campus. *The Boston Globe*. https://www.bostonglobe.com/2022/07/13/opinion/informers-campus/

Johnson, W. (1946). *People in quandaries: The semantics of personal adjustment*. Harper & Brothers.

Kissinger, A. (2020, April 3). The coronavirus pandemic will forever alter the world order. *Wall Street Journal*. https://www.wsj.com/articles/the-coronavirus-pandemic-will-forever-alter-the-world-order-11585953005

Korzybski, K. (1994). *Science & sanity: An introduction to non-Aristotelian systems and general semantics* (5th ed.). Institute of General Semantics.

Krauthammer, C. (2005, April 30). An Arab spring? *Hoover Institution*. https://www.hoover.org/research/arab-spring

Lakoff, G. (1996). *Moral politics: How liberals and conservatives think*. University of Chicago Press.

Latour, B. (2004). Why has critique run out of steam? From matters of fact to matters of concern. *Critical Inquiry, 30*. pp. 225–248.

Lee, I. (1941). *Language habits in human affairs*. The International Society for General Semantics.

Mercieca, J. (2020). *Demagogue for president: The rhetorical genus of Donald Trump*. Texas A&M University Press.

Moufee, C. (2005). *On the political*. Routledge.

Obama, B. (2016). Address by President Obama to the 71st session of the United Nations General Assembly [Transcript]. https://obamawhitehouse.archives.gov/the-press-office/2016/09/20/address-president-obama-71st-session-united-nations-general-assembly

Pilkington, E. (2008). Obama angers Midwest voters with guns and religion remarks. https://www.theguardian.com/world/2008/apr/14/barackobama.uselections2008

Postman, N., & Weingartner, C. (1969). *Teaching as a subversive activity.* Delacorte Press.

Reilly, K. (2016, September 10). Read Hillary Clinton's 'basket of deplorables' remarks about Donald Trump's supporters. *Time.* https://time.com/4486502/hillary-clinton-basket-of-deplorables-transcript/

Rosenberg, P. (2021). Conservatives claim to hate cancel culture – but it is the heart of the right wing agenda. *Salon.com.* https://www.salon.com/2021/05/01/conservatives-claim-to-hate-cancel-culture-but-its-the-heart-of-the-right-wing-agenda/

Sartre, J. (1984). *Being and nothingness.* Washington Square Press.

Soave, R. (2018). Some pundits say there is no campus free speech 'crisis.' Here's why they are wrong. *Reason.com.* https://reason.com/2018/03/19/some-pundits-say-theres-no-campus-free-s/

Tonn, M. B. (2005). Taking conversation, dialogue, and therapy public. *Rhetoric and Public Affairs, 8*(3), pp. 405–430.

United Nations. *Charter of the United Nations,* 1945, art. 1. https://www.un.org/en/about-us/un-charter

Woodward, C. (2011). *American nations: A history of eleven rival regional cultures of North America.* Penguin Books.

CHAPTER 10

MYLES HORTON AND THE HIGHLANDER FOLK SCHOOL: A SEMANTIC ENVIRONMENT OF POLITICAL ORGANIZATION, ACTIVISM, AND CHANGE

RYAN P. McCULLOUGH

F or most communication and media scholars who hear the term *political communication*, I think it reasonable to suggest that the approach of general semantics – and its scholarly counterpart, media ecology – might not come to mind. Those of us working those approaches probably find this development irksome because both general semantics and media ecology have been inspired by or respond to political developments and problems in political communication. Alfred Korzybski's *Manhood of Humanity* (1921) and *Science and Sanity* (1948), for example, developed a non-Aristotelian system of thought as a response to many of the failures in politics that led to the First World War. Similarly, S. I. Hayawaka's *Language in Thought in Action* (1972) – first published on the precipice of the Second World War – in many ways attempted to contend with the fraught political issues brought about by our two-valued orientation. Neil Postman (1976, 1988), a scholar who's work spans across general semantics and media ecology (Gencarelli, 2006), wrote about the stupidities that developed because of the sloganeering in political communication. Moreover, scholars aligned with media ecology, Postman, Marshall McLuhan, Lewis Mumford, Harold Innis, Jacques Ellul, and Daniel Boorstin shared a profound concern with the consequences of the media environment on our understanding of politics. In other words, those familiar with both approaches recognize the keen insights that general semantics and media ecology make about political communication and the nexus of politics and communication.

Much of the thinking about political communication rests on either the notion of understanding the effects of mass/public communication, critiquing the communicative practices of the politically powerful, or giving voice to communicators and communities left behind by traditional political machinations. My goal in this paper is not to discount or undermine any of the traditions of communication studies that seek to understand, critique, and give voice. Instead, my goal is to demonstrate and elucidate the value of general semantics in helping us to understand the connections between politics and communicative practices. Demonstrating the value of general semantics will help to both walk general semantics into the scholarly conversation centered on political communication and, through the case study I construct, provide political organizers and activists with the semantic resources to create a new sense of political consciousness.

To illustrate the value of general semantics to understanding political communication, I offer a case study of the educational philosophy of political activist Myles Horton (1905–1990). Horton and his collaborators at the Highlander Folk School in Tennessee developed an educational philosophy that illustrates the precepts of the semantic environment, even though they had no working knowledge of general semantics. While Horton's name does not appear within the tradition of general semantics, through a careful context analysis

(Postman, 2006) of Horton's educational philosophy practiced at Highlander, I argue that Horton's approach to education in support of political activism illustrates that careful attention to the semantic environment of learning can lead to results for political organization, activism, and change. By articulating his educational philosophy through the precepts of general semantics, we can see how general semantics can help us to understand, critique, and give voice within the context of politics. In addition, the case study provides a model-approach to creating democratic knowledge that inspired political activism and change. As such, those studying political communication would do well to in giving greater attention to general semantics and look to the semantic environment established by Horton and the Highlander Folk School as a model for giving voice to members of marginalized communities.

To develop this argument, this paper will proceed in three sections. First, I contend that Neil Postman's description of context analysis (2006) and semantic environment (1976) offers a way for scholars working within the tradition of general semantics to approach political communication that both corrects and extends upon dominant approaches to studying political communication. Second, I offer a context analysis on the semantic environment of the educational philosophy of Myles Horton and the Highlander Folk School to elucidate how attention to systems and environments leads to political change and the expansion of democratic practices. Finally, I conclude this essay by discussing how the context analysis of the Highlander Folk School expands our knowledge of general semantics scholarship, general semantics pedagogy, and political action.

Context Analysis: An Approach to Understanding Political Communication

Communication researchers concerned with political communication rely on a variety of methodological approaches. Political communication researchers use rhetorical-critical-interpretive analysis of communicative messages and structures, and, at the same time, much of political communication research grounded in socio-psychological theories like agenda setting and uses and gratifications depends on more quantitative methodologies associated with researching communication effects (Kaid, 1996, p. 445). Given the centrality of agenda setting and uses and gratifications, I do not think it a stretch to conclude that much of political communication research relies on content analysis. For most, the use of content analysis makes sense for theory building and research related to political communication. Content analysis, a methodology designed to pinpoint, quantify, and examine messages within a text, focuses on "studying mass-mediated and public messages" (Frey et al., 2000, p. 236). As an attempt to sway and influence voters, political communication invariably relies on mass and public communication, so it makes sense to study the effects of the messages embedded in these forms of communication.

I do not intend to deride much of the work related to political communication scholarship, but as someone working from the related perspectives of general semantics and media ecology, the reliance on content analysis becomes problematic approach to studying political communication. Content analysis works to describe the content of messages and make inferences about the people creating and receiving the content of those messages (Frey et al., 1992, p. 195). From the approach of media ecology, however, content analysis makes little sense because it treats each medium that delivers and spreads messages as essentially the same. One could conduct a content analysis of newspapers, radio, television, or digital media platforms, but the methodology remains constant. Content analysis focuses on the message, not the medium—on content, not form. Content analysis becomes frustrating because this approach ignores one of the central tenets of media ecology: the medium is the message (McLuhan, 2003). At the same time, from the approach of general semantics, content analysis runs the risk of confusing inference and fact, making this form of research a dangerous proposition (Hayakawa, 1972, p. 37). We inevitably make inferences, and content analysis produces inferences with statistical validity and reliability. Consequently, I do not suggest that the inferences made through the method of content analysis are inaccurate or morally wrong, but general semantics reminds us that we must make inferences with caution. Having been informed and influenced by media ecology and general semantics, it becomes difficult to cede confidence and control of the study of political communication to content analysis.

Neil Postman agrees with my perspective, or, to put it more accurately, I agree with him. Content analysis ignores environment, and Postman (2006) writes, "From the ecological perspective, content analysis, for example is viewed as either trivial or irrelevant" (p. 8). Postman encourages communication researchers – and this would also include political communication researchers – to adopt the environmental perspective grounded in a new metaphor for analyzing communication and developing theory. Postman calls this new perspective *context analysis*. Postman's (2006) emphasis on context and not content allows for a systems approach to communication:

> This [context analysis] implies looking at communication environments as systems within systems within systems. It means trying to identify significant characteristics of each system as a whole, the subsystems of which it is composed, the larger system within which it functions, and all the significant relationships among them. To make things even more confusing, context analysis takes as its subject matter the transactions between individual and reality, individual and individual, individual and group, group and group, group and culture, culture and culture and tries to see them all as functions of one another. (p. 8)

Context analysis calls for consideration of environment and systems, and context analysis reminds us that we embed messages within a larger system. Therefore, if we want to understand the message, we need to understand the context-system-environment that contributes to the creation of a message. Context analysis offers a corrective or addendum to studying political communication. If content analysis strips the message away from the medium to make inferences, then context analysis seeks to rejoin the message and medium. The medium necessarily informs the messages that arise out of the media system. Context analysis offers a re-focusing of our attention on environment.

Postman's context analysis and his increasing emphasis on language within environments-systems and language created by environments-systems led to his articulation and description of another metaphor, the semantic environment (Strate, 2014, p. 32). Although Postman (along with Charles Weingartner and Terrance Moran) used the term semantic environment previously (Strate, 2014, p. 32), the most complete articulation of the semantic environment came in Postman's (1976) book *Crazy Talk, Stupid Talk: How We Defeat Ourselves by the Way We Talk and What to Do About It*. *Crazy Talk, Stupid Talk* follows the tradition of general semantics and its attendant focus on personal development and growth, so the text mostly focuses on interpersonal communication (Strate, 2014, p. 32). Extending the context analysis metaphor, Postman asks us to think about how interpersonal communication results from the environment in which communication takes place and vice versa. Interpersonal communication is not simply a transmission of messages between interlocutors or individuals. Instead, interpersonal communication results from the larger environment. Postman (1976) writes, "It [the semantic environment] says that communication is not stuff or bits or messages. [...] Communication is a situation in which people participate" (p. 8). Communication – or the situation – results from the environment surrounding the communication much like "[g]rowth is a consequence of complex transactions among the plant, the soil, the air, the sun, and water" (Postman, 1976, p. 9). This perspective extends the context analysis metaphor in that communication occurs within a context—the semantic environment. Therefore, if we wish to understand interpersonal communication, then we must understand context and engage in context analysis of the semantic environment.

We should also remember that political communication does not take place entirely within the public sphere or within public communication. Certainly, interpersonal communication can involve a discussion of politics, but we would also do well to remember that much of our political education can happen within interpersonal communication. Much of the research conducted by sociologists at Columbia University's Bureau for Applied Social Research (see Lazarsfeld et al., 1944; Berelson et al., 1954; Katz & Lazarsfeld, 1966) acknowledge the role of relationships and interpersonal communication in opinion formation on political matters – the social influence model of mass media. In addition, rhetorical and persuasive communication scholarship acknowledges the importance of interpersonal influence within political and social movements (see Burgchardt, 2005; Crick, 2020; Simons, 1970; Stewart et al., 1984). While this essay does not subscribe to either the social influence or purely rhetorical approach, I do contend that communication research supports the relationship between interpersonal communication and political communication-education. Consequently, Postman's articulation of the semantic environment, although focusing mostly on interpersonal communication not directly tied to politics, does have implications for our understanding of political communication and politics.

Postman's emphasis on context analysis and his articulation of the relationship between the semantic environment and interpersonal communication allows us to rethink our approach to political communication. General semantics might seek to replace and extend traditional studies of political communication using content analysis with a form of context analysis of the semantic environments that allow political communication to grow and gestate. Again, those outside the traditions of general semantics and media ecology might not think we have much to contribute to the study of political communication, but the context analysis suggests that those traditions can offer much to the conversation on communication and politics.

In this sense, context analysis of the semantic environment dovetails nicely with Postman's (1999) desire to re-emphasize the importance of logic and rhetoric within education and teaching. Our education system still grounds itself in elements of the medieval trivium—grammar, logic, and rhetoric. However, there remains an overemphasis on the element of grammar, and this overemphasis comes at the expense of logic and rhetoric. As a solution to this development, Postman (1999) suggests that education systems should re-introduce logic and rhetoric through the study of language, particularly through the study of language from the perspective of general semantics (p. 163). Again, part of political communication research focuses on rhetorical-critical-interpretive analysis of communication messages and structures. If we think of general semantics as a type of logical-rhetorical study – a view that Postman embraces – then we can think of context analysis of the semantic environment as something akin to rhetorical analysis and/or criticism. Context analysis becomes a way to analyze the semantic-rhetorical contours of a communication situation, and context analysis, therefore, contributes to the rhetorical-critical-interpretive approach to studying political communication.

Thinking of context analysis as a form of rhetorical criticism becomes valuable for the study of general semantics and politics because the practice of criticism helps to build our theoretical approach and communicative practices. Rhetorical scholar, Roderick Hart (1997) claims that rhetorical criticism can fulfill four purposes. First, *"Rhetorical criticism documents social trends"* (Hart, 1997, p. 24, emphasis in original). Second, *"Rhetorical criticism provides general understandings via the case-study method"* (Hart, 1997, p. 25, emphasis in original). Third, *"Rhetorical analysis produces meta-knowledge"* (Hart, 1997, p. 26, emphasis in original). Fourth, *"Rhetorical criticism invites radical confrontation with Otherness"* (Hart, 1997, p. 28, emphasis in original). Taking these purposes articulated by Hart gives general semantics a new generative force, especially in the realm of political communication research. General semantics has always concerned itself with what is going on (WIGO) but thinking of context analysis as akin to rhetorical criticism reminds general semantics scholars that we have an obligation to document what is going on, especially in the realm of politics. By examining specific cases and specific semantic environments, we can start to build a working understanding of the semantic environments that produce political change and action. These case studies allow us to make inferences about the larger idea of the semantic environment and language use. Context analysis as rhetorical criticism allows for the theory-building – or if you prefer, the approach-building/tradition-building – of general semantics. Finally, thinking about context analysis as akin to rhetorical criticism allows us to move general semantics beyond the therapeutic and self-help elements of the tradition. This is not to say that this element of the tradition is wrongheaded, but criticism functions as "a wonderful way to get outside of oneself" (Hart, 1997, p. 28). Context analysis of the semantic environment invites us to see situations other than our own. It invites us to think about environments and communication not as a given but as a result or output of a system.

Hart fails to explicitly mention another purpose of rhetorical criticism: its pedagogical function (Frey et al., 1992, p. 168). Through a critical analysis of rhetoric, students of rhetoric learn about the uses of rhetoric and can apply those uses to their experiences as rhetors. If we think about context analysis of the semantic environment as aligned with rhetorical criticism, then we can think of what we learn from other semantic environments, and we can think about how to apply those lessons to different environments and situations. In the context of politics, if we think about the environments that create and sustain political change, we possess the ability to apply those lessons to what we do in other environments. How might we replicate that environment? How might we avoid the mistakes made in other environments, etc.? Context analysis opens a rhetorical space for the pedagogical goals outlined by Postman. We can reinvigorate our education about politics through general semantics as a form of rhetorical criticism.

Semantic Environment as Method of Analysis-Criticism

While one might bristle at the notion of *method* because method presumes a social scientific orientation toward communication, I believe method operates as an apt term. The map is not the territory, and method cannot accurately describe all the phenomenon under discussion. However, operationally, method suggests that we move through analysis in a systematic way. Scientific method, for example, grounds itself in empiricism. With the scientific method we create knowledge through experimentation, and certain processes exist within experimentation. In the same way, attending to the semantic environment offers a systematic way to express our knowledge about communication.

In *Crazy Talk, Stupid Talk*, Postman (1976) contends that the semantic environment consists of four elements: "first of all, people; second, their purposes; third, the general rules of discourse by which such purposes are usually achieved, and fourth, the particular talk actually being used in the situation" (p. 9). These four elements invite analysis of the context and semantic environment. To understand communication, we need to understand the people, the purposes, the rules and the talk in the situation. We cannot isolate one specific element as the cause of success or failure. Communication and talk become *crazy* or *stupid* only in the context of the semantic environment. Understanding the semantic environment helps us to grasp why and how language "does not or cannot achieve reasonable and humane purposes, either because the purpose is unreasonable and inhumane or the language will not do what it is supposed to do" (Postman, 1976, p. 75). Humane and reasonable language and communication (talk) only grows out of humane and reasonable purposes and rules of communication. People become humane and reasonable based on what the situation demands.

A thorough understanding of communication demands a systematic understanding of the semantic environment, and a systematic understanding of the environment demands a clear description of the four elements Postman articulated.

As mentioned previously, Postman's idea of context analysis stood as the intellectual forbearer to the semantic environment (Strate, 2014, p. 32). Consequently, I think of the semantic environment as a way to think through the context under analysis, scrutiny, and criticism. Let me apply an analogy. Rhetorical scholars utilizing Walter Fisher's (1984) narrative paradigm might use the qualities of narrative coherence and narrative fidelity to understand rhetorical texts and artifacts. In the same way, general semanticists utilizing context analysis might utilize the four elements of the semantic environment articulated by Postman to understand communication in situations. Elements of the semantic environment provide an analytical-interpretive-critical approach to the interpersonal communication and political communication that result from a system-environment of communication. Through the systematic analysis of the semantic environment, we understand the context that produced the communication. From understanding the context, we can then begin to build knowledge about social trends, produce theoretical knowledge, and understand the practices of others. Once we do these things, we can offer a communication pedagogy and/or a pedagogy about communication. However, to build our knowledge, we must have a case, and I offer that case in the next section: Myles Horton's educational philosophy and the practices at Highlander Folk School.

Myles Horton and Highlander Folk School: A Case Study

This section uses Postman's (1976) semantic environment as a form of context analysis to offer a case study of the communicative practices used in the Highlander Folk School. To develop this case study, I offer a brief biography of the school's founder and a brief history of the school and its successes to give a sense of the people and purposes of the semantic environment as a way to justify why this case deserves our attention. Then, I will discuss the educational practices (rules and talk) within Highlander Folk School as a semantic environment that allows for the development of political organization, activism, and change and how that organization, activism, and change are the outgrowth to the semantic environment.

The People in the Semantic Environment

Myles Horton was born in Savannah, Tennessee on July 9, 1905. Although both his parents were at one time schoolteachers, his parents did not have college educations and switched jobs and homes frequently, so Horton grew up poor (Horton, 1998, p. 1). The differences between the advantages of the rich and poor had a profound impact on Horton as a young child and teenager; it informed much of his thinking (Horton, 1998, pp. 2–3). Horton's parents still provided Myles an environment that valued education, reading, and a Christian sense of love for fellow man (Horton, 1998, pp. 13–14; Horton & Freire, 1990, p. 19). As a result of the environment provided by his parents, Horton decided to attend college, and he was able to attend Cumberland University in Lebanon, Tennessee through the help of his church and a football scholarship (Horton, 1998, p. 13). At Cumberland, Horton spent most of his time reading every book he could find, and during summers he would work at vacation bible schools in the smaller towns and hollows surrounding Cumberland (Horton, 1998, p. 23). One experience in Ozone, Tennessee taught him the importance of listening to the concerns of others and the value of having people develop solutions to their collective problems. Through talking, the families would build ideas and knowledge together (Horton, 1998, p. 23). Given the centrality of this moment – encouraging the folks at Ozone to talk through problems together – to Horton's life as an educator, I feel compelled to quote him at length:

Before the meeting was over I had made a very valuable discovery. You don't have to know the answers. The answers come from the people, and when they don't have any answers, then you have another role, and you find resources [...] So I became a resource person and started setting up follow-up meetings. (Horton, 1998, p. 23).

Horton discovered education need not be centered on the expertise of the teacher. Instead, the people themselves could be experts and identify their own problems and answers. The moment became so impactful to Horton that he began to connect everything he read to what he discovered in Ozone (Horton, 1998, p. 24).

The experience at Ozone inspired Horton to try to learn as much as he could about how he could teach people, especially poor adults, how to work together to resolve the issues brought on by poverty. To learn more, Horton decided to attend Union Theological Seminary in New York City. Horton (1998) wrote, "I went to Union Theological Seminary in the fall of 1929 to try to find out how to get social justice and love together" (p. 32). He studied with Reinhold Niebuhr, began to read Karl Marx, started to question the idea of individualism, and wanted to know more about collective action.

Wanting to know more about collective action, Horton moved on from Union and enrolled in the graduate program in sociology at the University of Chicago (Horton, 1998, p. 46). While at Chicago, encountered activist and social worker Jane Addams, and Horton had the opportunity to visit Addams's settlement houses that offered services for immigrants and the urban poor (Horton, 1998, p. 47). In Addams, Horton found a sympathetic ear, and she encouraged Horton to develop an analog to the settlement houses in the rural South and Appalachia (Adams, 1975, p. 19). However, despite his positive encounters with Addams and his desire to continue his education, Horton left the program at the University of Chicago because he did not see how the graduate program would help him to establish a school that matched his experiences at Ozone.

One book Horton encountered during his studies that connected to his experiences at Ozone was Joseph K. Hart's (1927) *Light from the North: Danish Folk Schools and Their Meaning for America*. Hart's text described Denmark's Bishop Nikolai S.F. Grundtvig's nineteenth-century Folk Schools. Grundtvig's schools focused on adult education to "enlighten and enliven the Danish peasantry after centuries of exploitation under a feudalistic system" (Glen, 1988, p. 4). Horton made his way to a Danish Lutheran Church in Chicago, and the ministers put Horton in touch with people and ministers in Denmark (Horton, 1998, pp. 50–51). With the support of Niebuhr, Horton left Chicago and moved to Denmark to study the folk schools (Adams, 1975, p. 20). In Denmark, Horton learned what made the schools so successful. Horton (1998) claimed, "The people would find their identity not within themselves but in relationship with others" (pp. 51–52). The success of the schools and finding identity with others created a movement in Denmark that led to a new constitution (Horton, 1998, p. 53). Thanks to his experience in Denmark, Horton felt that he was now ready to start an educational program for poor adults in Appalachia as a way to recreate his experiences at Ozone. When Horton returned to the United States, he solicited help from Niebuhr to build the finances to start what eventually became Highlander Folk School (Glen, 1988, p. 15).

Highlander Folk School opened on November 1, 1932, in Monteagle, Tennessee with Myles Horton and Don West, another southerner familiar with the folk school movement, as the co-directors of the school (Glenn, 1988, p. 17). Horton and West deemed Monteagle an appropriate location, not only because they had access to land in Monteagle, but because that area of Tennessee "had known poverty, disease, and illiteracy for many years. The coal and lumber industries, on which the [area] had based its prosperity, had collapsed well before the Great Depression, leaving only devastated resources and exhausted cropland" (Glen, 1988, p. 18). Especially for Horton the idea of folk schools illustrated how education did not have to function in a support of powerful ideologies. Folk schools, by placing poor people in space together to discuss their collective problems, could help to establish an environment that emphasized collective political action, not the specific needs of the individual.

Highlander's Success. The history of the Highlander Folk School requires a book-length treatment, so it is beyond the scope of this essay to offer the full history of the school[1], but I want to identify the importance of the school. Again, a purpose of general semantics is to document what is going on (WIGO), and a purpose of criticism is to document important social trends. Identifying the success of Highlander helps us to understand how social movements solve problems that respond to the demands of capitalism and racist policies. Locating the success of these movements comes with the hope that we can learn from their practices.

Highlander and Myles Horton became significantly involved in the labor movement of the American South and the Civil Rights movement of the 1950s and 1960s. The school and Horton achieved its most significant accomplishments between 1932 and 1962. While the first five years of the school did not produce many significant results (Glen, 1988, p. 21), Horton and Highlander staff helped workers during mine strikes in those first five years, and the Committee for Industrial Labor (CIO) noticed the efforts of the people at Highlander (Jacobs, 2003, p. xxii). The CIO called upon Highlander to help increase union membership (Glenn, 1988, pp. 46–47). Eventually, Highlander became the "unofficial training center for the CIO" (Jacobs, 2003, p. xxiii). However, by the early 1950s, Horton and Highlander began to disagree with the educational goals and practices of the CIO, and the relationship between Highlander and the CIO wrapped up in 1953 (Jacobs, 2003, p. xxiii).

Without the financial support of the CIO Highlander faced a precarious future, but Horton and Highlander crafted a partnership with people who would become centrally involved in the Civil Rights Movement. Despite having only spurious relationships with rural black southerners in its first twenty years, Highlander began to forge relationships with the black community, after the CIO dropped its affiliation, by building ties to famers' unions, unions with higher levels of black participation (Jacobs, 2003, p. xxiv). In addition, the school correctly predicted that desegregation was coming to the South, so they began holding workshops preparing for school desegregation (Jacobs, 2003, p. xxiv). With a level of trust established with the black community, Esau Jenkins and Septima Clark of Johns Island, South Carolina came to a Highlander workshop in 1954 (Jacobs, 2003, p. xxv). Jenkins and Clark, who became central figures in the Civil Rights Movement, worked with and at Highlander to create the now-famous Citizenship Schools to help black southerners pass literacy tests, giving black citizens access to the ballot (Jacobs, 2003, p. xxv). While the Southern Christian Leadership Conference eventually directed the Citizenship School program, the idea began in the environment set up by Horton and Highlander (Horton, 1998, p. 107). Before her involvement in the Montgomery Bus Boycott, Rosa Parks came to a training workshop held at Highlander in 1955 (Horton, 1998, p. 98). Dr. Martin Luther King Jr. spoke at Highlander at its twenty-fifth anniversary; Parks and Ralph Abernathy attended this event (Horton, 1998, pp. 118–119). Southern white supremacists labeled Highlander a "Communist Training School" and put a picture of King at Highlander on a billboard with the caption, "Martin Luther King at Communist Training School" (Horton, 1998, p. 121).

Because of its success and affiliation with the Civil Rights Movement, the state government of Tennessee wanted to disband the school, so through a court case and additional legal maneuvers, Tennessee rescinded the school's charter and Highlander's property in Monteagle was sold in 1962 (Glen, 1988, pp. 207–208). The school changed its name to the Highlander Research and Education Center, and eventually moved to New Market, Tennessee, continuing to operate to this day. Horton stepped down as director in 1972, but despite its continuing operation, Highlander has not enabled the type of region-wide success that it did in its first three to four decades. Highlander historian

John M. Glen (1988) aptly summarizes Highlander's impact; he writes, "Indeed, the history of the Highlander Folk School is in many ways the history of dissent and reform in Appalachia and the American South since the onset of the Great Depression" (p. 220). Because the labor movement of the American South and the Civil Rights Movement lost their influence, Highlander lost its influence.

The People's Approach to the Semantic Environment. Despite the fact that Highlander lost its influence in regional politics, we can draw lessons from Horton and the people working at Highlander. Fifty years have passed since Horton stepped down as director of Highlander, but the organization still acknowledges the centrality of Horton's philosophy to the practices and successes that grew out of Highlander (Highlander Research and Education Center, 2023). Horton had always been quick to acknowledge that other people became central to the creation of the environment at Highlander, including Septima Clark who became an instructor at Highlander (Horton, 1998; Horton & Freire, 1990). Having said that, if we are to think of communication as the outgrowth of the semantic environment that includes people, then we must consider the role of Horton in our context analysis of Highlander's semantic environment. Horton's vision of creating a space for people to learn about themselves in relation to others de-centers the individual. The people in the environment matter, but the individual identity of those people matter less than the relationships between the people. Creating identity through relationships was the lesson Horton took from the Danish Folk School movement. Highlander achieved its greatest success when the people at the workshop dealt with a collective problem like the exploitation of labor or white supremacy. At Ozone, Horton learned the value of de-centering himself; he was not an expert coming into a situation to solve a problem. The people were the experts. In Highlander, we find an environment where the "leader" is not really there to lead. The people are not there for themselves, but they are there to learn from one another – not the leader-teacher either.

Highlander's Educational Practices: Purposes, Rules, Talk

After stepping down as director at Highlander, Horton traveled and shared his educational philosophy with others (Horton, 1998; Jacobs, 2003). Horton believed that the educational philosophy practiced at Highlander would have purchase for other poor communities (Horton, 1998, p. 213). Horton did not share his educational philosophy in a traditional manner, and he did not author any books with a specific description of the philosophy (Jacobs, 2003). Instead, the educational practices and semantic environment of Highlander exist in the descriptions offered by Horton in his autobiography, *The Long Haul* (1998), and *We Make the Road by Walking* (1990), a "speaking book" that documents conversations between Horton and Paolo Freire, a Brazilian educational activist and author of *Pedagogy of the Oppressed*. Utilizing these texts, I hope to offer a clear sense of the semantic environment – the rules, purposes, and talk – of Highlander to understand the context that led to its successes in political organization and change. This analysis also points to the value of approaching political communication from the view of general semantics.

Circle of Learners. While Horton and Highlander's educational practices do not have a clear, coherent description, one practice became a through line for all of Highlander's workshops, the "circle of learners" (Horton, 1998, p. 150). The staff at Highlander would create a circle, and no one would sit at the front of the room (Horton, 1998, p. 150). This particular environment rejects both the "sage on the stage" and the "guide on the side" perspectives on teaching. Certainly, the circle of learners de-centers the notion that the teacher "starts" the learning by being the sage-expert who begins the session. At the same time, the educators at Highlander avoided guiding the conversation; instead, the Highlander staff focused on "creating a relaxed atmosphere in which the participants feel free to share their experiences. Then they are encouraged to analyze, learn from and build on these experiences" (Horton, 1998, p. 150). Staff members can add to the conversation, but they do not drive the conversation as a guide. The notion of a guide suggests that the circle of learners has a leader. A guide suggests that there will be someone who begins and ends the discussion. As Horton (1998) noted, "Each session had to take its own form and develop according to the students' needs" (p. 150). The circle of learners suggests that everyone, including the educator, comes to the circle to learn and share.

The circle of learners puts forth the rules of discourse that allow for productive conversations and learning to occur. The circle of learners works to establish a relationship where all members within the group stand on equal footing. Postman (1976) notes how relationships work to form the rules of discourse in the semantic environment, "By relationship, I am referring to the rules that define the emotional context of a semantic environment, the rules that form the container in which the content of our talk is presented" (p. 38). By de-centering the teacher and keeping the educator from being the sage or the guide, the people in the circle of learners can set the rules of discourse for themselves. With everyone on equal footing, no one becomes an expert, except being an expert in their own lived experience. The circle of learners places an equal relationship between all members at the forefront of the conversation. Although it is possible for someone to dominate a conversation, no one is in charge to shape the rules of the conversation and dominate how people relate to one another.

In addition, Horton and Highlander's focus on creating a specific atmosphere illustrates attention to the semantic environment. Conversation and talk emerge out of what Postman (1976) calls a "frame," and the frame emerges from the "tone" or "attitude and atmosphere" (p. 39). While frame, tone, attitude, and atmosphere all operate as fairly abstract terms, Postman (1976) clarifies the notion: "By atmosphere, I mean the ambience and texture of a semantic environment. This is something over which an individual rarely has any control" (p. 38). To clarify what he means, Postman offers examples of how stadiums, hospitals, trading floors, or churches influence the type of talk that takes place. The atmospheres created by these environments suggest that a certain type of talk will emerge. The goal to create a relaxed atmosphere at Highlander illustrates that, although Horton and Highlander do not use the term, they wanted to create an environment that allowed for a different type of talk than one might normally hear in traditional educational settings. As Horton puts it, "Instead of you getting on a pinnacle you put them on a pinnacle" (Horton & Freire, 1990, p. 146). The atmosphere of the circle of learners at Highlander means that education does not "start" with the educator getting up and sharing-delivering expertise. Instead, the atmosphere invites people to share their experiences. As an exception that proves the rule, the Highlander staff could exercise control over the environment and atmosphere, because the school was not subject to any of the traditional norms found in education.

Given how most individuals expect education to work, with a teacher sharing or offering expertise, students at Highlander were reluctant in sharing experiences. In addition, in traditional settings with the teacher acting as a guide on the side, instructors might want to summarize what others say to clarify a problem. However, the circle of learners and the atmosphere created at Highlander operated in a different manner. Horton offers an extended example of how this might work:

> In a class on union problems, the students would raise problems that they had, and we'd discuss them. And I knew the problems those people had because I'd dealt with the same kinds of people over and over again. I never, never put down a problem on the blackboard or listed a problem that they didn't list, even though I knew it was their problem, and I didn't do what I see some people doing today. I didn't put it in my own words to make it clear [...] That's a put-down to a worker to edit his or her way of saying things. So the workers worded the problems. First I would ask, "What do you know about that problem already?" Then they said, "I don't know anything" Well okay, you know how to survive, you're here. Your union sent you here. They thought you had some leadership ability. I would push them to name what they know, and they find right off, with a little struggle and a lot of embarrassment, that there are some things that they can articulate

[…] The one thing they know is their own experience. They don't need to homogenize it with other people's experience. (Horton & Freire, 1990, p. 167).

Essentially, the rules of discourse – the idea that students must build their knowledge instead of having knowledge dictated to them – created the type of talk that allowed people to articulate the problems they faced. By emphasizing a circle of learners, students came to identify their problems collectively rather than having their problems explained to them. Horton believed that this dynamic constituted a democratic type of learning because students can decide for themselves the problems that confront the union or social movement. The learning does not rest in the authority of the instructor. The people and students possess the authority.

Once students at Highlander in the circle of learning realized that their experiences and knowledge matter, an environment developed in which others feel confident to join in and share additional experiences (Horton & Freire, 1990, p. 168). This democratic experience within the circle of learners helped the students to not only identify a collective problem, but it also helped the students to come up with their own solution, not the solution handed to them by experts. As students came to this realization, Horton claimed, "Then, they planned: here's how we'll deal with this problem when we go back home" (Horton & Freire, 1990, p. 168). In this way, the semantic environment of Highlander and the circle of learners allowed students to use their own experiences as a vocabulary to understand a problem and solution. Postman (1976) states, "The vocabulary of any semantic environment defines the reality with which the environment is concerned" (p. 58). If Horton and the Highlander staff rephrased the problems and solutions for the student, then the students would have subsumed their knowledge with the knowledge of the staff at Highlander. By crafting their own ways to describe the problems, the students came to trust that they knew the problem and became confident in the crafted solution. The circle of learners prevented the students at Highlander from becoming what Postman (1976) calls "'locked in'" (p. 60) to the vocabulary of the experts. When people become locked in, Postman (1976) claims, "Their perceptions are completely controlled by someone else's vocabulary" (p. 60). The discussion and validation of experiences led to a feeling that the problems and solutions are authentic (Horton & Freire, 1990, p. 168). The problems and solutions were not controlled and dictated by someone else, so in this environment of the circle of learners, the people felt empowered by the decisions that they make, because the environment allowed them to make the decisions.

The circle of learners at Highlander rejected what Paulo Freire (2005) dubs in *Pedagogy of the Oppressed* "the banking concept of education" (p. 72). Freire's metaphor of the banking model of education lodges a critique of traditional forms of education. The banking model presumes that knowledge or information transfers from the teacher/expert to the student/inexpert. Freire (2005) explains why banking functions as an apt metaphor: "Education thus becomes an act of depositing, in which the students are depositories, and the teacher is the depositor. Instead of communicating, the teacher issues communiqués and makes deposits which the students patiently receive, memorize, and repeat" (p. 72). Instead of treating students as individuals with immanent value, the banking model of education treats students as individuals acted upon and managed by the instructor (Freire, 2005, p. 73). The banking model of education troubles Freire because this form of education simply replicates and repeats dominant structures that exist outside of the classroom. The banking model of education contains a hidden curriculum that encourages students to simply follow basic structures of power. Since the circle of learners at Highlander encouraged students not to conform to the locked-in patterns of communication and instruction by asking for students to look within themselves for the identification of problems and answers, the instructors and staff at Highlander did not deposit anything into the students. The students generated ideas for themselves. This democratization of knowledge and rejection of the banking model can only happen if one gives attention to the semantic environment. If one becomes committed to the idea that only the teacher possesses expertise, then the pattern of instruction will inevitably conform to the banking model and systems of domination. The circle of learners, by de-centering the teacher, allowed a different set of relations to develop out of the classroom. This new set of relations allowed a different form of education to form, a democratic form of education that allowed the students to develop and deploy their own expertise.

Collective Empowerment. While the democratic practices that emerged in the circle of learners stood central to the experiences of those who attended Highlander, Horton fundamentally believed that the work of Highlander did not end within the walls of the school. Horton wanted the experiences at the school to lead to collective action. In this sense, the work and learning completed at Highlander tried to move its students beyond individual achievements and individual action. The sense of collective empowerment and action, or the purpose, imbibed the semantic environment at Highlander.

Based on his experiences as a poor young factory worker, Horton learned about the importance of collective action. Horton's experiences led him to believe that most organizations tried to solve problems on an individual basis, not based on the collective good (Horton, 1998, p. 9). Individual action and/or solving problems individually meant that some people would become left out or left behind by an organization. Consequently, when Horton was in college, he started to learn about cooperatives (Horton, 1998, p. 14). Horton's knowledge of cooperatives helped him during his time at Ozone. At one point in time, Horton felt that one way to replicate his experiences at Ozone was to create a utopian community, so he traveled to and studied places like Black Mountain College that were adjacent to the utopian movement. At those utopian communities he found the same type of detachment that he found in individual solutions to problems (Horton, 1998, p. 30). To respond to the injustices of the world did not mean individual action or retreat into an insulated community. Responding to injustice meant acting in the world collectively. Horton (1998) wrote, "I understood that you couldn't act alone, and that you couldn't withdraw into a utopian community. To deal with injustice you had to act in the world. You had to share what you knew" (p. 30). Learning democratic practices and creating knowledge/learning democratically meant nothing if one retreated to individual action or into a community sheltered from the rest of the country. He felt that the democratic practices must move into the public sphere.

Perhaps Highlander's role in helping to establish Citizenship Schools best illustrates how the talk resulting in and from the semantic environment of the circle of learners helped to create and fulfill the purpose of collective empowerment and political action. Esau Jenkins of Johns Island, South Carolina and Septima Clark of Charleston, South Carolina came to a Highlander workshop on the United Nations, hoping the international organization could help combat the problems of racism and segregation in the United States (Horton & Freire, 1990, p. 67). However, a different issue emerged from that workshop; Jenkins and Clark wanted to help black folks living in Johns Island pass literacy tests to enable access to the ballot. While the literacy tests of the segregated South were inherently racist in their nature and deployment, Jenkins and Clark believed practical measures like adult education would improve access to the voting booth. Through discussion, Jenkins, Clark, and others felt that using trained teachers to help black adults would be counterproductive. Horton claimed, "Trained teachers would have to be thinking in terms of what they had learned, methodology, and they would identify illiterate adults with illiterate children" (Horton & Freire, 1990, p. 70). The discussion also led to a creative solution. The group in Johns Island decided that they should use black hair stylists to teach the literacy courses. Using black hair stylists made sense because of their level of education and because black hair stylists could work independently of the white community as they did not rely on whites for income (Horton, 1998, p. 102). Unlike the previous use of outside teachers who the black community mocked – rightly so – for trying to teach adults like children, black hair stylists knew the community and understood the community needs (Horton & Freire, 1990, p. 69). Led by stylist-cum-teacher Bernice Robinson, eighty percent of the students at Johns Island who attended what became known as Citizenship Schools passed the literacy test to gain access to the ballot.

The development and success of the Citizenship Schools illustrates how participants in the circle of learners created change outside of the walls of Highlander, and the circle of learners produced political results and change. What people in the circle of learners did have was an impact outside the walls of Highlander. In both his autobiography and his book with Paulo Freire, Horton was quick to give credit to the Jenkins, Clark, Robinson, and the people in Johns Island. The circle of learners allowed the black community to generate their own knowledge of what would work, but political action and change resulted from the environment found at Highlander. This analysis suggests that political action need not come from a central office directing the actions of the community. Instead, a semantic environment grounded in the purpose that people should develop their own solutions to collective problems allows political action to function as an output of the environment. In this sense, political activists would do well to take the lessons of Postman and Horton to heart by thinking about how they might create a semantic environment that allows democratic knowledge to grow into political action.

Highlander: An Exemplar Semantic Environment for Political Action

In thinking about a semantic environment, Postman encourages us to think about the people, purposes, rules of discourse, and the actual talk within them. The semantic environment of the Highlander Folk School demonstrated for us how talk within a thoughtfully constructed situation can produce political action. Guided by the educational philosophy of Myles Horton, the people at Highlander could meet to discuss collective problems. The rules of discourse fostered by the circle of learners allowed the people to rely on their own experiences to identify problems. In the specific instance of the formation of Citizenship Schools, members of the community could look to creating practical and successful solutions to what might seem like intractable problems. These rules of discourse allowed the people learning at Highlander to talk and produce democratic knowledge, and the democratic knowledge that they created did not simply replicate dominant structures of power. The knowledge produced at Highlander did not retreat from the public sphere; instead, the knowledge produced collective empowerment, political action, and change. Under a different set of circumstances, the ideas produced by the participants at Highlander could have slipped into or be derided as crazy talk or stupid talk. Fortunately, because the people in the situations committed to the circle of learners and its attendant rules of discourse, they could fulfill rational and humane purposes.

This analysis also suggests the importance of thinking about systems in relation to the semantic environment and political action. Certainly, Postman's articulation of context analysis and the semantic environment reflects his commitment to thinking about systems (Strate, 2014, p. 32). Continuing on this, grounding his work in both Postman and sociologist Niklas Luhmann, Strate (2022) claims, "The act of communication is the content inside of the system, while the medium exists on the level of the system itself" (p. 116). Consequently, we can think of the semantic environment as a system that produces a certain form of content. Now, since we commit ourselves to systems thinking, scholars working from the approach of general semantics cannot say that Myles Horton, or any other individual, produced the outcomes of Highlander Folk School. Instead, the collection of the people, purposes, rules of discourse, and talk led to the system output of political action and change. In addition, we can also think of the Highlander Folk School as a medium. In *Teaching as a Subversive Activity*, Postman and Charles Weingartner (1969) encourage educators to think of classrooms and schools as media. Building on the work of McLuhan and the medium is the message, Postman and Weingartner (1969) claim, "[T]*he critical content of any learning experience is the method or process through which the learning occurs*" (p. 19, emphasis in original). Because the Highlander Folk School emphasized producing democratic knowledge, the students did not just learn how to solve collective problems. They learned democracy itself. They learned that democracy is an act of beneficence, not demagoguery – following the demands of a single person. Therefore, the Highlander Folk School illustrates how a medium-system can generate change in the larger system. Democracy learned within the system of the school begets democracy outside the system, and we, as scholars and/or activists in the current moment, can reach this conclusion through context analysis of the semantic environment.

Conclusion

In the preceding sections of this essay, I argued that context analysis of the semantic environment produces knowledge about political communication. Through a case study, political communication scholars and general semanticists *as* political communication scholars learned that the educational philosophy of Myles Horton and the Highlander Folk School helped to create a semantic environment that allowed for political organization and collective empowerment to thrive and gestate. Based on this case study, a context analysis of the semantic environment shows itself as an appropriate method or approach to understanding political communication from the perspective of general semantics, and because of this case study, those working from the tradition of general semantics might think about how our approach to communication might contribute to the larger scholarly corpus on political communication. In addition, those committed to the practice of general semantics might think about how conscientious attention to the semantic environment has value beyond personal improvement or improving interpersonal communication. For those with a working understanding of general semantics, Highlander's circle of learners becomes an approach for thinking about political activism and collective action.

Hopefully, this essay demonstrates that analogizing context analysis to rhetorical criticism proves productive because the four purposes of criticism outlined by Hart (1997) offer ways for the tradition of general semantics to build knowledge grounded in our intellectual tradition. First, the above case on Highlander allows us to document a trend of communication and communicative environments. The semantic environment existed before the publication of *Crazy Talk, Stupid Talk*, but Postman gave a name to it. By documenting semantic environments of the past, the tradition of general semantics can begin to see how those environments shift over time, or we can find environments that run counter to larger environments as a way to document marginalized environments such as the environment of the rural, poor, southern Appalachia left out of previous scholarly discussion. Second, this case study helps us to expand our knowledge of the terms of the semantic environment set laid out by Postman. In particular, Postman suggests that certain physical environments – churches, stadiums, hospitals, etc. – have attendant atmospheres, purposes, or rules of discourse. While designers of these environments might think about how the design might lead to certain communicative outputs, the Highlander Folk School illustrates how interlocutors might actively work to create an atmosphere or rules of discussion. Another understanding that we might gain from this case study is that Myles Horton was an avid reader of printed material (Horton 1998; Horton & Freire, 1990). The print medium and reading instills rational thought (Postman, 1985), so we might tentatively conclude that if people in the semantic environment were informed by the rationality of print then we might see rational outputs from the environment. Third, this case study provides meta-knowledge about the semantic environment. Understanding the semantic environment does not just help us to avoid using crazy or stupid talk; rather understanding the environment can lead to active choices about how some might strive to educate and create political change. Fourth, Horton and the folks at Highlander worked with people and groups left behind by the larger body politic, or they worked with individuals who did not have a traditional education. This case study reminds us that if we want our students to learn about democracy then we need to think about how we invoke democratic practices in the classroom. Rather than thinking about how we can disseminate our knowledge to the students, the semantic environment enacted at Highlander demands that we allow students to frame problems themselves, not to impose our frameworks and demand that students lock into our semantic patterns and modes of discourse.

Finally, beyond these implications, the above case study of the semantic environment of Highlander illustrates the value of their pedagogy to political organizing. Political organizers would do well to look not only at Highlander, but they would do well to look at Highlander and the educational philosophy of Myles Horton from the approach of general semantics. In our current digital media environment, one might presume that the best way to organize is through the utilization of social media. I do not mean to suggest – in this space – that the method of organization through digital and social media is counterproductive, but Highlander serves as a valuable reminder of having people in a physical space together. In that physical space, people can learn about democracy. The moment an organizer employs digital and social media, they succumb to the technological imperative set up by those environments. Digital and social media create a different system and will produce different results. In addition, political organizers who have a background in general semantics must remember that they are not the experts. The circle of learners is set up for people to act on their own expertise. In this sense, political organizers who take lessons from this case study informed by general semantics would do well to allow people to act for themselves rather than impose strict lessons of general semantics. If one sets up an environment where people can trust themselves and work out issues together, then the lessons of trust and collaboration will become far more valuable than teaching any specific precept of general semantics.

Notes

1. There are many texts, all listed in the references that offer a complete history of Highlander (see Adams, 1975; Glen, 1988; Horton, 1998).

References

Adams, F. (1975). *Unearthing seeds of fire: The idea of Highlander*. John F. Blair.

Berelson, B. R., Lazarsfeld, P. F., & McPhee, W. N. (1954). *Voting: A study of opinion formation in a presidential campaign*. University of Chicago Press.

Burgchardt, C. R. (2005). *Readings in rhetorical criticism* (3rd ed.) (C. R. Burgchardt, Ed.). Strata Publishing.

Crick, N. (2020). *The rhetoric of social Movements: Networks, power, and new media*. Routledge. https://doi.org/10.4324/9780429436291

Fisher, W. R. (1984). Narration as a human communication paradigm: The case for moral public argument. *Communication Monographs, 54*(1), 1–22. https://doi.org/10.1080/03637758409390180

Freire, P. (2005). *Pedagogy of the oppressed: 30th anniversary edition* (M. Bergman Ramos, Trans.) Continuum. (Original work published 1975)

Frey, L. A., Botan, C. H., Friedman, P. G., & Kreps, G. L. (1992). *Interpreting communication research: A case study approach*. Prentice Hall.

Frey, L. R., Botan, C. H., & Kreps, G. L. (2000). *Investigating communication: An introduction to research methods* (2nd ed.). Allyn and Bacon.

Gencarelli (Ed.), T. F. (2006). Neil Postman and the rise of media ecology. In C. M. Lum, *Perspectives on culture, technology, and communication: The media ecology tradition* (pp. 201–254). Hampton Press.

Glen, J. M. (1988). *Highlander: No ordinary school 1932–1962*. University of Kentucky Press.

Hart, J. K. (1927). *Light from the north: The Danish Folk Schools and their meaning for America*. Henry Holt.

Hart, R. P. (1997). *Modern rhetorical criticism* (2nd ed.). Allyn and Bacon.

Hayakawa, S. I. (1972). *Language in thought and action* (3rd ed.). Harcourt, Brace, Jovanovich, Inc. (Original work published 1939)

Highlander Research and Education Center. (2023, May 18). *90 years of fighting for justice.* https://highlandercenter.org/our-history-timeline/

Horton, M. (1998). *The long haul: An autobiography* (J. Kohl, & H. Kohl, Eds.). Teachers College Press.

Horton, M., & Freire, P. (1990). *We make the road by walking: Conversations on education and social change* (B. Bell, J. Gaventa, & J. Peters, Eds.). Temple University Press.

Jacobs, D. (2003). *The Myles Horton reader: Education for social change.* The University of Tennessee Press.

Kaid (Eds.), L. L.. (1996). Political communication. In M. B. Salwen, & D. W. Stacks, *An integrated approach to communication theory and research* (pp. 443–458). Lawrence Erlbaum Associates.

Katz, E., & Lazarsfeld, P. F. (1966). *Personal influence: The part played by people in the flow of mass communications.* Transaction Publishers.

Korzybski, A. (1921). *Manhood of humanity: The science and art of human engineering.* E. P. Dutton & Company.

Korzybski, A. (1948). *Science and sanity: An introduction to non-Aristotelian systems and general semantics* (3rd ed.). The International Non-Aristotelian Library Publishing Company. (Original work published 1933)

Lazarsfeld, P. F., Berelson, B., & Gaudet, H. (1944). *The people's choice: How the voter makes up his mind in a presidential campaign.* Duell, Sloan, and Pearce.

McLuhan, M. (2003). *Understanding media: The extensions of man, critical edition* (W. T. Gordon, Ed.). Gingko Press. (Original work published 1964)

Postman, N. (1976). *Crazy talk, stupid talk: How we defeat ourselves by the way we talk and what to do about it.* Delacorte Press.

Postman, N. (1985). *Amusing ourselves to death: Public discourse in the age of show business.* Viking.

Postman, N. (1988). *Conscientious objections: Stirring up trouble about language, technology, and education.* Vintage.

Postman, N. (1999). *Building a bridge to the 18th Century: How the past can improve our future.* Vintage.

Postman, N. (2006). Media ecology education. *Explorations in Media Ecology, 5*(1), 5–14. https://doi.org/10.1386/eme.5.1.5_1

Postman, N., & Weingartner, C. (1969). *Teaching as a subversive activity.* Delacorte Press.

Simons, H. W. (1970). Requirements, problems, and strategies: A theory of persuasion for social movements. *Quarterly Journal of Speech, 56*(1), 1–11. https://doi.org/10.1080/00335637009382977

Stewart, C. J., Smith, C. A., & Denton, R. E. (1984). *Persuasion and social movements.* Waveland Press.

Strate, L. (2014). *Amazing ourselves to death: Neil Postman's brave new world revisited.* Peter Lang.

Strate, L. (2022). *Concerning communication: Epic quests and lyric excursions within the human lifeworld.* Institute of General Semantics.

CHAPTER 11

AMERICAN HATECORE: MUSIC, 'JOKES,' RACE
ROY F. FOX

The voice of Jolson is deep, resonant.

Its swirling waves flood the basement.

The concrete walls and wooden ceiling surrounding the phonograph echo the deep, sumptuous tones.

Then Jolson's voice stops. Right in the middle of the word, "happy." Something is not right. The boy lifts the needle just above the spinning Decca record. He freezes in thought as the album's purple label spins around and around just below his thumb and forefinger.

Now he knows what's not right and clicks the machine off.

He takes three steps toward the full-length mirror he'd taken from upstairs and sets it at a more upright position, alters the glass once more, and checks his reflection again.

He doesn't see the skinny nine year-old body in the glass wearing the white tee shirt and jeans. He doesn't see the dishwater blond crewcut that has grown a little, sticking out here and there, cowlicky. Instead, his leg muscles twitching and pulse rising, he sees only Jolson.

Two small windows provide dim light, so the bare bulb in the middle of the basement helps, since Jolson always insisted that the house lights at the Winter Garden Theater be turned all the way up so he could see every face that rode the crest of every electric syllable he sang.

And they couldn't be disappointed.

He discovers that his face needs fixing. His legs prickle with impatience as he hurries to the shelf at the opposite side of the basement. He picks up the chunk of cork from a Mogen-David wine bottle he'd earlier fished from the trash can.

He lights another match and carefully turns the cork right and left over the flame. He takes the blackened cork back to the mirror and dabs the gritty substance on the white spot showing just above his right eyebrow.

"Almost there," he thinks.

He clicks on the record player and jumps back in front of the mirror. Before the needle reaches the platter's first groove, he asks, "What would ya' like ta hear me sing?" And the throng inside his head all shouts back, "'You Made Me Love You'! 'Toot Toot Tootsie'!"

He jerks his head to the right to signal his bandleader and says," Okay, Lou, you heard the folks, 'Toot Toot Tootsie'!"

At that precise moment, the needle hits the first groove. And to the ensuing accompaniment of Lou Bring's peppery orchestra, the Jolson inside the phonograph and the Jolson inside the basement merge and explode.

For well or ill, this boy was me, circa 1958. For a few years, I was immersed in imaginative play, channeling Al Jolson. I discovered Jolson as he had been portrayed in old movies run on TV, "The Jolson Story" (1946) and "Jolson Sings Again" (1949), both starring Larry Parks. I watched these films each time they were rerun. I saved my allowances and lawn-mowing money to buy every Decca album of Jolson that was available.

I read everything I could about Jolson and memorized his recorded radio show banter with Oscar Levant. Decades earlier, a Black man advised Jolson to try performing in blackface. Jolson discovered that it worked like a "mask" that enabled him to set free *all* his emotions when performing – eyes, facial movements, voice power and range, hand and arm gestures, body movements, his skilled whistling, everything. His

AMERICAN HATECORE: MUSIC, 'JOKES,' RACE   259

blackface unleashed his talent at the same time as those with real black faces continued to be ground down.

How does all this relate to the 2020 killing of Ahmaud Arbery, a jogger who committed no crime? After months, three white men were arrested. To summarize, Arbery, a 25 year-old African American man, went for a jog, as he often did near his home in Brunswick, Georgia. He wore khaki shorts, running shoes, and a white tee shirt. When he reached a neighborhood, Gregory McMichael, 64, was outside working on his boat. He believed he recognized Arbery as the man he had earlier seen entering a nearby house under construction. McMichael told police later that he thought the jogger had been stealing from the site. He had not. McMichael assumed the worst and alerted his son, Travis McMichael. Both white men grabbed their weapons and headed out in their pick-up truck after Arbery. The elder McMichael grabbed his 357 Magnum revolver; Travis fetched his pump shotgun.

Arbery then jogged by William "Roddie" Bryan's house, who was outside. The McMichaels stopped Arbery in front of Bryan's house, who assumed that they had good reason to pursue Arbery, so Bryan started his own pick-up and joined the chase. Next, the two trucks split up, so the McMichaels could circle around and force Arbery between the two vehicles.

Throughout the chase, Arbery tried to run around the trucks to avoid a confrontation. Arbery, now only pursued by Bryan, was run off the road, into a ditch. Bryan's truck also hit Arbery, making a dent (I could find no photo of this dent, only a description of bits of white cotton cloth stuck to the truck's rear end, evidently from Arbery's white tee shirt).

Arbery again tried to escape when he was trapped between the two trucks. Travis McMichael drove the lead truck with his father in the back truck bed. Next, Travis got out of the truck, shotgun in hand, as Arbery tried to flee on the opposite side. Arbery decided to confront Travis, and they briefly grappled for the gun. Arbery is then shot in the chest, then once in his shoulder, and once in his wrist. Arbery tried to flee, took a few steps, collapsed face down on the road, and died ("Ahmaud Arbery Shooting: A Timeline," 2022).

These three men were not arrested until three months later, a delay which numbed the public's concern and allowed a "Let's wait and see" attitude to grow. However, there was another, nearly invisible reason for this patience: Gregory McMichael, his son, Travis, and their neighbor, Roddie Bryan, *appeared* to be so normal, so typical, so average, so harmless. In a sense, they were one-dimensional, like the suburban Texans, Hank and Peggy Hill, of the TV cartoon show, *King of the Hill*. The three suspects were so blah, that many people believed that this jogger must have been up to *something*. What made these mature men instantly throw their settled lives away to chase down and kill a jogger? This led me to speculate on their mental and emotional sources – their cultural histories. What forces nourished these white suburbanites' thinking and behaviors?

The socio-cultural forces of Jolson dominated me through my freshman year in college. My friends, a little puzzled, forgave me because they knew I was an art major. If they teased me, they risked my not answering their questions about the nude model in my drawing class. Jolson soon gave way to Bob Dylan and the Beatles. Until then, it was all Jolson's voice. It sounded like no other I had ever heard – deep, animated, true. The lyrics and music sparkled like crystal. Almost as powerful were the images of Jolson from the two biographical films, the photos, and illustrations of him on album covers, and what I could dig up elsewhere. Another image that I did not consider was that of myself, reflected in the mirror, miming the songs, complete with gestures, sometimes on one knee. Unknowingly I had unleashed the combustible powers of word, image, and music, even though Jolson had been dead for eight years, even at a time when Elvis and Buddy Holly reigned supreme.

When music makes words sing, visuality often reigns. According to Yong, "our species and our culture are so driven by sight that even people who are blind from birth will describe the world using visual words and metaphors.... When scientists describe senses that humans lack altogether, like the ability to detect electric fields, they talk about *images* and *shadows*" (2022, p. 11).

The "electric field" of my Jolson experience can be viewed through the lens of "Dual Coding Theory" (Sadoski & Paivio, 2013), which maintains that we store information in two kinds of codes: imaginal and verbal. Any experience we have is classified as a linguistic event or a nonlinguistic event, depending upon whether a logogen or an imagen is activated. *Logogens* are small bits, such as morphemes, syllables, or words arranged sequentially. An *imagen* is a pictorial representation. Regardless of which is activated first, further processing may occur in either system. As well, stimulation can cause either system to act on its own.

Imagery and perception account for thinking, at least as much as words. When I imitated Jolson as a kid, all pistons – music, words, internal and external images, physical movements – fired at once into the dusty basement air. It was sufficiently challenging to me but also pleasurable. I was not self-conscious, I did not judge my activity, I focused *only* on what I was doing – imitating, pantomiming, singing along – and I lost all sense of time. These experiences were *positive* – uplifting and satisfying. I was "in the zone."

I applied what I absorbed from Jolson – energy, love of words, images, music, focus, spirit – into other positive activities: reading, writing, learning, painting, hiking, and teaching. Eventually, though, I learned that not all image-word processes and outcomes are positive ones. That is, other people and contexts may give rise to what I call "hateflow," a kind of mutation or sub-variant of the more creative, positive mental state described by Csikszentmihalyi and others. One psychologist explains: "The Dark Side of Flow may result from the complete *absorption of self* and narrowing of attention which occurs when in flow-state. With the self gone, we can lose the emotional and behavioral flexibility needed to adjust effectively to our current context. Cognitive flexibility is the challenge" (Hogarth as cited in Csikszentmihalyi,

2013, p. 1). Another psychologist states that "flow can be experienced in anti-social behavior such as the act of killing another person" (Harari, 2008, p. 253).

Hateflow would likely occur during the few minutes of the actual killing. However, we do not know what the killers were thinking during this brief episode. We only have an imperfect video of the event and what the killers told the police who quickly arrived. What we do have is the white defendants' long-nurtured racism, as revealed by the trial investigators who collected songs, videos, texts, phone messages, and Confederate symbols on a license plate and bumper sticker.

First, the three defendants and their lawyers employed misleading and biased language. Second, Travis McMichael, one of the killers, favored a song by country-western musician, Jonny Rebel. A few of Rebel's other songs will provide more context. Third, the McMichaels and their neighbor, "Roddie" Bryan, often used racial slurs.

Travis McMichael's taste in country music opened a door into his cultural identity. An FBI analyst testified that Travis shared a video clip of a young Black boy dancing to the dubbed-in song of "Alabama Nigger," by musician Jonny Rebel (Goggin, 2022, p. 1). In these brief lyrics, Rebel uses the term, "nigger" 11 times.

Figure 1 *Realm of Deutschland: A Tribute to Jonny Rebel* CD cover (2019)

Titles of other Rebel songs include *Alabama Nigger, Leroy the Big Lip Nigger, Move Them Niggers North*, and *Kajun Ku Klux Klan*. Once I finally found the lyrics of his song *Damn, I Wish I Was a Nigger*, it used the word, "nigger" 26 times. Rebel's songs brim over with slurs, such as "jungle bunny," "kinky-top," "black ass," "jig-aboo," and "you-bangy." Black people are portrayed as welfare cheats, recipients of undeserved scholarships and jobs, lazy, illiterate, drug addicts, and prostitutes (*Lyrics Mania*, 2023).

Rebel, whose real name is, C. J. Trahan, has recorded "hatecore" songs for many years (*Lyrics Mania*). "This genre involves the embracing of taboo emotions such as hatred, anger, heartbreak, violent imagery, gore, homicidal tendencies, narcissism, and fear of rejection" (Hatecore, n.d.). Hatecore songs describe African Americans as living in dirt and garbage, drinking too much liquor, visiting and working as prostitutes, being lazy, cheating welfare, begging, sleeping and dozing, sweating, and smelling bad. In addition to the frequent use of "nigger," the narrator and songwriter Rebel refers to Black people as "spooks," "baboons," and "jigaboos" that have "big lips," "banjo lips," "monkey lips," and "Black face and bloodshot eyes / Crooked toes and crooked nose." Some of Rebel's songs call for violence—against the NAACP, African Americans, and Rev. Martin Luther King, Jr. (e.g., "Stick your black head out and I'll blow it!").

The following are a few of Rebel's songs that employ poetic devices to tap into affective or emotional communication and propaganda. All songs are delivered in a stereotypical rural Black dialect.

The song, "In Coon Town" uses repetition, refrain, and end rhymes such as "Up and down the street there ain't nothin' but trash/Nigger girls tryin' to get a Nigger boy's cash". *In Coon Town* is currently available on Spotify.com.

The song, "Nigger Hatin' Me" uses common childhood rhymes, such as "I like sugar, and I like tea / But I don't like niggers… no siree!"; two-valued orientations such as "we vs. you" and "me vs. you" and "I vs. NAACP." It also uses oppositions accomplished by changing the point of view, such as "Jig-A-Boo, jig-a-boo… where are you?" / "I's here in the woodpile… watchin' you"/.

The song "Some Niggers Never Die (They Just Smell That Way)" uses consistent appeals to the bodily senses: Sight – "He wasn't very dark, he was a / high steppin' yeller" and "fat nigger porter." Sound – "I coughed and I gagged all the way home"; Touch – "he was a-chokin' me to death"; Smell – "And up to my nose came a terrible odor / I looked around, tryin' to find something dead"; and Taste – "it was hot and that nigger was-a-sweatin' on my groceries."

Another key issue in the trial occurred when Gregory McMichael's defense lawyer told jurors that Arbery jogged through their neighborhood "in his khaki shorts with no socks to cover his long, dirty toenails." The lawyer, Ms. Hogue obviously assumed that Arbery was not wearing low-cut socks that would not be visible to bystanders. "Black people as dirty" has been a stereotype for eons. It's as if Ms. Hogue had been listening to Jonny Rebel songs on instant replay, which use the same "dirty and smelly" descriptions. Overall, because the phrase "long, dirty toenails" seems to have been calculated, it needs to be unpacked.

This lawyer's comment appears to be based on the autopsy of Arbery's body by the forensic sciences division of the Georgia Bureau of Investigation, which uses that exact language (Waldrop, 2021). Why was this detail necessary? It ignores any shred of context. In other coroner reports, I have not found such specific details, unless they were relevant to the cause of death. And why include the detail "with no socks"? Men around the world, joggers or not, wear shoes without socks. Hogue must have known this, so I view this detail as a clumsy attempt to steer jurors toward Arbery's feet – all so that she could lead jurors to again experience this vile phrase and associate it with Arbery and African American people. If the jury had been comprised of 11 Black people, I doubt that she would have included this phrase. Also, let's assume that Arbery's feet were indeed "dirty." He was reported to have worked at his father's truck wash and landscaping business. Maybe he had been planting a bush or a tree? Or shoveling compost into a hole? It's also true that many people prefer to put off showering until *after* they exercise.

Another issue is that McMichaels and Bryan believed that vigilantism was a good thing. Investigators found this quote on the elder McMichael's phone, posted just four months before the shooting: "A gun in the hand is worth more than the entire police force on the phone" (Goggin, 2022, p. 1). Here, two contrasting images make this maxim memorable, not to mention the fact that he who holds the weapon is hardly comparable – or should *not* be comparable – to the police force.

A more important element of this crime is that the three white defendants often slipped into racial slurs when speaking casually to others, even those they did not know. An FBI analyst said that "bootlip was Bryan's word of choice – a stereotype of a Black person's face." She also noted that Travis described Black people as "savages" and "monkeys" who would "ruin everything." Reacting to a video, Travis said he would "kill that fucking nigger." Travis also sent Jonny Rebel's song, "Always a Nigger," to a friend. Someone had dubbed this song over a video of a black child dancing (McKay, 2022). The "racist digital footprint of these men stretched back to 2013," soon after the 2012 re-election of Barack Obama.

At the trial's end, the judge quoted Gregory McMichael as saying to Arbery, "Stop or I'll blow your fucking head off." Maybe the judge wanted to emphasize the gulf between the defendants' racist language and behavior on the one hand – and, on the other hand, their very "average," even blah, appearance of normalcy, which brings us to another issue in this case that has not been sufficiently addressed, the appearance of the three defendants.

Travis McMichael looks like "Mr. Average American" – balding, bearded, glasses, conservative gray suit and tie, vanilla facial features. All three men look like people you see every day – at the Hy-Vee grocery store, at the Breaktime gas station, or milling about in Wal-Mart. They are *not* like the bug-eyed young men, such as Dylan Roof (who killed Black elderly people in their church) and Adam Lanza (who killed elementary school children in Newtown, Connecticut). In fact, the "alt-right" has worked to portray their followers as everyday people, as non-threatening and "normal" – as "just a growing movement of average American white men who happen to be obsessed with racism, xenophobia, anti-Semitism, and misogyny" (Kelley, 2017).

The textbook example of making groups appear normal (or "dressed to kill"?) is the 2017 "Unite the Right" rally in Charlottesville, Virginia. While chanting, "Jews will not replace us," these clean-cut young men sported beige khaki pants and white polo shirts. Hardly a beard, tattoo, or AK-47 in sight. When I first saw those guys, I did a double take, to make sure they were not headed to a tennis match.

Kelley observes that for those who are unaware of the alt-right's communication tactics, this crowd of choir boys looked harmless, even inviting. The goal here is the recruitment of new blood, the appeal for donations: "The core of marketing is aesthetic," said a leading alt-right organizer, "We need to *look* appealing. We want to hit the average. We want normal people. We must be hip, and we have to be sexy" (2017). The three defendants also wanted to appear "normal" – but only after the police arrived. One GBI agent testified that Bryan, the McMichaels' neighbor, heard Travis McMichaels say, "Fucking Nigger," *after* the shooting and *before* police arrived (Layne, 2020). That is, they spoke their truth when it was just them but censored themselves when the police arrived.

The primary characteristic of much literature, art, film, and propaganda is the image, whether interacting with language, thinking, memory, or actual experience. Arnheim's theory of cognition and Korzybski's "ladder of abstraction" point in the same direction: to persuade or emotionally affect people, get specific, and scale down the ladder of abstraction. Merely "telling" is never enough, as generalities are wispy filaments that waft away in a slight breeze. Instead, "showing" is everything – bone, brick, meat.

When considering the larger issue of how we think, it's not unusual to find cognition experts who value the word above the image, who consider language the province of so-called "higher-order thinking." However, Arnheim and others believe that mature thinkers do not rely solely upon language. Instead, thinking occurs in a visual medium and language, while helping us think, plays only a secondary role, "that we think by means of the things to which language refers – referents that in themselves are not verbal, but perceptual" (1986, p. 138). Many derogatory comments succeed because their imagistic language pierces our "defensive screens." We can see this in some direct quotes from the McMichaels and from Jonny Rebel's songs.

(1) *"Cracker Barrel should be called Nigger Bucket"* (Baker, 2022, p. 11). This is what Travis McMichael told a friend should be the new name of Cracker Barrel, the restaurant named for an old-timey camp snack which elicits images of doughy biscuits and thick sausage gravy. Travis's "Nigger Bucket," however, evokes a pail of pig slop that animals sink their heads into, as they noisily slurp every spot of grease.

(2) *Leroy, the Big Lip Nigger.* This Jonny Rebel song title seems designed to be pronounced as "Lee-Roy," to suggest an uncouth fellow. Zeroing in on his lips, a single characteristic – not just lips, but big lips—seems crafted to make us believe that this anatomical feature is a distasteful, primitive aberration. Also, the consecutive short "i" sounds of "big lip nigger" is a kind of half-rhyme that helps us see the man as well as remember the image.

(3) *"It was hot, and that nigger was-a-sweatin' on my groceries."* This line from another Jonny Rebel song uses the five bodily senses, in this case, odiferous perspiration dripping upon our lettuce and apples. The use of bodily senses, especially smell, helps convince readers of additional flaws of African Americans. This line was likely spawned by another slur from decades ago: "Sweatin' like a nigger at a convention" (Source unknown).

In sum, if we add the defense lawyer's comment about Arbery's "long, dirty toenails," we have an image of African Americans as sloppy and piggish brutes who bury their large lips into a bucket of scraps, while sweating profusely and never bathing. Each of these images indeed elicits other images – and also words that evoke other words – and images. Because they are so richly evocative, they function as a kind of abbreviated narrative or story. These mini tales may not be obvious or immediately apparent, but they lurk just below the text or image (or memories thereof) as shadow plays which can surface at any time, be they in fragmented or detailed form.

Songs like Jonny Rebel's hatecore music is also known as "white power music," now widely distributed by iTunes. Unsurprisingly, "Apple Inc., boasts the sale of more than 21 million songs every week, from a catalog of more than 26 million songs that, as of 2014, included at least 54 racist bands" (Kelley, 2017). A former insider of the white power movement explains how hatecore music helps recruit teenagers and young adults: "We hear the slogan, 'White people awake, save our great race,' twice per chorus, eight times in total through an entire song and, if they play that tape five times a week and just listen to that one song, they're listening to 'White people awake, save our great race' 40 times in that one week, which means 160 times a month and you do the math beyond that" (Kelley, 2017).

In addition to songs, another common vehicle of racism is "humor," as the following "jokes" illustrate (Kennedy, 2002, pp. 6–7). Like songs and other messages, they dehumanize and delegitimize African Americans.

(1) Q: What is the difference between a pothole and a nigger?
A: You'd swerve to avoid a pothole, wouldn't you?

(2) Q: How do you get a nigger to commit suicide?
A: Toss a bucket of KFC into traffic.

(3) Q: How do you stop five niggers from raping a white woman?
A: Throw them a basketball.

A common way to discuss jokes remains the "Sword and Shield" metaphor (Rappaport, 2005). Jokes such as "swords" are intended to insult or harm their targets, whereas jokes as "shields" may challenge and protect against prejudice. In short, racist jokes can be "bad, good, or misunderstood" (Hodson & MacInnis, 2016, p. 1). The "Sword" metaphor seems more common, as jokesters often express a "cavalier" attitude toward racist humor, insisting that they are "just jokes," that everyone else needs to lighten up. This response could be an attempt to cover up bias, to save face with listeners. The most successful way to conceal prejudice occurs when the jokesters accuse those who are uncomfortable with racist language of being "woke."

This term has become an all-purpose excuse for shaming those who express nearly any kind of humane values, an attempt to re-define morality as something trendy and shallow. Note this phrase from a website: "Brain Washed Science Nerd White Woketards" (Stormfront.com).

The word, "nigger," according to Kennedy (2002), has seeped into every aspect of American culture, noting that the number of Internet sites retrieved by using "nigger" as a keyword in his 2001 search was 241 (p. 150). When I did the same search in January 2023, this "protean" word resulted in 23,500,000 sites. As well, many people are unaware that data pools can be instantly flooded with racist language to help ensure that particular terms appear in machine learning searches.

These examples employ very common activities to help ensure they are clear to the largest audience – driving, eating, and watching a game. The Q and A format enables both actions to be brief and informal like neighbors talking over their backyard fence or waiting to use a copy machine. This format welds questions to their answers, forming an instant transition to completion and possible "satisfaction." Questions help guarantee some *participation* on the reader's part. Marketers know that getting consumers to actively participate within a message helps it stick. To boot, when the answer is *unexpected*, then its work is done, nesting within our memory at some level, where it may be recalled.

These examples are also very specific, residing cozily on the bottom rung of the ladder of abstraction. For many Americans, the "bucket of KFC" in #2 easily evokes an image of its red and white striped container.

Due to its strong verb, "toss," we may even visualize it tumbling out of a car window into heavy traffic, just as the verbs "swerve" and "throw" aid in our visualizing the scene. Potholes and basketballs are likewise concrete, with #3 relying on a common criticism, however unfortunate, of American basketball teams. The Australian Human Rights Commission provides a more distanced view of America's online life: "In many cases the information on the sites created outside of Australia is even more extreme than that contained on sites created locally. *This is particularly the case for sites created in America, where the First Amendment protects freedom of speech to the extent that racial vilification is lawful*" ("Examples of Racist Material," 2002).

Yes, here in the United States, racial vilification is lawful – and so common that we often fail to see its basic characteristics. The jokes noted here are definite assertions; the question-and-answer format leaves no room for discussion, which would demand an open-ended question, or no question at all. Closed-ended epithets are well suited for an authoritarian mindset.

Finally, if we are talking with others, and one person tells a racist joke, there exists a kind of *assumption* or "presupposition" on the speaker's part. If nobody in the group objects to the slur, it "slips into the common ground and changes what the participants… take everyone else to assume" (Cepollaro, 2017, pp. 5–7). When we quietly accept slurs, the speaker assumes we all share this negative view. Hovering there, unobjected to, it gains strength and more easily spreads. Therefore, if we object to a slur, it might be more productive to avoid arguing against the speaker's specific statement (e.g., that this person is filthy). Instead, we should reject the assumption that *all* the targeted people are filthy.

Allness orientations, language lodged low on the ladder of abstraction, internal and external imagery, and its interactions with words and music – all affect our internal maps and often lead us into making (among other issues) unwarranted assumptions – that wily trickster of general semantics. Being aware of these relationships and communicating about them is the best revenge. The white men pursuing Arbery may have misread true maps of actual reality. One true map was that Ahmaud was *not* stealing from the construction site. The police told Gregory McMichael this before the killing, which was verified by cameras. The three men acted upon a "larger" false map if they assumed Arbery was a thief because of his skin color. Allness indeed.

The three men likewise may have acted on a false map in their belief that Roddie Bryan's video would exonerate them, which it did not. Even though they were clearly the aggressors who grabbed their guns, pursued Arbery, and shot him dead, they evidently believed that Ahmaud was the aggressor because *he* attacked *them*. They must have believed that the video would reveal Arbery as the true aggressor. However, they again did not consider the entire context, the larger map that was revealed in court. One's map and memory can become distorted or "ruptured" during intense, quicksilver violence, a characteristic of hot symbolic environments. Nonetheless, the law does not and should not recognize this, unless a more complete context shows the aggressor feared for his own life. The jury did not believe that Gregory and Travis McMichael and Roddie Bryan feared for their lives. They were all sentenced to life in prison for state and federal convictions for "interference with rights" (a hate crime) and attempted kidnapping. The McMichaels have no chance for parole, but Bryan eventually does. We can only hope that this case is studied in law schools.

Ahmaud Arbery, too, may have acted upon a false map when he chose to jog in a white neighborhood, even though he had every legal right to do so. Arbery had an encounter with white police officers three years before his death, which *may* have influenced his decision to jog in a white neighborhood. At that time, a video from an officer's bodycam showed him talking to Arbery, who stood quietly near his own car as the officer called in for information from Arbery's driver's license (Burke, 2020). His car appeared to be parked in a field off the road. Arbery told the officer it was his day off from working six days a week, and that he was just trying to "chill." After several minutes Arbery began asking questions and became agitated, and, according to the officer, "jumpy," so the officer called in for backup. A second officer arrived and attempted to tase Arbery, but the device failed. Arbery was then ordered to get onto his knees. He obliged and calmed down. The first officer again assured Arbery that he (the officer) was not trying to "ruin" his day off and that he was trying to figure out what was going on. The officer repeated this explanation many times throughout their brief encounter.

This officer further diffuses the agitated Arbery by constantly talking to him, explaining his reasons for stopping Arbery because of drug activity in the area and the fact that his car's location was a bit unusual, adding that Arbery's irritability made him nervous. Overall, the first officer effectively neutralizes the situation by maintaining a constant dialogue, patiently explaining his own actions to Arbery. The officer's internal map is accurately aligned with reality. It's difficult to discern how this may have affected Arbery's internal map – his decision about where to jog. Because of the initial officer's work in "talking Arbery down," Arbery may have gained confidence that white men were decent people and he had little to fear from them.

Or, he could have become more distrustful of them, possibly motivating him to jog in a white neighborhood anyway, because that was his legal right. A major factor in our constructing of maps is our reliance upon outdated maps – even when they fail us time and again (Johnson, 1946).

So, too, do our adult life experiences heavily influence our internal maps. Gregory McMichaels worked in law enforcement for several years. The gun he grabbed was his work revolver. The elder McMichael's map could have been saturated with all things criminal for so long, that he would not or could not align it with the current territory. His son, Travis, appeared to have changed jobs. He stated to a co-worker that he "loved his new job because zero niggers work with me" (Goggin, 2022). This recent change could have created a positive shift in his map, or it could have reinforced his old map. In both cases, their maps could have alternated back and forth, with one map gaining or losing its dominant position. Unfortunately, the larger context, though, points to their reliance upon outdated maps.

As a 10 year-old, I knew nothing about "internal maps" – only that I was seized by an unusual voice I'd never heard before. I knew that Jolson had often appeared in "blackface." For decades Jolson has often been labeled as a "racist." But he also had African American friends and openly associated with them. In the 1930s, Black musicians Noble Sissle and Eubie Blake were refused service at a restaurant in Connecticut. Upon hearing about it, Jolson took them to dinner and promised them that he would "punch anyone in the nose who tried to kick us out" (Gioia, 2000, p. 1).

As well, in 1925, Jolson secured backing for a play titled, "Appearances," written by a Black bellhop. It twice ran on Broadway and went on tour. It was a courtroom drama about Blacks "passing" for whites. It was the first Broadway play to hire black actors who interacted with white actors, so Jolson broke the tradition of hiring whites to play black roles (Suggs, 2000). By many accounts, Jolson was an egomaniac (see his tombstone). Was he also racist? I don't think so. I understand, though, why people would think that, but it's harder to apply that label when we consider his actions within the larger context of his life and attitude in that bygone era.

What makes our current environment so unnervingly hellish is that racism can breed indefinitely in the shadows, seemingly invisible, until a flare-up reveals a pattern. One pattern—often hard to discern – is that created by the elusive "Trickster" of language and thought – in our habit of making *unwarranted assumptions*, whether pro- or anti-racist ideology. Especially in new situations, a rational response demands that some time should pass. We also need "cognitive flexibility" to adjust to our rapidly changing internal and external maps of reality, guides that can change on a dime.

Ahmaud Arbery's execution has simultaneously clarified and reminded us of another American pattern – that prejudice can arise from the calmest suburban homes where the most average, harmless looking people dwell, and then mutate in the maze of print and media symbols that saturate our information-gone-berserk landscape. Then, the cycle begins anew.

Language, imagery, race, violence, and symbols are necessarily baked into our American Pie. These issues reach deeply into nationalism, history, materialism, culture, learning and teaching, government, economics, poverty, identity, environment, and others. No easy answers exist here – just that we need to keep reminding ourselves of how fragmented our society is, which makes defining problems elusive, not to mention solving them. Today, neither sports nor religion nor myth provide a set of guidelines to which we can adhere during our time on this wild earth. Nor do we have a single language or body of literature to fill this void. Most of us no longer live within a community where almost everyone believes the same thing.

Without stable forces of social cohesion and psychic unity, what fills this yawning gap? We buy stuff. We entertain ourselves. We worship technology. We eat. We often do all of these at once. We also learn to love others – and to hate "others." And we kill them.

I only know that right now, we are teetering upon an exquisitely fine edge, seldom looking down to help us find a balance – a balance between people controlling meaning – and meaning controlling people. The former nourishes unity and agency; the latter fuels mobs that feast on ignorance. *

*From "Dover Beach" by Matthew Arnold (1851).

References

Arbery, A. (2022, August 8). Shooting: A timeline of the case. *The New York Times*. https://www.nytimes.com/article/ahmaud-arbery-timeline.html?smid=url-share

Arnheim, R. (1986). *New essays on the psychology of art*. University of California Press.

Baker, L. (2022, February 17). Racist, violent evidence presented in federal trial against Ahmaud Arbery's killers. *Health News Florida.* https://health.wusf.usf.edu/2022-02-16/racist-violent-evidence-presented-in-federal-trial-against-ahmaudarberys-killers

Burke, M. (2020, May 19). Ahmaud Arbery: A 2017 video shows police trying to use stun gun on him. *NBC News.* https://www.nbcnews.com/news/us-news/ahmaudarbery-2017-video-shows-police-trying-use-stun-gun-n1210326

Cepollaro, B. (2017, April 1). Slurs as the shortcut of discrimination. *Rivista Di Estetica.* https://journals.openedition.org/estetica/2063

Csikszentmihalyi, M. (2013). *Creativity: Flow and the psychology of discovery and invention.* HarperCollins.

Examples of racist material on the internet. (2002, October). *The Australian Human Rights Commission,* https://humanrights.gov.au/our-work/publications/examplesracist-material-internet

Gioia, T. (2000, October 22). Al Jolson: The megastar long buried under a layer of blackface. *The New York Times.* https://Jolson.org/Man/Racism/Nyt.html

Goggin, K. (2022, February 16). Racist social media posts, text messages revealed during hate crimes trial against Arbery's killers. *Courthouse News Service.* https://www.courthousenews.com/racist-social-media-posts-text-messages-revealedduring-hate-crimes-trial-against-arberys-killers/

Harari, Y. N. (2008). Combat flow: Military, political, and ethical dimensions of subjective well-being in war. *Review of General Psychology, 12*(3), 253–264.

Hatecore. (n.d). *Aesthetics fandom.* https://aesthetics.fandom.com/wiki/Hatecore

Hodson, G., & MacInnis, C. C. (2016). Derogating humor as a delegitimization strategy in intergroup contexts. *Translational Issues in Psychological Science, 2*(1), 63–74.

Johnson, W. (1946). *People in quandaries: The semantics of personal adjustment.* Harper and Row.

Jolson Sings Again, created by Henry Levin, performed by Larry Parks, Columbia Pictures, 1949.

The Jolson Story, created by Alfred E. Green, performed by Larry Parks, Columbia Pictures, 1946.

Kelley, B. J. (2017, October 9). The alt-right's new soundtrack of hate. *Southern Poverty Law Center.* https://www.splcenter.org/hatewatch/2017/10/09/alt-right%E2%80%99snew-soundtrack-hate

Kennedy, R. (2002). *Nigger: The strange career of a troublesome word.* Vintage Books.

Layne, N. (2020, June 4). White defendant used racial slur after shooting Ahmaud Arbery, investigator testifies. *Reuters.* https://www.reuters.com/article/us-usashooting-georgia-slur-idUSKBN23B2H4

Lyrics Mania. Website. https://www.lyricsmania.com./jonny_rebel_lyrics.html

Mckay, R. (2022, February 22). Prosecution, defense rest cases in Arbery hate crimes trial. *Reuters.* https://www.reuters.com/world/us/prosecution-defense-rest-casesarbery-hate-crimes-trial-2022-02-19/

Rappaport, L. (2005). *Punchlines: The case for racial, ethnic, and gender humor.* Praeger.

Realm of Deutschland: A Tribute to Jonny Rebel. (2019). Wotan Records, https://www.discogs.com/release/13979772-Various-Realm-Of-Deutschland-Tribute-To-Jonny-Rebel

Sadoski, M., & Paivio, A. (2013). *Imagery and text: A dual coding theory of reading and writing* (2nd ed.). Routledge.

Stormfront. https://www.stormfront.org/forum/index.php. Accessed March 1, 2023.

Suggs, J. C. (2000, November 5). Al Jolson; Hidden ironies. Section 2. *The New York Times.* https://www.nytimes.com/2000/11/05/theater/l-al-jolson-hidden-ironies-966215.html?searchResultPosition=1

Waldrop, T. (2021, November 24). Defense lawyer prompts outrage for bringing up Ahmaud Arbery's toenails in closing arguments. *CNN.* https://www.cnn.com/2021/11/22/us/ahmaud-arbery-trial-toenails-comment-outrage/index.html.

Yong, E. (2022). *An immense world: How animal senses reveal the hidden realms around us.* Random House.

CHAPTER 12

GREEN LIGHT: THE FACT THAT POLITICAL CANDIDATES MAY STRETCH THE TRUTH IN BROADCAST TELEVISION ADVERTISEMENTS

JEFFERSON SPURLOCK

In the 1950s, FBI informant and author Harvey Matusow served 44 months in prison after his conviction of lying to Congress. "He had falsely named 200 people as Communists or Communist sympathizers" (Shabad, 2018, p. 1). In the 1970s, President Richard Nixon's White House Chief of Staff H. R. Haldeman served 19 months in prison after being convicted of conspiracy, obstruction of justice, and perjury related to testimony he gave in connection with his role in the Watergate scandal (Shabad, 2018). In 1981, a Los Angeles jury ordered *The National Enquirer* to pay actress/comedienne Carol Burnett $1.6 million when it allegedly fabricated an article "depicting her [Burnett] as intoxicated at a Washington restaurant with Secretary of State Henry Kissinger" (Lindsey, 1981, p. 1).

These are examples of people in the public eye. A writer, a celebrity, and a White House employee. Two served prison time for lying; one sued a publication that lied and was awarded money. But none of these people were running for political office. So, what does this mean? Do candidates for public office have the green light to make false claims or statements in broadcast television advertisements? The answer is yes. Thomas (2016) writes: "Lying in politics is much a part of history as it is part of just about any political campaign. And the sad reality is it's perfectly legal" (p. 1). Tom Wheeler, former Chairman of the Federal Communications Commission under President Barack Obama, adds, "Unfortunately, you're [political candidates] allowed to lie" (Montanaro, 2022, p. 1).

Political Ads versus Non-political Ads

Advertising is a multi-billion dollar a year industry. Everything from toothpaste to used cars to skin care products are displayed on television daily. Montini (2020) insists, "Consumers are protected by truth in advertising laws administered by the Federal Trade Commission (FTC). The commission has the authority to do everything from fining a company to pulling the ads. It's different with political ads. While the Federal Election Commission requires TV and radio ads to provide information about who produced them, what is said in those ads has been deemed protected speech, even if it's not true" (p. 1).

For example, herbal supplement Airborne was ordered to pay $23.3 million in fines after its advertisement allegedly claimed that the product "helped ward off harmful bacteria and germs, preventing everyday ailments like the flu and common cold. There were no studies to support Airborne's effectiveness that met scientific standards" (Weinmann & Bhasin, 2011, p. 4). In another case, a New Jersey judge called Pennzoil's ads "misleading and repugnant" when they allegedly said their motor oil performed better than their competitors' products (Weinmann & Bhasin).

But when it comes to broadcast television ads involving candidates running for political office, it's a different matter. Bergmann (2019) contends: "The Supreme Court has ruled that such ads are protected by the First Amendment. In other words, the Constitution protects the right of political candidates to lie to their heart's content. The only risk to candidates is blowback from voters turned off by the half-truths and attacks in their campaign ads" (p. 1). For example, Katie Hobbs, the 2022 Democratic nominee for governor in Arizona, ran a TV ad lashing out at her Republican opponent, Kari Lake, calling her "not just radical. She's dangerous" (Doudna, 2022). Also in 2022, incumbent Republican Alabama Governor Kay Ivey appeared in her broadcast television ad saying, "Blue state liberals stole the election from President Trump" (Paepcke, 2022). In the race for the 2022 GOP nominee for governor in Idaho, incumbent Brad Little's television ads labeled his challenger Janice McGeachin "bad for Idaho and wrong for governor," while McGeachin struck back in her ad by calling Little a "RINO, a Republican in Name Only" (Russell, 2022, p. A1).

What do the Voters Think?

While political candidates hope that their rhetoric and messages will sway people to elect them to office, they wish that voters will believe what they are conveying in their broadcast ads, even if the truth has been stretched. But do all voters know that the First Amendment allows candidates to say whatever they wish in their broadcast television ads and that the TV stations cannot do anything about it? Probably not. That is why candidates say what they wish. As Thomas (2016) puts it: "Fact checking, in other words, is up to the voter, not the courts. If you think a politician is lying to you, then you are free not to vote for that politician" (p. 1).

References

Bergmann, R. (2019, October 21). First amendment protects right to lie, distort. *Asbury Park Press.* https://www.app.com/story/opinion/columnists/2019/10/21/politicalads-nj-first-amendment-protects-right-lie-distort/4015118002/

Doudna, M. (2022, August 9). Verify: Does, Kari, Lake, and want to legalize rocket launchers? *KPNX 12 News*. https://www.youtube.com/watch?v=ZheqtchdWYU

Lindsey, R. (1981, March 27). Carol Burnett given $1.6 million in suit against *National Enquirer*. *The New York Times*. https://www.nytimes.com/1981/03/27/us/carol-burnettgiven-1.6-million-in-suit-against-national-enquirer.html

Montanaro, D. (2022, March 17). The truth in political advertising: 'You're allowed to lie.' *National Public Radio*. https://www.npr.org/2022/03/17/1087047638/the-truthin-political-advertising-youre-allowed-to-lie

Montini, E. J. (2020, September 11). Yes, Vicki, politicians can lie in campaign ads. *Arizona Republic*. https://www.azcentral.com/story/opinion/op-ed/ej-ontini/2020/09/11/political-ads-can-lie-truth-advertising-not-apply/3464109001/

Paepcke, J. (2022, April 11). Governor Ivey defends 'stolen election' claim in campaign ad. *WVTM 13 News*. https://www.youtube.com/watch?v=FHbzgbhdhCk

Russell, B. Z. (2022, May 12). Gloves come off: Final ads of campaigns include attacks. *Idaho Press*, A1, A6.

Shabad, R. (2018, November 29). Five people who lied to Congress, and what happened to them. *NBC News*. https://www.nbcnews.com/politics/congress/5-people-who-liedcongress-what-happened-them-n941936

Thomas, G. (2016, August 12). Why is it legal for politicians to lie? *AvvoStories*. https://stories.avvo.com/news/politics/legal-politicians-lie.html

Weinmann, K., & Bhasin, K. (2011, September 16). Fourteen false advertising scandals that cost brands millions. *Insider*. https://www.businessinsider.com/falseadvertising-scandals-2011-9

ABOUT THE CONTRIBUTORS

Corey Anton (Ph.D., Purdue University) is Professor of Communication Studies at Grand Valley State University and a Fellow of the International Communicology Institute. He is author of *Selfhood and Authenticity* (2001, SUNY Press), *Sources of Significance: Worldly Rejuvenation and Neo-Stoic Heroism* (2010, Purdue University Press), *Communication Uncovered: General Semantics and Media Ecology* (2010, IGS Press), *How Non-being Haunts Being: On Possibilities, Morality, and Death Acceptance* (2020, Fairleigh Dickinson University Press), and *A.EYE CANDY: A Museum of Imaginary Robots and Other Digital Delights* (2023, IGS Press). He is the editor of *Valuation and Media Ecology: Ethics, Morals, and Laws* (2010, Hampton Press), the co-editor, with Lance Strate, of the collection *Korzybski And…* (2012, IGS Press), and co-editor, with Robert K. Logan and Lance Strate, of the collection, *Taking Up McLuhan's Cause* (2017, Intellect Publishing). A past Editor of the journal *Explorations in Media Ecology* and Past President of the Media Ecology Association, Anton currently serves as Vice President of the Institute of General Semantics, and on the editorial boards of *The Atlantic Journal of Communication, ETC, New Explorations,* and *Explorations in Media Ecology.*

Eva Berger (Ph.D., New York University) teaches media studies at the COMAS College in Israel where she has also served as Dean. She is the Secretary and a member of the Board of Trustees of the Institute of General Semantics. She is the author of multiple articles and books. Her latest is *Context Blindness: Digital Technology and the Next Stage of Human Evolution* for which she received The Erving Goffman Award for Outstanding Scholarship in the Ecology of Social Interaction from the Media Ecology Association in 2023. She is also the 2024 recipient of the J. Talbot Winchell Award for Indispensable Contributions, Accomplishments and Timebinding Efforts in Service to the Field of General Semantics.

Joshua Clements is a doctoral student and adjunct instructor at Duquesne University. He also serves as the tutoring services coordinator at Abraham Baldwin Agricultural College. His research interests are broad but generally involve the convergence of education, media ecology, and general semantics.

Susan Drucker (Juris Doctor, St. John's University) is a Distinguished Professor of Journalism in the Department of Journalism/Media Studies, School of Communication, Hofstra University. She is an attorney, and Treasurer of the Urban Communication Foundation. She is the author and editor/co-editor of 13 books and over 200 articles and book chapters including the *Urban Communication Reader* (Volumes 1, 2, & 3), *Voices in the Street: Gender, Media and Public Space,* and *Urban Communication Regulations: Communication Freedoms and Limits.* Her work examines the relationship between media technology and human factors, particularly as viewed from a legal perspective.

Etai Eshet is a graduate student in Science, Technology, and Digital Culture at The Cohn Institute for the History and Philosophy of Science and Ideas at Tel Aviv University. He has a B.A. in media studies. His professional experience includes years in social media management, both commercial and news media. Currently, he is a writer on Internet culture for multiple websites.

ABOUT THE CONTRIBUTORS

Roy F. Fox is Professor Emeritus and former Chair of the Department of Learning, Teaching, and Curriculum at the University of Missouri. He formerly served as Director of Writing at Boise State University. His long-time work in verbal and visual literacy has produced numerous publications, ranging from research articles to book chapters, editorials, and poetry. His several books include *Harvesting Minds: How TV Commercials Control Kids; MediaSpeak: Three American Voices; Images in Language, Media, and Mind;* and *Facing the Sky: Composing through Trauma in Word and Image.* In 2016, he served as a Fulbright Scholar to Ireland. He continues his life-long habit of painting and drawing.

Thom Gencarelli (Ph.D., New York University) is Professor of Communication, Sound & Media Arts at Manhattan University in Riverdale, New York. He is a Past President of the Media Ecology Association, the New York State Communication Association, and the New Jersey Communication Association, Treasurer and member of the Board of Trustees of the Institute of General Semantics, and the current Editor of the IGS journal *ETC: A Review of General Semantics.* He is co-editor (with Brian Cogan) of *Baby Boomers and Popular Culture: An Inquiry into America's Most Powerful Generation* and author of the forthcoming *Searching for the Right Notes: Essays on Media, Music, and Meaning.* He is a recipient of multiple awards including, in 2023, the J. Talbott Winchell Award for Outstanding Contributions and Service to the Cause of General Semantics from the IGS. He is also a songwriter, musician, and producer, and has released four albums with his ensemble bluerace: *World is Ready* (2009), *Beautiful Sky* (2013), *Mistral* (2019), and *INDYeGO* (2024).

Gary Gumpert (Ph.D, Wayne State University) is Emeritus Professor of Communication at Queens College of the City University of New York and was one of the founders of the Urban Communication Foundation, of which he is President Emeritus and remains on the Board. His creative career as a television director and his academic career as a scholar span over 60 years. He is series editor of the Urban

Communication Series for Peter Lang Publishing, the co-editor of several books on urban public space dealing with issues of gender, immigration, and sports, and co-editor of *The Urban Communication Reader* Volume 1. His research focuses on the impact of communication technology upon social and urban space.

Martin H. Levinson (Ph.D., New York University) is a Past President of the Institute of General Semantics, Book Review Editor for *ETC: A Review of General Semantics*, and a contributing editor to *The Satirist, A Critical Online Journal*. He has published dozens of articles and six books on GS subjects. He is currently a faculty member with the Osher Lifelong Learning Institute at Stony Brook University, a teacher for the United Federation of Teachers' Si Beagle Learning Program, and a lecturer on topics of historical interest for schools and public libraries.

Jermaine Martinez (Ph.D., University of Illinois Urbana Champaign) is an Associate Teaching Professor at Northern Arizona University and recipient of the Sanford I. Berman Award for Excellence in Teaching General Semantics.

Christopher W. Mayer is an independent scholar and the founder of Woodlock House Family Capital, a private investment partnership based in Mount Airy, MD. He is a member of the Board of Trustees of the Institute of General Semantics, and author of *How Do You Know?*, which received the S. I. Hayakawa Book Award from the Institute of General Semantics in 2019, and the more recent *Dear Fellow Timebinder: Letters on General Semantics*.

Ryan McCullough (Ph.D., Duquesne University) is a Professor of communication and Chair of the Department of Media and Visual Arts at West Liberty University, a small public institution located in West Liberty, WV. He teaches courses in media theory, media law and ethics, social media, public relations, and public speaking. His most recent research has appeared in *Explorations in Media Ecology* and *Communication Research Trends*. He currently serves as the Executive Council Representative for the Kenneth Burke Interest Group at the Eastern Communication Association and as the Media Ecology Association's liaison to ECA.

Jefferson Spurlock (Ph.D., University of Southern Mississippi) is the current Associate Chair of Integrated Media in the Department of Media at Boise State University. A former professional radio and television journalist, Dr. Spurlock also served as the Director of the Hall School of Journalism and Communication at Troy University where he holds the rank of Professor Emeritus.

Lance Strate (Ph.D., New York University) is a Professor of Communication and Media Studies at Fordham University; President, Trustee, and former Executive Director of the Institute of General Semantics; Secretary and Past President of the New York Society for General Semantics; a founder and Past President of the Media Ecology Association; and Past President of the New York State Communication Association. He is the author of eleven books, including *Media Ecology: An Approach to Understanding the Human Condition*; *Diatribal Writes of Passage in a World of Wintertextuality*; *Concerning Communication: Epic Quests and Lyric Excursions Within the Human Lifeworld*; *First Letter of My Alphabet*; and, most recently, *Not A, Not Be, &c*.

INDEX

Abrams, Floyd: 165, 169
Abstraction: 6, 15, 20, 44, 59, 70, 71–73, 97, 108–110, 112, 115–116, 185, 186, 216,
 –Levels of Abstraction: 15, 59, 66, 187, 205, 266, 270
 –Orders of Abstraction: 205, 219
Abstractions: 10, 11, 15, 24, 71, 73, 97, 108, 110–112, 113, 115, 117
Administrative state: 48–49, 96
Airborne: 278
Agonism: 195, 217–221
Ailes, Roger: 127, 132
Alexander the Great: 50, 52
Allness: 140, 182, 270–271
Allness attitudes: 139–140, 182, 187
Alpha Fold: 31
Alphabetic Literacy: 73–74
Alphabetic Writing: 72,
American Revolution: 53
Amusing Ourselves to Death: 43, 81

Antagonism: 7, 178, 195, 200–201, 204–205, 207, 209, 213, 215, 218–220
Antisemitism: 147
Anton, Corey: xv, 16, 219
Appalachia: 237–238, 241, 252
Arab Spring: 55, 159, 197
Arendt, Hannah: 85–86, 88–89, 93, 101
Argentina: 114, 174
Aristotelian: 54, 55, 64, 74, 79, 183, 205
 –Biology: 50
 –Logic: 49, 53, 55, 61, 73, 84
 –Politics: 50, 61, 80
Arnheim, Rudolf: 266–267
Arnold, Matthew: 274
Assumption: 68, 133, 270
Assumptions: 6, 12–13, 18, 110, 112, 215, 273

Baker, Liz: 267
Beavin-Bavelas, Janet: 134
Berger, Eva: xi, 206, 212

Biden, Joseph: 143, 154, 162
Bill of Rights: 124
Bois, Samuel: 5
Bolshevik Revolution: 46
Boston Globe, The: 207,
Boorstin, Daniel: 88, 125, 226
Bragg, Alvin: 166
Brandenburg test: 164–165
Brandenburg v. Ohio: 164
Bridgman, P. W.: 143
Building a Bridge to the Eighteenth Century: 83
Burke, Minyvonne: 271
Burnett, Carol: 277

Cancel culture: 57, 206–208
Capital: 21–22, 26, 37, 116,
Capitalism: 38, 47, 63, 123, 239
Capitalist: 21, 24, 47, 116,
Cassirer, Ernst: 20
Carter, Jimmy: 83, 126
Cepollaro, Bianca: 270
Ceteris Paribus: 112
Chase, Stuart: 45, 47
Chemistry-binding: 20
Civil Rights: 91, 121, 216
—Civil Rights Act: 121
—Civil Rights Movement: 239–241
Civil War: xv, xvi, xvii, 54, 121, 124, 161
Clinton, Bill: 128
CNN (Cable News Network): 127
Codified law: 63, 71, 77
Code of Hammurabi: 60, 72

Communications Act of 1934, The: 126
Consciousness of Abstracting: 6, 15, 220
Conspiracy: 132, 155–157, 161–163, 168, 176, 185, 189, 277
—Theories: 7, 173–177, 180–183, 187
Conspiratorial thinking: 173–179, 182, 184–185, 187
Content analysis: 228–231
Context analysis: 226–227, 229–233, 235, 241, 250–252
Context blindness: 206
CPI (consumer price index): 110–115
Conversational avoidance: 208, 210, 212–213, 216–218
Crazy Talk, Stupid Talk: 230, 234, 252
Critical thinking: 174–175, 184
Csikszentmihalyi, Mihaly: 261

Dating: 5–6, 111, 143, 184–185, 220
Declaration of Independence: 62, 124, 177
de Saint-Exupery, Antoine: 37–38
Dehaene, Stanislas: 29
Delayed evaluation: 138–139
Democracy: 7, 43–45, 47, 49, 52–57, 59–63, 72, 76, 78–81, 84, 86–87, 89–90, 92, 94–98, 100–102, 120, 125, 129, 132–134, 156, 158, 173–175,

177, 179, 188–189, 196–197, 200, 207, 218, 251, 251
Democratic Party: 121
Democratic-Republicans: 120–121
Derrida, Jacques: 201, 204
Dewey, John: 20, 29
Disagreement: 199–200, 205, 208, 210, 212–214, 219, 221
Dixiecrats: 121
Double bind of democracy: 84, 89
Dual coding theory: 261

Economy: 21, 28, 107–109, 113, 115
Einstein, Albert: 47, 49
Eisenstein, Elizabeth: 75, 78
Either/or thinking: 5, 14–17, 122–123, 134
Either-or thinking: 128, 139
Elementalism: 6, 16, 140
End of Education, The: 83, 91, 173
Enlightenment, the, or Age of Reason: 44, 46, 53–54, 66, 76, 80, 86, 92
Epistemology: 45, 98, 178, 188
Etc.: 6, 141, 184–185, 200
Extensional: 6, 9, 11–14, 17, 21–23, 28, 38, 76, 79, 183–184, 200, 220–221
–Extensional theory of happiness: 37

Facebook: 1, 38, 132, 148
Fairness Doctrine: 126–127

Federal Reserve: 112–113
Federalist Papers: 120
Federalist Party: 120
First Amendment: 124, 131, 164–165, 167, 270, 279
First World War: 45–46, 225
Flash mobs: 7, 158–161, 163–165, 168
Flow: 261–262
Fourth Estate: 79, 124,
Fox News Channel, The: 127
Freedom Caucus: 128
French Revolution: 54
Freire, Paolo: 236, 241–242, 244–246, 248–249, 252

Gabor, Dennis: 37
Georgia Bureau of Investigation: 264
Goffman, Erving: 282
Great Depression: 47, 54, 126, 238, 241
Green Party:
Gutenberg, Johannes: 124

Habermas, Jurgen: 100, 197
Haldeman, H. R.: 277
Hamas: 147–151
Happiness formula: 138
Harari, Yuval: 16, 262
Hashtag activism: 148, 150–151
Hatecore: 263, 268
Hateflow: 261–262
Hayakawa, S. I.: 5, 45, 228
Herder, Johann Gottfried: 29

Highlander Folk School: 226–227, 235–236, 238–239, 241, 249–252
Hobbs, Katie: 279
Hodson, Gordon: 269
Horton, Myles: 226–227, 235–253
Hyphens: 6

I.F.D. (Idealization – Frustration – Demoralization): 206, 219
Identity politics: 206, 209, 216–217
Illiberal democracy: 54, 90
Incitement: 156–157, 160, 162–166, 168
Indexing: 5–6, 79, 140, 184–185, 220
Infantilism: 195, 200, 204–206, 208, 210, 212, 216–217
Inflation: 34, 107, 110–116
Intensional: 4–5, 9–14, 76, 183
Internal and external: 261, 270, 273
Intersectionality: 149
Is of identity: 6, 141, 181, 210
Isegoria: 60
Isonomia: 60
Israeli-Palestinian conflict: 149
Ivey, Kay: 279

Jackson, Don: 62, 134
Jefferson, Thomas: 53, 62, 120
Johnson, Kenneth G.: 142–144
Johnson, Wendell: 5, 74, 99, 205, 272
Journalism: 124
Judeo-Christian values: 96

Kahneman, Daniel: 180, 182
Kelley, Brendan: 266, 268
Kennedy, John F.: 83
Kennedy, Randall: 268–269
Kinetic use-value: 22, 26–30, 32, 34–35, 39
Klapp, Orin: 58
Kodish, Bruce: xvi, 2
Korzybski, Alfred: xvi, 5, 13–22, 24–27, 29, 37, 45–49, 59, 61–62, 66–69, 74, 79, 91, 95, 98, 107–113, 115–117, 138, 141, 175, 179–187, 189, 195–196, 198, 201–206, 208, 210–217, 219–220, 225
Korzybski: A biography: xvi
Korzybski And…: 219

Labor: 23, 27, 33, 38, 92, 114, 116, 239, 241
Labor unions: 239, 241
Lacan, Jacques: 215
Lake, Kari: 279
Langer, Ellen: 10
Langer, Susanne: 20, 28, 88
Language: 16, 20, 22, 28–29, 45, 67–70, 74, 76, 98, 122, 139, 144, 156, 165, 178, 180–181, 201, 203–204, 220, 230, 232–234, 262, 265–267, 269–270, 274
Language crimes: 155–156, 168
Language Habits in Human Affairs: 142, 202
Language in Thought and Action: 225

INDEX

Lazarsfeld, Paul: 130, 231
Lee, Irving J.: 5, 142, 202
Levinson, M.: 2, 182, 185
Libertarian: 4, 16, 90, 186
Libertarians: 120
Limbaugh, Rush: 127
Lincoln, Abraham: 44–45, 121
Little, B.: 279

MacInnis, Cara: 269,
Madison, James: 53, 120
Manhood of Humanity: 2, 46, 107, 115–117, 225
Map vs. territory: 4–5, 11, 15–16, 108, 117, 179–181, 183, 185, 189, 202, 218, 234, 270–273
Marx, Karl: 47, 53, 237
Matusow, Harvey: 277
McGeachin, Janice: 279
McLuhan, Marshall: 36, 52, 72, 74–76, 78, 80, 82, 101, 125, 209, 226, 228, 251
Media ecology: 2, 43, 68, 76, 98, 225–226, 228–229, 231
Merchan, Juan: 166–167
Meta: 132
Meta levels: 59, 61–66, 86, 93
Meta-knowledge: 232, 252
Metacommunicate: 134
Money: 21–22, 26–27, 31, 34, 37, 51, 108–109, 111–112, 114–116, 166, 258, 278
Moran, Terence: xiii, 45, 81, 83, 125, 230
Moynihan, Daniel Patrick: 93
Mr. Average American: 265
Multi-valued approach: 139

Mumford, Lewis: 48, 226
Murdoch, Rupert: 127
Musk, Elon: 130–133

New Deal: 45, 49, 126
New York Times, The: 131–132
New York Times Magazine, The: 157
Newspapers: 78, 82, 100–101, 124–125, 228
Nixon, Richard: 83, 122, 277
Non-aristotelian:
 –Politics: 61, 79–80, 95
 –Rhetoric: 93–94
 –System: 4, 49–50, 181–183, 219, 225
Non-El: 197–198, 200, 207, 220
Nystrom, Christine: xiii, 5

Oath Keepers, The: 155, 161–163
Obama, Barack: 95, 148, 197, 212, 265, 278
Occupation: 149–151
October 7th massacre: 147–149, 151
O'Neill, Tip: 82
On the Political: 195–196
Open Society Pyramid Model: 59, 61–62, 64–65, 76–77, 101

Paivio, Allan: 261,
Paradox of democracy: 56–57
Para-rational: 198, 200, 212, 219–221
Pedagogy: 227, 235, 242, 253

Pedagogy of the Oppressed: 242, 246
Pennzoil: 278
Peterson, Valerie: xii, 41, 209
Phillips curve: 113
Plato: 50–53, 55–56, 59, 73–74, 76, 79, 84–85, 92, 188
Polarization: xvii, 14, 120, 122, 165, 199, 205
Political:
 –Activism (organizing): 7, 120, 130, 148, 155, 157–159, 162, 168, 227, 236, 242, 249–250, 252–253, 279
 –Communication (scholarship): 46, 48, 62, 79, 86, 137–138, 144, 200–201, 205, 210–211, 216, 219, 221, 225–229, 231–233, 235, 251
 –Parties: 3–4, 24, 78, 82, 87, 120–122, 141, 144, 196
Popper, Karl: 50–51, 53, 64, 74, 79–80, 84–85, 89–90, 95, 179
Post-political: 196–200, 205–220
Postman, Neil: xiii, xvii, 5, 33, 43–45, 54, 56, 74, 76, 81, 83, 87–88, 90–91, 96, 133, 173, 209, 226–227, 229–232, 234–235, 243, 245–246, 249–252
Potential use-value: 22, 26–27, 29–30, 34

Power, Jerome: 113–114
Pragmatics of Human Communication, The: 134
Press-Radio War: 124
Protected speech: 164, 278
Proud Boys, The: 154–155, 163
Pula, Robert: 13, 108, 184
Pula's Guide for the Perplexed: 13, 108

QAnon: 173, 183–184, 188

Racist material, examples of: 270
Rappaport, Leon: 268
Rationalism: 74, 86, 209–211, 219
Reagan, Ronald: 83, 127
Reality tunnel: 18, 186–188
Rebel, Jonny: 262–265, 267–268
Republican Party: 83, 121, 123
Rheingold, Howard: 130, 158
Rhetoric: 4, 60–61, 84–85, 92–94, 167, 197, 213, 232–233, 279
Rhodes, Stewart: 161–162
Right-to-life Party: 120
Roosevelt, Franklin Delano: 45, 48–49, 82, 126
Roosevelt's New Deal: 45, 49, 126
Russian Revolution: 55

Sadoski, Mark: 261
Sanders, Bernie: 38

Schwartz, Barry: 38
Science and Sanity: 45, 225
Seditious conspiracy: 155–157, 161–162, 168
Semantic:
 –Environment: 20, 44, 63, 120, 122–123, 125, 129–130, 133–134, 196, 199, 203, 205–206, 210–211, 214, 219, 226–227, 230–236, 241–243, 245, 247–253
 –Reactions: 6, 60, 189, 198, 203, 205, 208, 210, 212, 217, 219–221
Shannon, Claude: 123, 127, 129
Smart Mobs: The Next Social Revolution: 130, 158
Space binding: 20
Social media: 1, 33, 44, 56, 88, 123, 129–133, 148–149, 162–163, 165–167, 206, 253
Social media trends: 147
Socialist: 24, 49, 116
Soviet Communism: 46
Stock Market Crash of 1929: 47
"Stop the Steal": 155
Strate, Lance: xi, xii, 2, 44, 46–47, 52, 58, 68, 73–74, 76, 80, 84, 87–88, 101, 107, 133, 181–182, 185, 189, 219, 230, 235, 250
Suggs, Jon-Christian: 273
Superabundance: 27–28, 30–32, 34–36, 38
Sword and shield metaphor: 268

Symbolic inflation: 34
Systems: 31, 49–50, 58, 66, 70, 72, 77, 94, 98, 116, 178, 185, 227, 229–230, 232, 247, 250

Talmud: 79
Tea Party movement: 128
Technologies of secrecy: 155, 168
Technopoly: 83, 96
Philadelphia Evening Post, The: 124
Tiananmen Square: 55
TikTok left: 149–150
Time-binding: 14, 16–18, 20–29, 37, 48, 68–69, 75, 116, 198, 201–202, 218, 221
Torah: 61, 63, 72, 79
Trahan, C. J.: 263
Tribalism: 80, 206, 212–213, 216–217
Truman, Harry: 82
Trump, Donald: 100, 131, 154–155, 157, 159, 166–167, 279
Truth in advertising: 278
Twitter: 130–131, 148
Two-party system: 7, 120, 122, 128
Two-valued orientation: 122, 133–134, 226, 263

Understanding Media: 36
U. S. Constitution: 120, 124
Uscinski, Joseph: 173–178, 182

Vaidhyanathan, Siva: 132
Veblen, Thorstein: 46–47

Washington, George: 120,
Watzlawick, Paul: 62, 91, 134
Wealth: 14, 20–31, 34, 36, 38–39,
    63, 108, 115–117, 121, 124,
    132, 134
Weaver, Warren: 123, 127, 129
Weimar Republic: 114
Wheeler, Tom: 278
Whigs: 121
Wiener, Norbert: 123, 129
WIGO: 233, 239
Wilson, Robert Anton: 175,
    186–189

Wisdom economics: 27
Woke influencers: 149

X: 130–132

Yong, Ed: 260

Zimbabwe: 114,
Žižek, Slavoj: 215
Zuckerberg, Mark: 132–133

#FreePalestine: 147–148

www.ingramcontent.com/pod-product-compliance
Lightning Source LLC
Chambersburg PA
CBHW032034150426
43194CB00006B/279